D0439105

The Ethnic Eye

The Ethnic Eye

Latino Media Arts

Chon A. Noriega *and*
Ana M. López, *editors*

University of Minnesota Press

Minneapolis / London

Copyright 1996 by the Regents of the University of Minnesota

Lillian Jiménez, "Moving from the Margin to the Center: Puerto Rican Cinema in New York," first appeared in *Jump Cut* 38 (June 1993), reprinted by permission; Ana M. López, "Greater Cuba," first appeared as "The 'Other' Island: Cuban Cinema in Exile," *Jump Cut* 38 (June 1993), reprinted by permission; a longer version of Claire F. Fox, "Mass Media, Site Specificity, and the U.S.-Mexico Border: Guillermo Gómez-Peña's *Border Brujo* (1988, 1990)" appeared in *Social Text* 41 (January 1995).

All rights reserved. No part of this publication may be reproduced, stored in a retrieval system, or transmitted, in any form or by any means, electronic, mechanical, photocopying, recording, or otherwise, without the prior written permission of the publisher.

Published by the University of Minnesota Press
111 Third Avenue South, Suite 290, Minneapolis, MN 55401-2520
Printed in the United States of America on acid-free paper

Library of Congress Cataloging-in-Publication Data

The Ethnic eye : Latino media arts / Chon A. Noriega and Ana M. López, editors.
    p.   cm.
    Includes bibliographical references and index.
    ISBN 0-8166-2674-X (hc)
    ISBN 0-8166-2675-8 (pb)
    1. Latin Americans in motion pictures. 2. Hispanic Americans in motion pictures. 3. Motion pictures—Latin America. 4. Motion pictures—United States. 5. Motion picture producers and directors—Latin America. 6. Hispanic American motion picture producers and directors. I. Noriega, Chon A., 1961–   . II. López, Ana M.

The University of Minnesota is an equal-opportunity educator and employer.

Contents

v

Acknowledgments

The idea for this book came out of the conference "Latino Media Arts: Theory and Culture," held at the Whitney Museum of American Art on November 13–15, 1992, and organized by Chon A. Noriega, Ana M. López, and Lillian Jiménez, in collaboration with John G. Hanhardt, curator of film and video at the Whitney Museum. Earlier versions of many of the essays collected here were presented at the conference. The editors wish to thank John G. Hanhardt for his generous support and encouragement in this project. The Whitney Museum conference was funded by the John D. and Catherine T. MacArthur Foundation.

Chon A. Noriega wishes to acknowledge the UCLA Office of the Chancellor, Academic Senate, and Department of Film and Television for their research and faculty support in the preparation of this book.

Earlier versions of two essays appeared in a special issue of *Jump Cut* edited by Chon A. Noriega. Grateful acknowledgment is made for permission to reprint the following essays: Lillian Jiménez, "Moving from the Margin to the Center: Puerto Rican Cinema in New York," *Jump Cut* 38 (June 1993): 60–66; Ana M. López, "The 'Other' Island: Cuban Cinema in Exile," *Jump Cut* 38 (June 1993): 51–59. Luisela Alvaray provided invaluable assistance in compiling the index.

Introduction

While attempting to develop a critical discourse on Latinos and cinema, filmmakers and scholars (mostly historians and social scientists) initially placed an emphasis on Hollywood representation.[1] In the 1960s and 1970s, these efforts provided a historical rationale for concurrent demands for access to the mass media to ensure Latino self-representation in film and television. Taken as a whole, this critical discourse mostly circulated within ethnic studies programs and in those social spaces where the idea of a Latino cinema could take hold and develop: film festivals, film student groups, and media advocacy groups.

Since the mid-1980s, a new generation of Latino film scholars trained in film theory and history have turned increasingly to issues of self-representation. Such a shift relies upon the accumulation over twenty-five years of a significant and diverse body of Latino film/video, from early work related to civil rights struggles to the so-called Hispanic Hollywood of *La Bamba* (1987) to recent video explorations of gender and sexual identities *within* Latino culture. But this new work also reflects a significant generational distance from the social and political movements that gave rise to the various Latino cinemas. Indeed, most of the contributors to this collection were graduate students at the time they wrote their essays; or, to put it another way, many were born as these movements came to an end. Whereas an intermediary generation of scholars, working under the umbrella of cultural studies, sought to reform Latino cultural nationalism by divesting it of its patriarchal, homophobic privileged agency, the new generation is more likely to be critical of the underlying nationalist premises themselves—that is, of the discourses of belonging. In many ways, this produces critical work that oscillates between a number of disciplinary locations—body-specific (ethnic, gender, queer), media-specific (film, video, multimedia), and discourse-specific (genre, identity, reception)—without a secure mooring in any one camp. Likewise, the object of study—Latino media—no longer marks the site of a simple oppositional practice vis-à-vis Hollywood, but must be seen through the filter of a number of competing disciplines, traditions, histories.

ix

For example, Cheech Marin's *Born in East L.A.* (1987), produced and distributed by Universal Pictures, has been discussed as an example of Hollywood production, Chicano cinema, and New Latin American Cinema; and, in fact, the film provides a rare instance in which these antithetical practices overlap to some degree. Multimedia artist Ela Troyano, on the other hand, occupies different points in the histories of the American avant-garde film (as a protégée of Jack Smith), lesbian cinema (as star of Su Friedrich's *Damned if You Don't* [1984]; and director of *Carmelita Tropicana: Your* Kunst *Is Your* Waffen [1993]), Cuban cinema-in-exile (as what Ana M. López identifies as a third generation), and Latina film and video. Needless to say, these multiple and conflicting constituencies—not to mention Troyano's refusal to take up a partisan identity—make her a problematic denizen of any one category.

Herein lie both the premise and the problem of this collection: How do we define Latino in relation to other identity markers of race, ethnicity, gender, sexuality, and politics? This book is the first to deal with a wide range of Latino groups and media practices rather than focusing on one subnational group and its relationship to a "dominant" or "hegemonic" national culture. Toward that end, we understand "Latino" as a form of panethnic politics designed to redefine the national for the benefit of the specific ethnic groups subsumed under that term. Thus, we have brought together film scholarship on the major Latino cinemas—Chicano, Puerto Rican, Cuban (exile and American)—while exploring the discourses and strategies that traverse Latino cinemas as well as imbricating them in the national culture, as in the idea of Latino gay and lesbian media arts. But, at the same time, how do we acknowledge the desire of many of the media artists themselves to occupy those generic registers usually precluded by a body identification—that is, the default arenas of nation, medium, and mode within which all media artists operate? There are, after all, filmmakers and *Latino* filmmakers, just as there are women video artists and *Latina* women video artists, and gay and lesbian documentary filmmakers and *Latino* gay and lesbian documentary filmmakers. In each instance, these distinctions have practical consequences, determining how and to what extent the *Latino* media artist enters into competition for festivals, grants, fellowships, and so on.

Historically, Latino cinema defines the cinematic expressions of three distinct communities with shared experiences of discrimination yet different historical trajectories in the United States: Chicano, Puerto Rican, and Cuban American. In the past two decades, what were once distinct ethnic communities have become heterogeneous due to an influx of South American exiles in the 1970s and massive immigration from the Caribbean and Central America throughout the 1980s. For all Latino groups, one can point to historical experiences rooted in the increased control of the United States over the former Spanish colonies in the Americas. In 1848, the Mexican-American War resulted in the conquest of the northern half of Mexico; and, in 1898, the Spanish-American War initiated colonial control over Puerto Rico and Cuba, among other "strategic" territories. The first half of the "American Century" witnessed a complicated and ambiguous positioning of Puerto Ricans and Chicanos, with their legal status as citizens balanced against the simultaneous dispossession of communal landholdings in the name of economic development. Since the 1930s, Chicanos have faced various repatriation and deportation programs. For Puerto Ricans, an industrialization program on the island resulted in massive migration to the United States, an insidious female sterilization program aimed at population control, and an exodus of agricultural contract labor. Since the 1870s, Cubans have had a presence in the United States—especially Florida and New York—both as migrants and as exiles from the various independence struggles. However, it was the 1959 revolution that produced the exilic core of the Cuban American experience.

For Latinos in general, the generation that came of age in the 1960s and 1970s was the first to gain access (albeit limited) to the means of self-representation in film and television. Born in the post-World War II decade, these filmmakers grew up in the contentious ideological and political terrain of the Cold War, civil rights movement, and Third World struggles against the remnants of U.S. and European colonialism. But rather than formulate a connection between Chicano, Puerto Rican, and Cuban American cinemas that then leads to an overinvestment in ethnic or cultural "naming"—the numerous debates over "Latino" versus "Hispanic"—we want to raise the question of the use value of such a panethnic identification. After all, the debate over "Hispanic" versus "Latino" is never over who is or is not included in the category (both refer to the same aggregate), but rather over the proposed cultural and political function of each term. It is here that distinctions are made that exclude some groups: for example, most liberal-to-progressive definitions of "Latino" exclude Cuban Americans, albeit implicitly.[2]

The reason for the debate over these two terms lies in the different political traditions they describe. "Hispanic" emerges both as a professional self-designation within middle-class political and professional activities and as a U.S. census category, and reflects various attempts to acquire institutional, economic, and political power through homogenization. "Latino" emerges out of the efforts of civil rights struggles and grassroots social movements to achieve "radical" change at the national level through the articulation of a collective identity by the Latino intelligentsia. Thus, while "Hispanic" is founded in a socioeconomic politics, "Latino" tends more toward a cultural politics. In either case, however, a panethnic group is more imagined than real. There are too many contradictions within the diverse cultures and political strategies grouped together under the term "Hispanic" or "Latino."[3] This is not to say that Latino does not exist as an available cultural identity, political affiliation, or expressive genre (as in Latino media arts), but rather that such a category is, in the final analysis, a highly conflicted one that is the product of a racial politics played out at the national level. Rather than search for a common denominator—that ineffable essence around which all Latino groups can be mobilized as voters, consumers, or radical subjects—we want to draw attention to the fact that "Latino" has been used for competing purposes at various levels of social organization. Latino, then, is a politically constructed category, or at least more transparently so, while in some ways it has also been a highly effective one, albeit in contradictory ways. On the one hand, it has generated a critical space for films and videos produced by artists of Latin American and Caribbean descent; on the other hand, it has provided the rationale for isolating these texts from other films and videos. Latino media has become a genre onto itself, explainable only in relationship to itself, as has also happened with Black film, women's cinema, queer media.

Although this book can't help but to contribute to both tendencies, we want to question the boundaries that trap individual texts within these categories. We want to look beyond the usual question—how do these films and videos express an identity?—to the question of the multiple locations within which these texts may be inscribed. As we have already suggested, some filmmakers and films are difficult to locate in any one category. What we want to propose as a general rule, however, is that all Latino films and videos should be approached through the matrix of differential histories; and that, in particular, these texts fluctuate among various interrelated histories: the ethnic or subnational (Chicano, Puerto Rican, Cuban American); the interethnic and interminority (relations across communities of gender, race, sexuality, and so on); the panethnic or national category for minorities (Latino, Hispanic); the mainstream or national (American); and the hemispheric or international (Latin American). Toward that end, we have divided the book into two sections: "Critical Mappings" and "Close Readings." The first provides thematic histories for Chicano, Puerto Rican, and Cuban American cinemas, concluding with a history of Latino gay and lesbian independent film/video. The second provides a series of close readings of individual texts, drawing upon diverse critical discourses and historical sources. The critical attention to the specificity of these texts reveals the extent to which they necessarily emerge from and exceed the categories posited in the first section.

Critical Mappings

The essays in this section represent recent attempts to write a particular "Latino cinema" into history. Obviously, the essays are guided by multiple objectives. First of all, from the perspective of the academy, Latino film and video scholars have felt the urgent need to promote the inclusion of "Latino" and subnational cinema and video in the canon that is taught and reproduced in film courses and history textbooks. Simultaneously, the historical inscription of such categories has been—correctly—perceived as a precondition for access to media arts funding for noncommercial projects. There is a paradox at work here that speaks to the dynamic for racially marked expression and its circulation within popular and academic discourses. The articulation of an essential ethnic category created the possibilities for subsequent production and reception. It is not too much of a stretch to argue that, for example, Chicano-produced films did not exist—in either film festivals or college courses—until "Chicano cinema" was named, providing a category that defined prior exclusion and subsequent inclusion in pretty much the same terms. As such, "Chicano cinema" became *the* category, implicit or not, through which Chicano filmmakers and video artists entered the museum, film festival circuit, grant opportunities, and college curriculum. An individual text or filmmaker, then, was read in relationship to "Chicano," and perhaps "Latino," but little else. Thus the essays in this section engage in a potentially polemical historicizing project: the construction of distinct, internally coherent histories as a way of inserting ourselves into History.

However, as the essays themselves often suggest, there are dangers implicit in this historicizing move. For one, the wish to locate historical coherences often drives the authors to posit problematic, but unavoidable, temporal relationships that seem to exclude other causal forces. Thus, for example, when individual filmmakers are identified with a generation (precursor, first, second, third) within the history of Chicano, Puerto Rican, Cuban American, or Latino gay and lesbian cinema, the specific ethnic genealogies being established effectively ignore "other" film/video/art histories that these artists have participated in but been excluded from. This happens, however, even as the artists are also recuperated through the newly constituted Latino category. This is the Catch-22 of this project: it is necessary to posit subnational histories in order to locate texts and, thereby, incite discourse; but, at the same time, any specific text will necessarily exceed the history within which it then circulates, and within which it is, more or less, contained.

Chon A. Noriega's "Imagined Borders" unpacks the already much-discussed category of "Chicano cinema" to tease out the nuances of its relationships to the multiple and contradictory discourses of Chicano cultural resistance, egalitarianism, and nationalism. Noriega demonstrates the need to consider Chicano cinema as a category as well as a practice in order to reveal how the play between these two registers created new terms for negotiating access within the film and television industry. This was done through an argument that located Chicano cinema "in opposition to Hollywood and in alliance with the New Latin American Cinema." But, in order for this binarism to serve reformist ends at the level of practice, it had to remain "tightly coupled," resulting in "the disavowal of an avant-garde tradition *within* Chicano cultural production" that questioned its bipolar terms.

In "Moving from the Margin to the Center," Lillian Jiménez argues that although it is rarely recognized as a distinct group or movement, Puerto Rican media production in New York emerged out of the concrete struggle for civil rights in the late 1960s and is intimately tied to the community's radicalization. Thus, while always linked to the island, albeit other, Nuyorican videos "came out of a movement for voice." Jiménez traces the history of the emergence of this voice in documentary, narrative, and experimental work, and traces its interrelationships with other voices from the island and the Latino community itself through the 1990s.

Ana M. López's "Greater Cuba" provides a detailed history of the rather different phenomenon of Cuban exile and Cuban American film and video. Unlike Chicano and Puerto Rican cinema, Cuban exile cinema is linked neither to a civil rights movement nor to the fluid migratory experience of the "airbus" to Puerto Rico. The various waves of Cubans who left the island after the 1959 revolution were not immigrants but exiles who dreamed of the possibility of return and often refused to assimilate. In this context, Cuban exile cinema is differently inscribed in the spectrum of Latino political filmmaking, often speaking against the very revolution that other Latino groups identified as a precursor for their own struggles. Nevertheless, the work of "newer" generations — the Cuban Americans — participates in and often aggressively speaks with a "Latino" rather than an exclusively "Cuban" voice.

The last essay in this section, Frances Negrón-Muntaner's "Drama Queens," also tells a history, but a differently constituted one, that of Latino gay and lesbian independent film/video. Negrón-Muntaner's essay cuts across the subnational categories to argue for the existence of a small, recent, but coherent category of Latino film and video that is constituted through a discourse on gender and sexuality. Her analysis carefully details the "structure of feeling" of these works by tracing how they invoke and rework Latin American and Latino cultural forms such as the melodrama/*telenovela*, autobiography/*testimonio*, music (bolero, *rancheras*), and camp.

Close Readings

This section covers mainstream feature films, experimental narratives, documentaries, and short experimental and multimedia videos. The goal here is to cover a wide spectrum of video- and filmmakers, with attention to their location within the so-called media arts: industry, independent, alternative, gallery/museum. By focusing on either individual films or filmmakers, these essays collectively provide the contextual specificity and detailed textual analysis necessary to question the very categories and "master narratives" posited in the first section. Here, then, the "canon" is recentered in other directions.

The first three essays of this section analyze mainstream feature films—produced in and on the margins of Hollywood—that explicitly address questions of Latino identity and that have contributed to the constitution of a Latino filmmaking "canon" (alongside the already well-analyzed features of "Hispanic Hollywood" such as *Zoot Suit* [1981], *Born in East L.A* [1987], and *La Bamba* [1987]).[4] Overall, they question and analyze how these Latino mainstream films intervene in the generic, aesthetic, and ideological conventions of contemporary narrative cinema. Analyzing one of the "key" films of the Hispanic Hollywood boom of the late 1980s, *Stand and Deliver* (1987) by the Cuban-born filmmaker Ramón Menéndez, Ilene S. Goldman's "Crossing Invisible Borders" demonstrates how the film inflects the "neophyte teacher" film (such as *Blackboard Jungle* [1955], and *To Sir, with Love* [1967]) with a specifically Chicano/Latino thematic. She argues that although *Stand and Deliver* uses traditional generic patterns and mainstream distribution channels, it also strikes a balance between "affirming and maintaining Chicano identity and participating in a larger dominant culture." In contrast to Goldman's thematic and ideological reading, Kathleen Newman's "Reterritorialization in Recent Chicano Cinema" analyzes Edward James Olmos's directorial debut, *American Me* (1992), from the perspective of State theory. Applying theories of the State developed in Latin America to her close reading of the film, Newman is able to argue that, despite its questionable political message and gender roles, the film contributes to a much-needed reterritorialization of the United States as a neutral site of equality and justice for all citizens. Finally, Charles Ramírez Berg's "Ethnic Ingenuity and Mainstream Cinema" analyzes Robert Rodríguez's award-winning student short film *Bedhead* (1990) and his $7,000 feature *El Mariachi* (1993), two critically acclaimed genre films by the latest entrant into the roster of Latino mainstream filmmakers. According to Ramírez Berg, Rodríguez's films are exemplary of how the "new" wave or generation of Chicano filmmakers negotiates the impasse between mainstream media and ethnic identity. He concludes that *El Mariachi* effectively combines "entertainment" and "ethnic ingenuity" while bemoaning the loss of cultural memory and questioning dominant notions of masculinity, the U.S.-Mexico border, and cinema itself.

While the above feature-length narratives attempt to infiltrate and subvert the "mainstream," the next two essays examine recent experimental and nonmainstream narratives—Ela Troyano's *Carmelita Tropicana* and Felix Rodriguez's *One Moment in Time* (1992)—that appropriate and mix commercial film and television genres in order to address questions of ethnic, racial, gender, and sexual identity. Given their attempt to explore the relationships between these different registers, these works also problematize any simple "genealogical" or subnational model for Latino film and video. Questioning Celeste Olalquiaga's erasure of sexual difference from the concept of Latino kitsch, José Esteban Muñoz identifies Ela Troyano's *Carmelita Tropicana* as a decidedly campy, Cubano, lesbian, and Latino film that references a number of genres: music, comedy, prison film, and melodrama. His detailed reading and theoretical elaboration of the interconnections among ethnicity, camp/kitsch, and sexual identity extend the categories outlined in Negrón-Muntaner's essay in the first section. In particular, Muñoz locates Troyano's Latino milieu vis-à-vis the influence of Jack Smith and the American avant-garde film and performance art of the 1960s. Finally, Marcos Becquer and Alisa Lebow offer an extensive and theoretically rich analysis of Felix Rodriguez's rarely seen video *One Moment in Time*. Becquer and Lebow identify the tape as a "docudrag," a "fiction in documentary clothing" and a documentary about drag. Akin to "vogueing," docudrag articulates "realness" in a way that questions the very notion that there is any real to reveal. The film—in a move echoed by Becquer and Lebow's nuanced reading—exemplifies and comments upon transgendered practices, skirting/subverting the codes of fiction, documentary, homosexual, transsexual, and Latino urban identity.

As with the New Latin American Cinema, Latino film and video has had a strong "documentary impulse" that—concurrent with other civil rights struggles—spoke against the prevailing stereotypes in the U.S. news and entertainment media. Although, at one extreme, this resulted in a counterdiscourse rooted in either an "authentic" essence or compensating "positive images," Latino documentary filmmakers have for the most part proceeded on assumptions similar to those of Becquer and Lebow's docudrag. But rather than disavow a "real" altogether, these filmmakers acknowledge instead that what documentary does is to make a political argument *about* the real and *within* the social and aesthetic conventions for nonfiction media discourse. In "From Exile to Ethnicity," Marvin D'Lugo argues that *Improper Conduct* systematically disavows the controversial denunciation of homophobia and repression in Cuba (which is the putative "topic" of the film) in order to address and refigure the Cuban exile audience as an emergent ethnic community. D'Lugo's analysis traces a series of textual instabilities that point to an evolution from the exilic fetishization and containment of the past to the necessary restaging of identity—in the slippage from sexuality to nationality—in the present and in the new *patria*.

Experimental and multimedia video is perhaps the most prolific and provocative area of contemporary Latino media production, emerging at precisely that moment when two events—the federal deregulation of television and the rise of consumer video equipment—brought about a discursive and aesthetic shift from public affairs television to an activist-oriented video art.[5] The final five essays range, chronologically, from Raphael Montañez Ortiz's "deconstructivist" digital/laser/videos to Frances Salomé España's mythopoetic feminist videos. These essays can be divided into two major, though overlapping, tendencies: those dealing with video that incorporates or supports other art forms, and those dealing with freestanding texts engaged in identity politics. With respect to the former, Scott MacDonald's "Media Destructivism" examines the recent video work of Raphael Montañez Ortiz, a forgotten pioneer of avant-garde film/video whose "destructivist" work spans four decades. In the late 1950s, Ortiz produced a number of recycled or compilation films before turning to performance, sculpture, and installation, as well as founding El Museo del Barrio in New York City. Since 1985, he has returned to the earlier project of appropriating and deconstructing the Hollywood text. But, as MacDonald notes, these new multimedia works are unique in that they are "neither films, nor videos, nor computer art, nor laser art—though each of these four technologies is a crucial dimension of the process that produces the works." C. Ondine Chavoya points to another dimension of video that pushes at the limits of current film and video scholarship and its focus on the audiovisual *text*: public art performance that depends on mass media discourse (television, radio, newspaper), and video as part of multimedia installation within the art gallery or museum. In "Collaborative Public Art and Multimedia Installation," Chavoya provides a discursive and textual analysis of David Avalos, Louis Hock, and Elizabeth Sisco's controversial "public art ambush," *Welcome to America's Finest Tourist Plantation* (1988), a bus poster project whose extensive television coverage subsequently became part of an art exhibition. In addition to its pivotal role in the "new" public art and installation of the past decade, video has also had a long relationship with performance art. In "Mass Media, Site Specificity, and the U.S.-Mexico Border," Claire F. Fox compares two versions of *Border Brujo*—Guillermo Gómez-Peña's 1988 performance and Isaac Artenstein's 1990 video—to chart and critique the process in which the "border" goes from a signifier of a specific place to a metaphor for both global cultural changes and the artist's intervention. Fox argues that although it is undoubtedly true that the "border" has invaded the metropolis, it is essential not to forget the specificity of the border as *place* and the important functions served by an "art of place."

In contrast to the previous video artists' concern with other art forms and with deconstructing mass media and subverting public space, the last two essays place their own concerns with representation and social space in relation to the articulation of liminal and hybrid identities. In "The Forbidden Kiss," Christopher Ortiz's close analysis of Cuban American multimedia artist Raúl Ferrera-Balanquet's 1990 video *Mérida Proscrita* carefully positions the work at the intersection of a critique of "white" filmic representation of Latino gays and the Latin American specificity of melodrama, boleros/music, and the city of Mérida, Mexico. Ortiz also outlines the artist's own complicated artistic history, which combines exile through the Mariel boat lift, familiarity with New Latin American Cinema, formal training in film and multimedia art at the University of Iowa, and a variegated activist persona. Finally, Carmen Huaco-Nuzum's "(Re)constructing Chicana, Mestiza Representation" provides a close reading of Frances Salomé España's *Spitfire* (1991). This richly textured five-minute video manipulates and interrelates images of a young Chicana, la Virgen de Guadalupe, and Mesoamerican female deities in order to introduce notions of time, memory, history, and desire into a feminist sociopolitics. For Huaco-Nuzum, *Spitfire* must be read in relation to both the Hollywood representation of Latinas—the *Mexican Spitfire* series (1939–43), starring Lupe Vélez, and alluded to in the title—and Mexican female archetypes. It is from this position, as the image used for the "phallocentric racial pleasure and fantasy" of two nations, that the mestiza subject must renegotiate the terms of knowledge, power, and pleasure.

If we were to be perverse, at this point we might suggest that, given the range of work analyzed in the second section, perhaps the term "Latino" is not, after all, the most consistently appropriate category. Certainly it is hard to conceive of a category that can account for texts as diverse as *El Mariachi, Improper Conduct,* and *Spitfire.* In many ways, one could even argue that any one of the films and videos discussed here would fit better in other categories, particularly ones foregrounding formal characteristics (such as narrative, documentary, and experimental). Such an argument looks ahead to a future moment when "Latino" works might be fully integrated into these and other established modes and thereby become open to a broader range of inter- and intratextual associations. If so, however, this suggests that Latino media arts is a category based on exclusion alone, a mere catchall for all the overlooked works by artists who happen to be of Latin American and Caribbean descent. Indeed, Latino *cannot* carry the weight of identification as do Chicano, Puerto Rican, Cuban American, and so on. But, as the articles in the first section suggest, beyond their cultural specificity, the subnational groups share historical and socioeconomic affinities that coalesce as a political strategy articulated in the U.S. public sphere rather than in the barrio. Even more perversely, while this seems to provide an ideological rationale for our collection, we are left with a final irony: the media artists themselves have rarely ever made "Latino" works, preferring instead to work at the level of either the subnational or the national itself, speaking either as ethnics or as Americans to both their communities and the nation. Indeed, as a number of articles point out, the artists are often highly aware of constructing hybrid texts — mixing genres, languages, cultural codes — for diverse audiences or interpretive communities. Like these artists, we are caught trying to have it both ways, engaging in a willful ambivalence about critical location, textual classification, and spectatorship/reception — in short, about the need to name. So perhaps in closing we should name perversity — the contrariness of refusing fixity, essences, secure locations, singular affiliations — as the critical strategy under which this project has been undertaken.

Notes

1. This was often in conjunction with federal reports on minority employment in the industry. For more on Latino scholarship and media policy reports, see Chon A. Noriega, "El hilo latino: Representation, Identity, and National Culture," *Jump Cut* 38 (June 1993): 45–50, and "The Numbers Game," *Jump Cut* 39 (June 1994): 107–11. Early articles circulated within Chicano and Hispanic journals as well as professional newsletters such at that of the Chicano Cinema Coalition. See, for example, Thomas M. Martínez, "Advertising and Racism: The Case of the Mexican American," *El Grito: A Journal of Contemporary Mexican-American Thought* 2.4 (summer 1969): 3–13; and Francisco J. Lewels, "Racism in the Media—Perpetuating the Stereotype," *Agenda: A Journal of Hispanic Issues* (1978): 4–6.

2. Portions of the preceding two paragraphs first appeared in Chon A. Noriega and Lillian Jiménez, "La Indirecta Directa: Two Decades of Chicano and Puerto Rican Film and Video," *New American Film and Video Series 61,* program note (New York: Whitney Museum of American Art, 1992).

3. As one recent study revealed, the various claims about the Latino population—whether from Republicans, Democrats, or the Latino intelligentsia—are at best "suspect" generalizations: "A surprisingly small percentage of each group prefers to identify in pan-ethnic terms such as Latino or Hispanic," preferring to use "American" instead. The study upset many cherished notions about the cultural characteristics of each group (the relative importance of Spanish-language maintenance, religion, identity) and about a panethnic identification based on social interaction and common culture. At the same time, however, it found common views on many "domestic policy issues" that could be the basis for a "unified Hispanic agenda," although one that moved between liberal, moderate, and conservative positions within the mainstream of the nation's politics. See Rodolfo O. de la Garza et al., *Latino Voices: Mexican, Puerto Rican, and Cuban Perspectives on American Politics* (Boulder, Colo.: Westview Press, 1992), 13–16.

4. See, for example, Chon A. Noriega, "Chicano Cinema and the Horizon of Expectations: A Discursive Analysis of Film Reviews in the Mainstream, Alternative, and Hispanic Press, 1987–1988," *Aztlán: A Journal of Chicano Studies* 19.2 (fall 1988–90): 1–32; Rosa Linda Fregoso, "*Born in East L.A.* and the Politics of Representation," *Cultural Studies* 4.3 (October 1990): 264–80; Rosa Linda Fregoso, *The Bronze Screen: Chicana and Chicano Film Culture* (Minneapolis: University of Minnesota Press, 1993); Eddie Tafoya, "*Born in East L.A.*: Cheech as the Chicano Moses," *Journal of Popular Culture* 26.4 (spring 1993): 123–29; Chon A. Noriega, " 'Waas Sappening?': Narrative Structure and Iconography in *Born in East L.A,*" *Studies in Latin American Popular Culture* 14 (1995): 107–28; as well as essays in Gary D. Keller, ed., *Chicano Cinema: Research, Reviews, and Resources* (Binghamton, N.Y.: Bilingual Review/Press, 1985), and Chon A. Noriega, ed., *Chicanos and Film: Representation and Resistance* (Minneapolis: University of Minnesota Press, 1992).

5. For more on this shift, see Chon A. Noriega, "Talking Heads, Body Politic: The Plural Self of Chicano Video," in *Resolutions: Contemporary Video Practices,* ed. Michael Renov and Erika Suderburg (Minneapolis: University of Minnesota Press, 1996), 207–28.

Critical Mappings

Imagined Borders:
Locating Chicano Cinema in America/América

Chon A. Noriega

In this essay, I will examine the articulation and development of a "Chicano cinema" as an expression of the Chicano civil rights movement. To some extent, this is a history that has been told a number of times already, first by the filmmakers themselves, and later by programmers and scholars.[1] And it is a history that has been told within a metanarrative of cultural resistance that defines *lo chicano* according to its oppositional "experience," "expression," and "identity." Nonetheless, in these accounts, my own included, Chicano cinema inevitably occupies an ambiguous location within the national culture, caught between the conflicting egalitarian and communitarian goals of both its practitioners and its academic critics.[2] This conflict marks the underlying conditions for the production of both Chicano films and the critical discourse on them (in short, race relations), while the metanarrative of cultural resistance requires that, as a practical matter, such social contradictions be addressed at the allegorical level. Although an institutional critique of either Chicano cinema or Chicano studies is beyond the scope of this essay, I do want to raise the ambiguous location of Chicano cinema to the level of historiographic operation. One can find a precursor in Coco Fusco's writings on Black and Latino media in the late 1980s.[3] Working not as an academic but as a media professional actively involved in the object of her study—curator, writer, and program officer—Fusco voiced pragmatic concerns as she sought to define a historical moment of "minority" intellectual or cultural production. If more academic accounts necessarily diverted these concerns to an allegorical level, Fusco bristled against her location as the representative for the underrepresented, as the insider for the outsiders, and, consequently, as the outsider who was inside. This ambiguous or dual location, then, became the very methodology by which she read against the grain of oppositional thinking and of "minority" texts. In a similar fashion, I want

3

to raise several questions about the function of "Chicano cinema" within various discourses—nationalist, postnationalist and American, pan-American—in order to make a distinction between the idea of "Chicano cinema" (as category) and its practice. In some respects, the category preceded the practice insofar as it created the possibilities for special admissions, trainee programs, public affairs series, production grants, distribution agencies, exhibition slots, and so on. From this discursive origin, "Chicano cinema" constructed itself in opposition to Hollywood and in alliance with New Latin American Cinema.[4] Although framed as a matter of either/or choice, this strategy actually provided new terms within which access could be negotiated. As a final matter, I want to suggest that "Chicano cinema" developed not just vis-à-vis Hollywood and New Latin American Cinema (as well as cinema and television), but through the disavowal of an avant-garde tradition within Chicano cultural production. The focus of this essay will be on the period of the Chicano civil rights movement (1965–75), during which the first generation of Chicano filmmakers went from student activists to film and television professionals. I will pay special attention to Jesús Salvador Treviño and his pivotal role as filmmaker, organizer, advocate, and polemicist.

The Chicano Civil Rights Movement

As the story is told, the first generation of Chicano filmmakers emerged out of the context of the farmworkers' struggle and the student movement. In the first years of the Chicano movement, the farmworkers' struggle would in some sense define its political, class, and rhetorical orientations, providing the basis for a categorical shift away from the perceived middle-class, accommodationist, and integrationist strategies of the Mexican American Generation.[5] Under the leadership of César Chávez, the United Farm Workers (UFW), founded in 1962, gained national attention when it joined the grape strike in Delano, California, on September 16, 1965, the anniversary of Mexican independence from Spain in 1810. Both Mexican-based historical references and cultural production played a pivotal role in these social protests (and their political resonance), incorporating more subtle allusions to American political history. Luis Valdez, writer and director of *Zoot Suit* (1981) and *La Bamba* (1987), was especially important in developing this bicultural political rhetoric in the mid-1960s.

In 1965, he founded El Teatro Campesino in order to rally striking farmworkers, developing collaborative agitprop *actos* (skits) that were performed on the flatbeds of trucks. Then, in March 1966, he wrote the influential "Plan of Delano," a manifesto that announced the grape strike as the start of a "social movement" — done in the rhetorical style of the U.S. Declaration of Independence and Black gospel à la Martin Luther King Jr. — which it then rooted in the Virgin of Guadalupe, Benito Juárez, and the Mexican Revolution of 1910.[6] In this manner, Valdez created a unique expression that coupled together seemingly opposed egalitarian and communitarian goals, so that the call for equal justice within the United States justified an affirmation of a Mexican past and culture that then made such equality its inevitable outcome. As a Chicano rhetorical strategy, Valdez's "Plan of Delano" would have a direct impact on other plans ("El Plan Espiritual de Aztlán" and "El Plan de Santa Barbara"), epic poems ("I Am Joaquin"), films (in particular, Valdez's *I Am Joaquin* [1969] and *Los Vendidos: The Sellouts* [1972]), and — in a more indirect fashion — film manifestos.[7]

By the late 1960s, the emphasis of the Chicano movement shifted from rural to urban issues, and from farmworkers to students, and Los Angeles became a major focal point. In East Los Angeles, some ten thousand high school students undertook a series of "Blow Outs" (or walkouts) in March 1968 to protest institutional racism and poor education. The Blow Outs were initiated by high school teacher Sal Castro, who joined the students, and were coordinated by members of United Mexican American Students (UMAS), including UCLA students and future filmmakers Moctesuma Esparza and Francisco Martinez. In June, Castro and Esparza were among the "L.A. Thirteen" indicted on conspiracy charges for their organizational role in the Blow Outs, an act that resulted in increased Chicano student activism and radicalism within the next year.[8] In March and April 1969, student conferences in Denver and Santa Barbara consolidated the student movement, uniting the four major Mexican American student groups under one banner: M.E.Ch.A., or El Movimiento Estudiantil Chicano de Aztlán (The Chicano Student Movement of Aztlán). The rejection of the self-designation "Mexican American" in favor of "Chicano," and the fact that *mecha* is vernacular Spanish for "match," underscored the student movement's militant nationalism.

The first Chicano film, *I Am Joaquin* (1969), embodies these transitions in the Chicano movement and represents the culmination of an intertextual dialogue between the movement's rural and urban visionaries: Luis Valdez and Rodolfo "Corky" Gonzales. Like Valdez, Gonzales had been actively involved in the Democratic Party, but became disenchanted in the early 1960s. In 1965, Gonzales resigned from the party and founded the Crusade for Justice, a civil rights organization located in Denver. The film is Valdez's adaptation of Gonzales's epic poem of the same title, written in 1967, and widely distributed through chapbooks and mimeograph copies.[9] The poem itself, however, draws upon the rhetorical style of Valdez's "Plan of Delano," ending with the first person singular expression of phrases that punctuate the earlier manifesto: "I SHALL ENDURE. I WILL ENDURE."[10] The major shift between plan and poem occurs in terms of the subject of their "poetic consciousness."[11] The "Plan of Delano," although grounded in key figures and moments from Mexican history, addressed a multiethnic membership (mostly Mexican and Filipino), then focused on one class-based social movement rooted in the farmworkers' struggle, but ultimately aimed at uniting "all of the races that comprise the oppressed minorities in the United States," including "poor whites." Furthermore, in defining the role of theater and other cultural expressions within that movement, Valdez himself made a clear-cut distinction between its symbolic politics (both theater and demonstrations) and "actual hard-ass, door to door, worker to worker organizing."[12] If community had to be imagined for a national audience, local politics required an interpersonal expression and organization of that community. In contrast to the "Plan of Delano," Gonzales's "I Am Joaquin" envisioned a mestizo historical genealogy for the broad-based Chicano movement, articulating a series of bipolar parameters for Chicano identity—of race, religion, class, and, more insidiously, gender—that could be subordinated to nationalism. For Gonzales—as echoed in the words of "El Plan Espiritual de Aztlán"—"nationalism as the key to organization transcends all religious, political, class, and economic factions" within the Chicano community.[13] Nationalism, then, gave a singular political meaning to *mestizaje*. Whereas Valdez used nationalist icons in order to argue for historical justification as well as internal unity within a working-class struggle, Gonzales turned nationalism itself into the "key" for uniting an admittedly heterogeneous group of Mexican descent.

By the time "I Am Joaquin" was written, Valdez had realized the need to develop the aesthetic and political dimensions of El Teatro

Campesino beyond direct involvement with the United Farm Workers. At stake for Valdez was a question of professionalism and the potential for a national audience for an artistic practice that had begun as a component within grassroots politics. Valdez's film adaptation exemplifies his own artistic shift from community-based organizing to addressing a mass audience for which community must be imagined. Before the adaptation, El Teatro Campesino had developed a slide show that combined the photographs of George Ballis, who worked with the United Farm Workers, with a dramatic reading of the poem. Shortly thereafter, Ballis's photographs were shot and edited together into a film, with Luis Valdez's narration and Daniel Valdez's improvised music recorded in a sound studio in Los Angeles.[14] The film was shown at both farmworkers' rallies and within the urban barrio (as with earlier dramatic readings of the poem and the slide show), but it also reached classrooms, festivals, and a national television audience. Thus, the film—like the poem—brought together the diverse aspects of the Chicano movement, while it also expanded the domain for Chicano expressions into the mass media of film and television.[15] In this manner, the film adaptation of "I Am Joaquin" signaled both the professional reorientation of El Teatro Campesino (and Chicano arts in general), Luis Valdez's own shift from rural/local/grassroots to mass media forms, and "a new era in Chicano self-determination in film and television."[16]

From Protests to Trainee Programs, 1967–69

Although *I Am Joaquin* is symptomatic of the struggle for Chicano self-representation within film and television—both as an organizing tool and as a means of representing the Chicano movement to a national audience—more structural changes would come about as a result of the combined efforts of social protests, federal regulation, and foundation initiatives. From these efforts emerged a number of industry trainee programs and film school admissions policies that brought in the first generation of would-be Chicano filmmakers. In the summer of 1968, for example, the U.S. Office of Economic Opportunity funded a program called New Communicators that was designed to train minorities for employment in the film industry. With a board of directors comprised of various progressives within Hollywood, the program "recruited about twenty students, largely

Blacks and Chicanos, with a few Indians and one or two token hip-pie-type white guys."[17] Through intensive hands-on training with film graduates from the University of Southern California, the students were to advance from Super-8 to 16mm over the course of one year. Although the program fell apart within eight months because of internal conflicts, it nonetheless provided several Chicanos with their first exposure to the film industry: Jesús Treviño, Esperanza Vásquez, Francisco Martinez, and Martín Quiroz. Treviño, who by this time had become involved in the Educational Issues Coordinating Committee (EICC) formed within the Chicano community after the Blow Outs of March 1968, used a Super-8 (and later a 16mm) camera from the New Communicators to document subsequent Blow Outs as well as EICC activities. In particular, he documented the Sal Castro hearings before the board of education, and the EICC sit-in and arrests after the board refused the appeal to reinstate Castro.[18] In addition to the ten to twelve hours of unedited footage collected, Treviño edited together several films in early 1969 as part of his training at New Communicators. These include *La Raza Nueva* (The new people), on Super-8 with sound and narration on a separate tape cassette, and *Ya Basta!* (Enough already!), on 16mm. *La Raza Nueva* documents the March 1968 Blow Outs, the conspiracy trial of the "L.A. Thirteen," and the Castro hearings and sit-in. In *Ya Basta!*, Treviño experiments with jump cuts, dramatic recreations, and multiple story lines, which reemerge in Treviño's later television documentaries such as *Yo Soy Chicano* (1972). The "free-form" docudrama intercuts blown-up footage from *La Raza Nueva* with a dramatic sequence about a teenage boy with troubles at home and school. By the end of the film the boy's death is coded as a direct outcome of the board of education's refusal to reinstate Castro. Although these films appear "primitive" and incoherent according to mass-media conventions, their effective use within the EICC and the Chicano community at the time suggests another way of understanding early artistic expressions within the movement. As Treviño himself argues, the "free-form" style of *Ya Basta!* relied upon the fact that "so much of this was self-evident to the audience."[19] Thus, the film served the needs of an audience whose main concern was the organization of a "community" and not the craft of an autonomous, objective, or artistic statement. To that extent, watching a "Chicano" film about an event experienced firsthand by many of the audience members played a role in community building, becoming more important than the actual form and content of the film, and more important than its ability to function within the mass media.

Chicano Public Affairs Series, 1970–74

The limited or distorted media coverage of social protests and community concerns motivated a number of student activists to become filmmakers able to work within the mass media itself. Meanwhile, Chicano media advocates and activist groups, including Carissma and Justicia, aggressively pushed for Chicano-produced local television shows in the Los Angeles area.[20] Overall, these local television shows or specials provided initial, albeit contested, outlets for Chicano-produced film related to the issues, protests, and goals of the Chicano movement. But as producers attempted to address these issues within the television industry, they confronted both economic and ideological constraints. In fact, program budgets did not provide for more than a "talking heads" format, while station managers suppressed their efforts to use television for social critique. An examination of two series produced by Treviño reveals the extent to which Chicano filmmakers were able to subvert these constraints.

The *Ahora!* series—funded by the Ford Foundation as part of an initiative at PBS affiliate KCET in Los Angeles—was perhaps the first television show to document and discuss current issues within the Chicano community. Given the prior absence of local media coverage on Chicanos, members of the community were hostile to the series, then in development, even though politically active Chicanos were in the role of producers. Various community meetings were held, and at one such meeting some two hundred people voted on whether or not to support the program. Treviño attempted to intervene: "I gave this impassioned plea, like, at least give us a chance, don't you trust me, et cetera. And the vote ... there were four people who voted for me: my wife, two friends and myself! [Laughing] It was really tense in those days."[21] In the first week, the program featured "every single major [Chicano] group," and by the end of the year, "whenever we would have a major news event happening, the local news stations would come to our studio, because we would have the people there. We would get them before anyone else."[22] Because of the close relationships Treviño established within the community, *Ahora!* could also provide immediate coverage for planned protests and other events. Treviño quickly became the associate producer, writer, and on-air host for the show, which aired live weeknights at 7:00 P.M. for 175 episodes. In addition to the political issues dealt with in talk-show format or documented through live remotes, *Ahora!* scheduled regular episodes on cultural and historical dimensions of the Chicano experience. These included a three-part series on Mexican Americans in Hollywood.[23] Treviño also hired Luis Torres, a high school senior (later a producer for the National Latino Communications Center), to research and write a weekly episode on "la raza history." On Fridays, the show usually aired live performances of Latino music and drama. In this manner, in its weekly programming, *Ahora!* wove together current events, history, culture, and entertainment, providing an integrated vision of the Chicano community and its political struggle.

Taken as a whole, Treviño's programming on *Ahora!* can be seen as congruent with "El Plan Espiritual de Aztlán" and its demand for cultural expressions that would "strengthen our identity and the moral backbone of the movement." The Plan made explicit the movement's assumption about the role of cultural production within political struggle, and, more generally, the way in which cultural nationalism mediated between the Chicano family and dominant society: "our culture unites and educates the family of La Raza towards liberation with one heart and one mind." The Plan then articulated seven "organizational goals" for the movement, calling upon "writers, poets, musicians, and artists" to assist this process by defining the "cultural values" of the family and home as a "powerful weapon" against the "gringo dollar value system." But while the role of cultural expression was central to the organization of the movement, it was also the only "organizational goal" that was absent from the "action" or public sphere portion of the Plan. To some extent, this can be explained by the way in which the Plan equated cultural expression with the private domain of the family and home. Thus, although the Chicano family served as a model for political organization and "nation" building, its patriarchal and hierarchical structure served to keep the issues associated with family *entre familia* (literally, "between family members," or not for public discussion). These issues were, namely, those of gender, generation, and sexuality. Within the terms of the Plan, cultural production was expected to maintain this status quo—to reaffirm the traditional family—as a central element within an oppositional Chicano politics.

Despite its location within mass media, *Ahora!* worked within the terms of the Plan, since the public affairs series used broadcast television to reach the homes of Chicano families just after dinner, informing that audience about political events, but also cultivating cultural and historical awareness that was, in the words of the Plan, both "appealing" and "revolutionary." As an example of prime-time access programming, *Ahora!* was situated between the six o'clock news and prime-time entertainment, drawing upon both forms of television discourse, but serving a specific segment of the station's market. Thus, although ratings were generally above average for its time slot, the viewership was constituted along the lines of local and ethnic needs (what would now be called narrowcasting). As such, this type of show was at odds with commercial television, which sold advertising time based on reaching a percentage of a broadcast audience. This narrowcasting strategy would typify minority public affairs series throughout the 1970s until deregulation brought an end to prime-time access, shifting the few remaining shows to Sunday mornings.

When Ford Foundation support ended in 1970, Treviño had to apply activist strategies within the station in order to secure another show that addressed the concerns of the Chicano community. He organized the fifteen to twenty "Spanish surnamed" employees of the station—janitors, secretaries, and various technicians— "to sign a petition that said, unless the Chicano community had a weekly television show, we were all going to resign en masse.... and that was the birth of *Acción Chicano* [*sic*]."[24] By the time *Acción Chicano* first aired in 1972, Treviño had decided that "the problem with our programming was that it kept being ghettoized and relegated to the corner." His response was to reproduce the "high production values" of the station's other shows, even though this meant that he had to stick to a talk-show or performance format given the limited budgets (about fifteen hundred dollars per week/episode). Even with these limitations, however, Treviño and other Chicano filmmakers could draw upon various strategies in order to introduce political commentary, and to find alternative ways to "run the whole spectrum of programming."[25]

One effective strategy used by Treviño and others was to speak from behind the mask of a "folk" ethnicity, in particular through *teatro* performances that included variations on the folk music of the Mexican Revolution. In this manner, the "folkloric" appearances satisfied station managers who might otherwise have been concerned

Chicano Poets Ricardo Sanchez *(left)* and Alurista *(right)*, backed up by music from the Con Safos music group, are featured on an episode of *Acción Chicano.* The weekly public and cultural affairs series was broadcast over KCET, Los Angeles from 1972 to 1974. Series was executive produced and hosted by Jesús Treviño; associate producers were Rosamaria Marquez and Antonio Parra. (Photo courtesy of Jesús Salvador Treviño.)

about the unsubtitled Spanish. In one episode of *Acción Chicano,* Treviño featured a performance by Los Mascarones (The Masquers), a Mexican *teatro* group similar in style and politics to El Teatro Campesino. The episode was sent to PBS for national release, and, "they thought this was a nice folkloric kind of stuff . . . and went along with it." It was during the national airing that PBS discovered the content of the Spanish-language episode (with no subtitles), since numerous Cuban exiles in Miami called in to protest. The Los Mascarones performance ends with the theme song of the Cuban Revolution, with added lines that place the civil rights struggles of Chicanos, Puerto Ricans, and Blacks within its radical framework.[26] In the 1970s, many of the Chicano and Latino television series and specials would use Spanish as a way to communicate ideas and information that might have been censored in English.[27] Other examples of *teatro*-based programs that relied on Spanish-language dialogue and code switching, included *Los Vendidos: The Sellouts* (1972), *Guadalupe* (1976), and *El Corrido* (1976).

Host Jesús Treviño interviews three Chicano legislators on an episode of *Acción Chicano*. (Photo courtesy of Jesús Treviño.)

Using *Acción Chicano* as a base from which to pool resources and expand his audience, Treviño was also able to produce some of the first film documentaries. "I would tape two or three shows and make them all talk shows so that I could take that budget and invest it in film stock." These films included *La Raza Unida* (1972), *Yo Soy Chicano* (1972), *Carnalitos* (1973), and *Somos Uno* (1973). Treviño also used these films as a way to train other Chicano filmmakers, such as Bobby Páramo, who coproduced *Carnalitos*.[28] Finally, in a move that would have national repercussions, in 1972 *Acción Chicano* pooled resources with a new Puerto Rican series in New York City, *Realidades*, wherein the two shows traded five episodes each for local rebroadcast. This became a first step in the development of pan-Latino advocacy and organization at the national level.

"Our Own Institutions"

In 1975, *Realidades* became the first national Latino television series, and subsequently commissioned numerous Chicano films, including Severo Perez's *Cristal* (1975), Susan Racho's *Garment Workers* (1975), José Luis Ruiz's *Guadalupe* (1976), Bobby Páramo's *Salud and the Latino* (1976), Ricardo Soto's *Cosecha* (1976), *Migra* (1976), and *Al Otro Paso* (1976), and Adolfo Vargas's *Una Nación Bilingüe* (1977). The program stood in contrast to the earlier occasional national feeds of local material, and provided a pan-Latino forum for Chicano and Puerto Rican films. Several works dealt with national Latino issues, with footage shot on both coasts and in the Midwest: *Garment Workers,* Jay Ojeda's *De Colores* (1975), *Salud and the Latino*. *Realidades* was created in 1972, when members of the Puerto Rican Education and Action Media Council took over the studio of PBS affiliate WNET-TV (New York) during the station's pledge drive. In its first two years, the series was similar to the concurrent *Acción Chicano* (also created through protest), with which it exchanged programs.[29] In 1974, the Corporation for Public Broadcasting (CPB) awarded *Realidades* sixty thousand dollars to produce a one-hour pilot for national broadcast. In its two years as a national series, *Realidades* received $553,687 from the CPB, and produced twenty-three half-hour programs. The monies from CPB represented less than 3 percent of the CPB total production budget; after the series ended, that level dropped to 1 percent for Latino projects.[30]

Despite its short-lived success, *Realidades* revealed the need for a national pan-Latino organization in order to secure greater continuity of reforms, while it also provided a national network of producers associated with the series. With the waning of public protests in the early 1970s, Chicano/Latino filmmakers began to develop national institutions within the industry. These included the Latino Consortium (since 1974; now, National Latino Communications Center), which syndicates Latino-themed and -produced works on public television; the Chicano Film Festival in San Antonio, Texas (since 1975; now, CineFestival), which provides a national forum for public exhibition, as both a community-based event and a professional one; and the National Latino Media Coalition (1975–80), formed by Humberto Cintrón, executive producer of *Realidades,* which lobbied for federal funding. Echoing "El Plan Espiritual de Aztlán," Treviño identified these various efforts as an attempt to create "our own institutions."[31] These were, however, institutions that attempted to speak on behalf of both the community and media professionals from within the mass media, rather than institutions whose domain was that of the community itself. In contrast to *Ahora!* and other eclectic-format series whose primary audience was the Chicano community, these "institutions" worked at the crossroads of a Chicano/Latino audience and a national one, primarily within the domain of educational programming rather than that of entertainment. Overall these efforts represented a significant shift from social protest strategies to professional advocacy within the industry and the independent sector. But, as Treviño and other filmmakers have noted, Hollywood studios and television networks remained intransigent in the face of these internal pressures.[32]

Locating Chicano Cinema

The move to professionalism, however, did not occur in a political vacuum; rather, despite limited success with studios and networks, it represented a significant maneuver within a larger strategy to locate Chicano culture. Throughout the 1960s and 1970s, contacts with Latin America via postrevolutionary Cuba provided an essential framework for the development of the movement's radical politics as well as its reformist achievements. Even before the Chicano movement, in 1964, Luis Valdez traveled to Cuba as a member of a Progressive Labor Party delegation. Valdez, like many Chicano student activists, had been involved in reformist efforts directed at the Democratic Party, such as the Mexican American Political Association (MAPA), and had been active in the "Viva Kennedy!" clubs. Upon his return from Cuba, however, Valdez coauthored one of the first radical student manifestos, "Venceremos! Mexican American Statement on Travel to Cuba," which anchored its rejection of reformist politics in a pan-American solidarity.[33] Chicano political discourse continued to look to Mexico, Cuba, and, more generally, the "Bronze Continent" as the necessary backdrop of its efforts to imagine an ethnic community within the political, socioeconomic, and legal structures of the United States. This "imagined" location in the Americas became the context for local political action as well as professional reform within the U.S. film and television industries.

Perhaps the most lasting impact has been the result of Treviño's involvement with New Latin American Cinema. In 1974, Treviño was recruited into the Cuban-sponsored Comité de Cineastas de América Latina (Latin American Filmmakers Committee), an international committee of a dozen filmmakers committed to the advancement of New Latin American Cinema. The committee met six times between 1974

and 1978, and worked toward the organization of the Annual Festival of New Latin American Cinema, which premiered in December
1979 in Havana, Cuba. At its sixth meeting (in Havana, July 12–17,
1978), the committee issued a declaration about the festival, and, in
the second paragraph, spelled out the relationship of the Chicano
filmmakers to New Latin American Cinema:

> We also declare our solidarity with the struggle of Chicano cinema, the
> cultural manifestation of a community that combats the oppression
> and discrimination within the United States in order to affirm its Latin
> American roots. This reality remains almost or entirely unknown by
> most of our people, or reaches them through the distortions of the im-
> perialist news media. Yet today the Chicano community has its own
> filmmakers and films, and demands of us the commitment to strengthen
> the cultural-historical ties that join us together, by contributing to the
> dissemination of their films, their experiences, and their struggles.[34]

Treviño and the Chicano Cinema Coalition led a delegation of Chicano filmmakers and media advocates to the first festival. As he explains, "It was a real eye-opener experience for a lot of Chicanos
that went, because for the first time they were seeing a lot of Latin
American, not just Cuban, cinema."[35] Although the experience seemed
to confirm the predictions of the earlier film manifestos, the social context for racial and radical politics in the United States had changed
quite a bit since the heyday of the Chicano movement and New Latin
American Cinema. Nonetheless, the contacts with Cuba and Latin
America did foster an increased international political perspective in
the 1980s, although it is difficult to separate this from the filmmakers' increased awareness of and attention to the international film
market and festival circuit.[36] In this respect, the festival served an important symbolic role in doubling the "location" of Chicano cinema,
making it into a movement that was at once reformist and revolutionary. But rather than constitute a contradiction, this dual location
provided Chicano filmmakers with an effective political strategy within
the United States. Clearly, many of the early successful reforms came
about as a result of shifting the center leftward during public protests
and press statements, providing filmmakers with a vantage point from
which to negotiate.

By the late 1970s, this strategy rang hollow after national and international "movement" politics came to a violent end. Chicano filmmakers would, for the most part, shift to a politics of "professional-

ism" within the industry and the independent sector. Still, "Chicano cinema" persists as a quasi-national category within international film festivals in Latin America and Europe, and is generally tied to a "minority" cultural politics.[37] Since the late 1970s, Chicano filmmakers have continued to articulate and develop connections to New Latin American Cinema as well as Spanish-language cinema in general. These filmmakers also initiated various efforts to integrate both Hollywood and the independent sector in order to produce and distribute Chicano-themed feature films and documentaries. Thus, if Treviño and others located "Chicano cinema" within both New Latin American Cinema and Hollywood, it was as the functional synthesis of ostensible contradictions, one that allowed the practice to follow upon the idea and the possibilities it created.

What stands outside these efforts to walk the line between reform and revolution—the bipolar terms of the Chicano movement—was the simultaneous emergence of a Chicano avant-garde in the mid-1960s and early 1970s, one split between the modernist aesthetics of a personal, visionary cinema and the postmodern parody of an alienated television generation.[38] Taking this work into account challenges the prevailing history of Chicano cinema with its equivalence between body, politics, and aesthetics as well as its ambivalence about institutional location. Indeed, *I Am Joaquin* is not the "first" Chicano film in the strict sense of the word, since there are at least two earlier avant-garde films: Ernie Palomino's *My Trip in a '52 Ford* (1966), also a film poem, but one that follows in the tradition of Beat counterculture rather than the neo-indigenist *floricanto* (Chicano poetry); and Severo Perez's *Mozo: An Introduction into the Duality of Orbital Indecision* (1968), a pot-induced send-up of the trance film that circulated as part of the Texas Underground National Tour. Most filmmakers and critics, however, continue to identify *I Am Joaquin* as the "first" Chicano film, in the same manner that poets and literature scholars identify Gonzales's "I Am Joaquin" as the "first" Chicano poem: both are seen as the first articulations of a political, historical, and poetic consciousness about the "Chicano experience." Unlike the experimental films with their interracial, cross-cultural, and transcendental concerns, *I Am Joaquin* contributed to the idea of a "Chicano cinema" that operated within clearly marked borders (for community, for identity) that were defined by the exigencies of the Chicano civil rights movement. Like Gonzales's poem, which recontained its

ambivalence within stable bipolar terms, Chicano cinema both juxtaposed and straddled two locations: America and América. Again,
this was not so much a matter of an either/or choice (even though it
was presented as such), but rather an attempt to define tightly coupled oppositional terms—nationalism and assimilation; revolution
and reform—so that the one would inevitably produce the other.
Without a doubt, such a strategy put Chicano cinema on the map in
both a literal and a figurative sense, constructing an alternative to
Hollywood. But it was an alternative in both senses of the word,
something different from Hollywood, yet something that also aspired
to take its place.

Notes

1. Of the filmmakers, Jesús Salvador Treviño has been the most prolific
and influential, publishing in Europe and the Americas, and in some ways
setting the terms for subsequent scholarship. See, for example, Treviño's articles "Cinéma Chicano aux Etats-Unis," in Les Cinémas de l'Amérique La-
tine, ed. Guy Hennebelle and Alfonso Gumucio-Dagron (Paris: Nouvelles
Editions Pierre Lherminier, 1981), 493–99; "Chicano Cinema," New Scholar
8 (1982): 167–80; and "El desarrollo del cine chicano," in Hojas de cine:
testimonios y documentos del nuevo cine latinoamericano (México: Fun-
dación del nuevo cine latinoamericano, 1986), n.p. Books on Chicano cinema include Gary D. Keller, ed., Chicano Cinema: Research, Reviews, and
Resources (Binghamton, N.Y.: Bilingual Review/Press, 1985); Chon A. Noriega, ed., Chicanos and Film: Representation and Resistance (Minneapolis:
University of Minnesota Press, 1992); Rosa Linda Fregoso, The Bronze Screen:
Chicana and Chicano Film Culture (Minneapolis: University of Minnesota
Press, 1993); and Gary D. Keller, Hispanics and United States Film: An Overview and Handbook (Tempe, Ariz.: Bilingual Press, 1994).
2. I draw upon Mario Barrera's insightful analysis of the historical role
of egalitarian (integrationist) and communitarian (cultural nationalist) goals
in the Mexican-origin community. See Mario Barrera, Beyond Aztlán: Ethnic Autonomy in Comparative Perspective (Notre Dame, Ind.: University of
Notre Dame Press, 1988), chapters 1–6.
3. Coco Fusco, "Fantasies of Oppositionality: Reflections on Recent Conferences in Boston and New York," Screen 29 (autumn 1988): 80–93; and "Ethnicity, Politics and Poetics: Latinos and Media Art," in Illuminating Video:
An Essential Guide to Video Art, ed. Doug Hall and Sally Jo Fifer (New York:
Aperture/BAVC, 1990), 304–16.
4. Chon A. Noriega, "Between a Weapon and a Formula: Chicano Cinema and Its Contexts," in Noriega, ed., Chicanos and Film, 141–67.
5. See Carlos Muñoz Jr., Youth, Identity, Power: The Chicano Movement
(New York: Verso, 1989).

6. The "Plan of Delano" is reprinted in Armando B. Rendon, *Chicano Manifesto* (New York: Macmillan, 1971), 327–30. Rendon reprints the "Plan of Delano" with three other manifestos under the appendix title "Four Declarations of Independence."

7. As I discuss later, this can be seen in the use of specific phrases as well as rhetorical strategies. The "Plan Espiritual de Aztlán" is reprinted in Rudolfo A. Anaya and Francisco Lomelí, eds., *Aztlán: Essays on the Chicano Homeland* (Albuquerque, N.M.: Academia/El Norte Publications, 1989), 1–6. The "Plan de Santa Barbara" is reprinted in Muñoz, *Youth, Identity, Power,* 191–202. Three film manifestos from the 1970s are reprinted in Noriega, ed., *Chicanos and Film,* 275–307.

8. The charges against the "L.A. Thirteen" were dismissed as unconstitutional after two years of appeals (Rodolfo Acuña, *Occupied America: A History of Chicanos,* 3d ed. [New York: HarperCollins, 1988], 338).

9. *I Am Joaquin* was later annotated and reissued by Bantam Books in 1972. Film and poem appear in Spanish and English versions.

10. "I/WE SHALL ENDURE" appears in capital letters in both texts.

11. See Tomás Ybarra-Frausto, "The Chicano Movement and the Emergence of a Chicano Poetic Consciousness," *New Scholar* 6 (1977): 81–109.

12. Luis Valdez, "Notes on Chicano Theater" (1970), in *Luis Valdez—Early Works* (Houston: Arte Público Press, 1990), 8.

13. "El Plan Espiritual de Aztlán," in Anaya and Lomelí, eds., *Aztlán,* 2. See also Gonzales, "Chicano Nationalism: The Key to Unity for la Raza," *Militant,* March 30, 1970.

14. The production dates cited for the film range from 1967 to 1970. In his article "Cinéma Chicano aux Etats-Unis," Treviño—based on interviews with the Valdez brothers—states that the film was shot and recorded "[o]n a hot summer evening in 1967," the same year the poem was written. The film itself has a 1969 copyright, which may indicate that the film was shown before it was copyrighted, or that it took over a year to edit the film.

15. See Rolando Hinojosa's comments on the changes made in the film in order to make it more commercial (Hinojosa, "*I Am Joaquin*: Relationships between the Text and the Film," in Keller, ed., *Chicano Cinema,* 142–45). The United Farm Workers Service Center continued to document events on film, and produced at least two Spanish-language documentaries for internal use: *Nosotros Venceremos* (1971; *We Will Overcome*), which uses photographic stills to relate UFW struggles and goals; and *Sí, se puede* (1973; *Yes, We Can*), on César Chávez's hunger strike in Arizona.

16. Jesús Salvador Treviño, "Chicano Cinema Overview," *Areito* 37 (1984): 40.

17. Personal interview with Treviño, May 28, 1991.

18. Ibid.

19. Ibid.

20. Treviño, "Chicano Cinema": 170–71; and Harry Gamboa Jr., "Silver Screening the Barrio," *Equal Opportunity Forum* 6.1 (November 1978): 6–7.

21. Personal interview with Treviño, May 28, 1991.

22. Ibid.

23. An unauthorized reprint appears in Cine-Aztlán, "The Treviño/Ahora Survey: A Historical Profile of the Chicano and Latino in Hollywood Film Productions," in *La Raza Film Bibliography* (Santa Barbara, Calif.: Cine-Aztlán, 1974), 9–16.

24. Personal interview with Treviño, May 28, 1991. In Spanish, adjectives usually conform to the gender of the noun. Thus, the correct title would be *Acción Chicana*. Treviño, however, "purposely changed it to *Chicano*," since "I basically, at that time, thought that *Chicana* would read that it was a show only for women, and I wanted to make it clear that this was for the whole community." That there would have been such confusion owes more to the decreased Spanish-language maintenance within the Chicano generation than to sexism. In fact, Treviño himself was not fluent in Spanish at the time.

25. Ibid.

26. Ibid.

27. In Lubbock, Texas, for example, the Spanish-language series *Aztlán* (1976–79), produced by Hector Galan, "got away with murder, because the station didn't understand" (statement by Hector Galan during the roundtable "In the Public Eye: A Dialogue on Chicano Media Arts," Dialogues in Movement: A Chicano Media Arts Retrospective, San Antonio, Texas, July 13, 1991).

28. Bobby Páramo, "*Cerco Blanco, The Balloon Man*, and *Fighting City Hall*: On Being a Chicano Filmmaker," *Metamorfosis* 3.2 (1980–81): 77–82.

29. José García Torres, "José García Torres & *Realidades*," interview by Aurora Flores and Lillian Jiménez, *Centro Bulletin* 2.8 (spring 1990): 30–43.

30. "Pensamientos: Latinos and CPB," *Chicano Cinema Newsletter* 1.6 (August 1979): 2–3, 2.

31. Quoted in Antonio José Guernica, "Chicano Production Companies: Projecting Reality, Opening the Doors," *Agenda: A Journal of Hispanic Issues* 8.1 (January–February 1978): 12–15, 13.

32. Jesús Salvador Treviño, "Lights, Camera, Action," *Hispanic* (August 1992): 76.

33. Luis Valdez and Roberto Rubalcava, reprinted in Luis Valdez and Stan Steiner, eds., *Aztlán: An Anthology of Mexican American Literature* (New York: Alfred A. Knopf, 1972): 215–16.

34. "Declaración del Comité de Cineastas de América Latina," *Cine Cubano* 8.3 (1977–78): 45–46; translation mine. The declaration was translated by Ralph Cook and reprinted in *Cineaste* 9.1 (fall 1978): 54. In Cook's version, he inserts references to the Chicano movement. The original text, however, refers to the Chicano "community," and not the "movement," whose militant phase had already come to an end.

35. Personal interview with Treviño, May 28, 1991.

36. See, for example, David Rosen's chapter on *The Ballad of Gregorio Cortez* in *Off-Hollywood: The Making and Marketing of Independent Films* (New York: Grove Weidenfeld, 1990), 1–22.

37. See my forthcoming article, "On Curating," *Wide Angle* 17.1–4.

38. These two tendencies are exemplified by the work of Willie Varela and Harry Gamboa Jr., respectively. See Chon A. Noriega, "Willie Varela," *New American Film and Video Series 72*, program note (New York: Whitney Museum of American Art, 1994); and the section on Gamboa in my article "Talking Heads, Body Politic: The Plural Self of Chicano Video," in *Resolutions: Contemporary Video Practices*, ed. Michael Renov and Erika Suderburg (Minneapolis: University of Minnesota Press, in press). For the filmmakers' own accounts, see Gamboa, "Past Imperfecto," *Jump Cut* 39 (June 1994): 93–95, and Varela, "Chicano Personal Cinema," *Jump Cut* 39 (June 1994): 96–99.

Moving from the Margin to the Center: Puerto Rican Cinema in New York

Lillian Jiménez

Without a doubt, in order to stand on our own two feet Puerto Ricans of all generations must begin by affirming our own history. It is as if we are saying—we have roots, therefore we are!

Bernardo Vega[1]

For many Puerto Rican film- and videomakers, picking up the camera was equivalent to "picking up the gun" in defense of civil and human rights in the United States after the civil rights movement. The beginning of this "coming to self," as bell hooks describes it, was a burning desire to expose the terrible conditions under which Puerto Ricans of this generation had been raised; challenge the assumptions under which these conditions thrived; and re-create the societal institutions that had engendered them. In this war, *images* were a potent and vital weapon. Through popular culture, distorted images of spitfires and Latin lovers (oversexed and irresponsible), brutish farmworkers (substandard intelligence), *bandidos* (untrustworthy), petty tyrants, welfare recipients, or drug addicts (undisciplined children) had burned deep into the collective consciousness of Puerto Ricans and the broader society. In effect, the dominant ideology and its cultural machinery indicted Puerto Ricans as responsible for their own conditions. In this paradigm, American institutional benevolence was necessary in order to protect Latinos from themselves. In the late sixties and early seventies, a new generation of Puerto Ricans responded to these assumptions with "Fuego, fuego, fuego ... los yanquis quieren fuego" (Fire, fire, fire, the Yankees want fire). In Newsreel's *El Pueblo Se Levanta* (1972), Iris Morales, a member of the Young Lords Party, a Puerto Rican political activist organization, says, "I always thought it was my parents' fault; that my parents were the ones who had made this oppression; that they had made everything so dirty ... but then I started thinking."[2] Puerto Ricans took up the struggle to discover their history, and to expose, challenge, and change their reality. Images were key in this life-and-death struggle.

Although it has not been widely known, the first Puerto Rican migrants to the United States (during and after World War II) were deeply concerned with their depiction in the media. By creating a wide network of civic, cultural, and political organizations, these *pioneros* organized against all forms of discrimination, including media stereotypes. In 1940, *Scribner's Commentator* ran an article entitled "Welcome Paupers and Crime: Puerto Rico's Shocking Gift to the U.S.," which said "all Puerto Ricans were totally lacking in moral values, which is why none of them seemed to mind wallowing in the most abject moral degradation." While forty Puerto Rican organizations, including the Asociación de Escritores y Periodistas Puertorriqueños,[3] organized against this article, seven years later the *World Telegram* ran a series of equally vitriolic articles. These, too, were met with a vociferous demonstration that stretched for several blocks.[4]

An instrumental component of this resistance was the hometown clubs that Puerto Rican immigrants formed in New York. These clubs celebrated common roots and created a necessary support system and vital network for housing, jobs, moral support, and cultural maintenance. Here, members could speak their own language and associate freely with Puerto Ricans of different classes and "colors" who shared a similar economic and social status. Contrary to commonly held beliefs, Puerto Ricans did not passively acquiesce to exploitative conditions in these early years. There were numerous left-leaning and mainstream political organizations composed of working-class *puertorriqueños* that fought injustice. In addition, many Puerto Ricans were active in union organizing and international solidarity work, especially with Nicaragua and the Republicans during the Spanish Civil War.

Although thousands of Puerto Ricans migrated to the United States prior to World War II, it was not until the advent of intensive industrialization of Puerto Rico through Operation Bootstrap policies (late 1940s to mid-1950s) that hundreds of thousands of Puerto Ricans migrated to the United States in search of employment. Settling in large metropolitan areas on the East Coast like New York and cities in New Jersey and Connecticut, they occupied low-income housing readily available as Irish, Jewish, and Italian immigrants moved up the economic ladder and away to the outer boroughs and suburbs. Unlike other immigrants, Puerto Ricans were citizens and anticipated

benefits from that legal status. Racially mixed, they were more toler-
ant of behavior and relationships deemed inappropriate in race-con-
scious United States. Confronted by abject discrimination in spite of
their citizenship and because of their racial mixture, they developed
a survival strategy that relied on the existing infrastructure of hometown clubs, civic associations, and political clubs. To achieve educational and political objectives, they created new organizations like
the Puerto Rican Forum and Aspira of America.

Although these first generations of migrants paved the way through
internal and external forms of resistance, their survival strategies were
varied and fraught with contradictions. Years of ideological and political domination by Spain and then the United States had instilled
the culture with a deep-rooted sense of nationalism coupled with political ambivalence. Some quickly seized the opportunity to remake
themselves in the model of the assimilated "American" citizen.

The third generation of Puerto Ricans, who reached their late teens
during the volatile and empowering civil rights movement, affirmed
their cultural and political identity with the emergence of new community and political organizations in New York. Raised on television,
propelled by ideas of empowerment and an unremitting rage against
a social order that denied their existence, they repudiated the "com-
placent" and "accommodationist" strategies employed by mainstream
Puerto Rican political leaders of the day. Educated in American schools,
many young Puerto Ricans had served as intermediaries for their
families with educational, health, and social-service agencies. Having
weathered the full fury of institutional racism, accommodation as
such was the last strategy they wished to employ. Asserting their presence in militant and forceful terms, theirs was the strategy of direct
confrontation. The Young Lords, the Puerto Rican Student Union, the
Movimiento Pro Independencia (the precursor of the Puerto Rican
Socialist Party), El Comité-M.I.N.P., Resistencia Puertorriqueña, and
El Pueblo del Vladic in the Lower East Side, just to name a few, were
engaged in re-creating the Puerto Rican community, using as role
models Puerto Rican labor figures like Luisa Capetilla and Juana
Colón; nationalist leaders like Don Pedro Albizu Campos and Lolita
Lebrón; and international leaders like Che Guevara. Involved in local,
national, and international issues, they galvanized the Puerto Rican
community by traveling to socialist countries, taking up the issue of
Puerto Rican independence, creating support committees for nation-

alist leaders imprisoned since the early 1950s, and worked closely with similar organizations within the Black, Asian, and white communities. This generation picked up the camera in spite of and in defense of the ones they loved.

Cultural revitalization based on nationalism was an integral component of this political ferment and awakening. As "cultural workers," artists of all disciplines collaborated to create a new image of Puerto Ricans. Utilizing the visual arts, Taller Boricua created enduring posters for the arts and political movements of the late 1960s and early 1970s. Through poetry, Pedro Pietri and Sandra María Estévez created a new voice for a young generation of defiant Puerto Ricans. A distinct Puerto Rican identity, tied to the island, rooted in the New York experience, and shaped by the anti-imperialist ideology of the period, had emerged. Yet, there were no film and video images produced by Puerto Ricans that represented the history, culture, and daily reality of the majority of Puerto Ricans.

To fill this void, *Realidades,* a local series on public broadcast station WNET/Channel 13, was created through community pressure. In 1972, community activists Gilberto Gerena-Valentín, Esperanza Martel, Diana Caballero, Julio Rodríguez, and others formed the Puerto Rican Education and Action Media Council to protest negative depictions of Puerto Ricans and advocate increased employment of Puerto Ricans within the industry. Joined by filmmaker José García, they successfully pressured WNET — by taking over the studio during an evening pledge drive — to establish *Realidades* with discretionary station money. Humberto Cintrón, a community activist, became executive producer. José García, who had established several community film workshops throughout the country (including Appalshop in Appalachia) for the National Endowment for the Arts, became producer. The series provided the focus and center for Puerto Rican involvement in the broadcast industry and later in the independent film and video field. Retaining its local focus for two years, several important cultural and public affairs documentaries were produced and acquired, including *Angelitos Negros,* an in-studio dance piece about a *baquiné,* the African-based burial ritual of a young child; *Towards a Collective Expression,* the first documentary by Marcos Dimas about the philosophy and work of Taller Boricua, the visual arts group he cofounded; and *Los Nacionalistas,* a documentary that reclaimed the history of Don Pedro Albizu Campos and the Nationalist Party of

Puerto Rico. An important developmental leap was made when programming exchanges with KMEX, a local public broadcast station in Los Angeles, elevated *Realidades* to national prominence. Chicano filmmaker Jesús Treviño's important *Yo Soy Chicano,* about the political consciousness of the Chicano movement, was the first film exchanged and it opened a dialogue between Puerto Ricans and Chicanos. This dialogue and working relationship with Chicano directors in the West and Southwest was instrumental in the formation of the National Latino Media Coalition, which legally challenged the broadcast industry nationally. In 1974, the Corporation for Public Broadcasting funded *Realidades* as a national series and Lou de Lemos, a Dominican with experience in commercial media, took over as series producer.

During this period, *Realidades* served as one of the principal creative magnets within the Puerto Rican community, attracting artists from different disciplines to collaborate and brainstorm on a myriad of projects. Furthermore, contact was made with Sandino Films, a collective of filmmakers in Puerto Rico, resulting in José García's *Julia de Burgos,* a film about the life and death of revolutionary poet Julia de Burgos. Writers, visual artists, poets, and film- and videomakers like Diego Echevarria, working at Channel 13 on another show, and Diego de La Texera, cofounder of Sandino Films in Puerto Rico, gravitated to the series as a creative wellspring. However, a precarious funding base, uneven progamming schedule, and internal problems caused the *Realidades* series to end in 1975. Initiated by a core group of activists and makers with varying levels of skill and experience in response to the exclusionary practices of the media industry, *Realidades* launched the careers of many producers still working within the broadcast, advertising, and independent film industries: Raquel Ortiz, independent producer, formerly executive producer of public affairs at WGBH in Boston; Larry Varas, independent producer, formerly with CBS in New York; Livia Pérez, independent producer; Felipe Borerro, sound recordist; Eulogio Ortiz, assistant director with the *MacNeil/Lehrer News Hour,* WNET, New York; Mercedes Sabio, program manager, WOSU, Athens, Ohio; and Lou de Lemos, Children's Television Workshop, New York.

As a consequence of the *Realidades* series and the advocacy and litigation waged by the National Latino Media Coalition against the stations, José Rivera, the coalition's attorney, was the first and only Puerto Rican named to the board of directors of the Corporation for Public Broadcasting in the late 1970s. In addition, several Latino-based public affairs shows were spawned at commercial stations—many of which are still in place today, such as NBC's *Visiones* and ABC's *Imágenes Latinas*.

The Documentarians: The Media Guerrillas

Many film- and videomakers chose to remain independent of the corporate media structures. The earliest wave of Puerto Rican filmmaking concentrated on the documentary format because of its relative low cost, accessibility, and efficacy in representing the external conditions in which the majority of Puerto Ricans lived. Newsreel, an alternative media organization patterned after the Film and Photo League of the 1930s, espoused the theory that anyone could "pick up the camera and shoot" to create films that empowered people. Generally influenced by the democratic underpinnings of the media movement, a small cadre of Puerto Rican documentarians slowly emerged. Profiles of three Puerto Rican documentarians illustrate the motivation and problems faced by these independent producers.

Carlos de Jesús started out as a photographer until German television asked him to direct a film on housing in New York in the early 1970s. This collaboration produced his first film, *The Devil Is a Condition* (1972), a lyrical ode to Latinos and Blacks fighting to improve their housing conditions throughout the city. Made with a cache of liberated film, a borrowed camera, editing facilities, and lab processing provided by German television, and an otherwise no-money budget, it was presented at the Whitney Museum and garnered awards at festivals in Paris. Lacking personal resources and thereby requiring an institutional base, he helped found *Imágenes* at New Jersey Public Television and went on to make *The Picnic* (1976), a celebration of cultural values by Puerto Rican inmates and their families in a New Jersey prison. He continued to work in Latino series within public broadcasting throughout the country because the infrastructure for independent film was in a nascent stage. He currently teaches at New York University, and continues to work in photography and video.

On the other hand, **Beni Matías** received formal training in film production at La Escuela Oficial de Cinematografía in Madrid, Spain. On her return to the United States, she worked at Young Filmmakers Foundation, a film resource center on the Lower East Side that provided equipment access to independent filmmakers. Lacking experience and knowledge about funding for film, she collaborated with Marci Reaven, a New York University student who shared her values and vision about documentary film as a tool for social change. They made *In the Heart of Loisaida* (1979), a black-and-white documentary about early housing takeovers on New York's Lower East Side by Latino tenants. It was made essentially through in-kind contributions of equipment and labor and a small grant from Adopt-A-Building, a not-for-profit housing organization. On the basis of the first film, she and copartner Marci Reavens received governmental support to produce *Through Young People's Eyes* (1981), a color documentary about low-income Black and Latino children in Philadelphia.

Although this film was a significant breakthrough for Matías because she now had greater access to resources, she nonetheless chose a "holistic" approach to independent film by working with other makers and in other areas of the field. She worked as a sound recordist, associate producer, and production assistant to survive and refine her skills. Continuing production, she codirected (with Billy Sarokin) *Housing Court* (1984), a documentary that explored the complex and arcane machinations of the Bronx Housing Court, on a New York State Council on the Arts grant and Sarokin's equipment. By teaming up with people who had access to equipment and common interests, she pragmatically solved the persistent equipment problems of independent producers. In addition to production work, she worked with Women Make Movies' *Punto de Vista Latina,* an exhibition presentation of Latin American women's films in Latino communities throughout New York, and coedited a catalogue on Third World media. Seeking a more stable creative outlet, she secured a job at WNET/Channel 13 on the *Metroline* series as an associate producer and worked her way up to producer. Beni later worked as the first senior producer of the Independent Television Service (ITVS), based in Minneapolis. She is now the executive director of a not-for-profit organization in Minnesota, and has recently completed a documentary on a Native American artist for KTCA in Saint Paul.

Pedro Rivera, a history student from San Juan, Puerto Rico, was referred by members of Sandino Films in Puerto Rico to Jaime Barrios, a Chilean filmmaker and cofounder of Young Filmmakers Foundation. With his interest in history, education, and film, he began teaching filmmaking to Latino children at Young Filmmakers Foundation, now Film/Video Arts. There he met his longtime collaborator, Susan Zeig, and together with Jaime Barrios and the Centro de Estudios Puertorriqueños (Hunter College) embarked on the production of a historical compilation film about the impact of the Operation Bootstrap industrialization program on Puerto Rico, *Manos a la Obra* (1985). Continuing his collaboration with the Centro and Zeig, he completed *Plena Is Work, Plena Is Song* (1989), a documentary about working-class Puerto Rican culture expressed through the African-based music and singing of *plena*. Upon completion of that film, he taught in the public school system and began work on a series of videotapes about Puerto Rican community life in New York and a film on the economic status of Latinos. He is now completing a Ph.D. in cultural studies.

Scene from Pedro Rivera's *Manos a la Obra*. (Photo courtesy of the Cinema Guild.)

In addition to these three documentarians who, without personal financial resources and experience, made their mark on Puerto Rican film and video on the East Coast, there were a number of other makers on the scene dealing with issues of labor organizing, Latino music, and the political status of the island: *What Could You Do with a Nickel* (1981), a documentary film about Black and Latino domestic workers forming a union in the South Bronx, was coproduced by the author of this essay; Carlos Ortiz completed *Machito: A Latin Jazz Legacy* (1986), a documentary film about Frank "Machito" Grillo, the Cuban Latin jazz composer and bandleader; Zydnia Nazario, an architect by profession, directed *The Battle of Vieques* (1986), a documentary about naval maneuvers on the island of Vieques off the coast of Puerto Rico, and is currently fund-raising for *Linking Islands,* a documentary film about the evolution and intersection of New York-based Puerto Rican art and politics. One of the few formally trained filmmakers of this era, Vicente Juarbe, directed *Puerto Rico: Our Right to Decide* (1984), a documentary film on the political status of Puerto Rico, for the Methodist Church. He worked in commerical television in Philadelphia and currently resides in Puerto Rico, where he is an active member of the film and video community.

These documentarians were committed to illustrating the history, social issues, and culture of Puerto Ricans so long ignored by the dominant social institutions. They attempted to find a form for representing the complex survival strategies developed by Puerto Ricans in the midst of abject racism and poverty. Although some of these films suffered from low production values—as people struggled with the language of the form, limited funding, and lack of experience—they more than made up for their limitations by their passionate quest for validating images. Possessed with an insider's knowledge of the culture and an unswerving need to express themselves, they created celluloid images that were more reflective of the multiple experiences of Puerto Ricans in the United States and Puerto Rico. Their overriding contribution was to defy conventional assumptions and assert that Puerto Ricans should and could occupy the center of cinematic discourse. Further, they privileged poor people relegated to the margins of society with validating images that reflected the variety of implicit and explicit responses to oppression. Some subjects internalized their oppression, others fought against it, and yet others, determined to survive, got around it. These multifaceted responses to oppression gave a name and face to the invisible "other." The women in *In the Heart of Loisaida,* poor and uneducated, found their "voice" as community heroes for thousands to "see."

The Storytellers

The documentary form had its advantages, but it also had its limitations. A maker could only work with the material retrieved from the field — if subjects proved inarticulate about an issue, then they were forced to rely on narration, as a voice of authority. Hence, most of the aforementioned films utilized narration to a greater or lesser degree. Eschewing the ebb and flow of the interview and talking heads format, a small group of makers chose the narrative form to visualize their stories about Puerto Rican experiences. These films, for the most part, expressed the subtle and complex fabric of the internalization of racism. For example, Pablo Figueroa directed his first narrative piece for NBC in 1974 about the dilemma of a fifteen-year-old girl who is compelled to take the reigns of the family. *We, Together* presented the interweaving nature of one family, the centrality of family life in the Puerto Rican culture and its dissolution in the face of economic and psychological hardship. Deciding to work outside the television format, with its inherent formulaic limitations, Figueroa embarked on independently making *Cristina Pagan* (1976), a short narrative about a young mother who accepts the death of her child through spiritualism. Working with a core of Latino technicians at commercial equipment houses, he painstakingly made the film through free labor and his own money.

Discovering film through theater, his natural affinity for fiction was realized in the narrative form, where he could visualize the inner reality of oppression, while the documentarians had chosen to show its outer manifestations. Unable to secure the financial wherewithal to produce a feature film in the late 1980s, he collaborated with the Committee on Hispanic Families and Children to direct *Dolores* (1988), a short narrative, shot on film but edited on video for economic reasons, about domestic violence within the Latino community.

While Figueroa felt alone in his solitary quest to fictionalize Puerto Rican realities, Luis Soto — formerly with Sandino Films in Puerto Rico and *Oye Wille,* another Puerto Rican series produced by Lou de Lemos for PBS — was collaborating with Angela Fontañez, who started out with WNET's *Black Journal* in 1968. They made *Reflections of Our Past* (1979), a short drama that featured young people traveling back in time to discover their history and culture, through a state education contract. Originally part of a series of television programs for young children on Puerto Rican history and culture, only one video was produced. Soto established his own production company making promotional films and commercials, and became the first Puerto Rican to direct a film for *American Playhouse,* formerly a PBS dramatic series, now an independent entity. His *The House of Ramón Iglesias* (1982) is a feature-length film adapted from a play about an educated Puerto Rican man who reconciles his love/hate relationship with his janitor father. The film handled the self-hatred faced by many people of color head-on while not sacrificing the dynamic bonds of love within the family. In 1987, Maria Norman directed *The Sun and the Moon,* a narrative feature film about a Puerto Rican woman's personal odyssey into her identity.

Searching for a Mode

The most prolific maker to emerge during the late seventies was Edin Vélez. Influenced by Marshall McLuhan while studying fine arts at the University of Puerto Rico, he journeyed to New York to study video at Global Village. He became involved with the early downtown video scene of Woody and Stein Vasulka in Soho. He escaped the burgeoning commercial video industry to teach at Young Filmmakers Foundation, and began working on his independent work in earnest. Although he experimented with video synthesizers for a while, his first piece to receive attention was *Tule: The Kuna Indians* (1978), a representational documentary about the Kuna Indians of the San Blas Islands off Panama. His later work, *Meta Mayan II* (1981), was a visceral and evocative personal essay of his trip to Guatemala. Not wanting to become "pigeon-holed as the Puerto Rican making Latino tapes,"[5] he solicited and received funding from the New York State Council on the Arts to make *The Oblique Strategist Too* (1984) about the composer Brian Eno and *As Is* (1984), a meditation on New York. In 1984, Edin, his wife and partner Ethel, and the author of this article produced *Sanctus,* the first video installation by a Puerto Rican artist at El Museo del Barrio. Years later, living in Japan on a National Endowment for the Arts Fellowship, he directed *The Meaning of the*

Interval (1987), a personal essay on Japanese culture, and the critically acclaimed video *Dance of Darkness* (1989), about Butoh dance. In an effort to define himself artistically and create his own cinematic language, Edin has used his self-imposed status as "outsider" to explore other cultures and experiment with time, location, and the boundaries of the frame within video art. He has just completed his first film project on Columbus's "discovery" of the Americas, *Memory of Fire* (1994; edited on video), and has yet to complete *Signal to Noise,* a videotape about Puerto Rico, the birthplace he fled in the late sixties. If completed, the tape will represent a synthesis of his high aesthetic sensibility and all the ambivalence of a Puerto Rican living in self-imposed exile.

A Grounding in Self

Missing from the outlining of Puerto Rican filmmakers are several imporant non-Puerto Rican contributors. Cuban-born and Puerto Rican-raised filmmaker Ana María García made the seminal *La Operación* (1982), about the massive sterilization abuse of Puerto Rican women, and *Cocolos y Roqueros* (1992), a documentary about how race and class are played out through popular music in Puerto Rico. Diego Echevarria, a Chilean-born and Puerto Rican-raised filmmaker who worked at WNET and NBC for many years, directed two independently produced documentaries: *Puerto Rico: A Colony the American Way* (1981), a short film about the political status of Puerto Rico, and *Los Sures* (1984), a beautifully crafted film about a Puerto Rican community in the Williamsburg section of Brooklyn, New York. *Los Sures* premiered at the New York Film Festival but was not well received by many members of the Puerto Rican community because of its focus on marginalized members of the community and its omission of stable working-class families from Williamsburg. Affonso Beatto, a Brazilian cinematographer based in New York during the late seventies and early eighties, established the Latin Film Project as a support system for Latin American filmmakers. During that time, he directed *Paradise Invaded,* an early documentary film about the colonialization of Puerto Rico, in collaboration with José García and other Puerto Rican filmmakers. *Los Dos Mundos de Angelita* (1978), a feature-length film about the dissolution of a Puerto Rican family after its arrival in New York, was directed by Jayne Morrison, a white woman

Scene from Diego Echeverria's *Los Sures*. (Photo courtesy of the Cinema Guild.)

from New York, and written by a Puerto Rican. It featured an all-Puerto Rican cast and many Puerto Rican/Latino crew members.

National and cultural affirmation occupied the center of these cinematic propositions as film- and videomakers struggled to represent and legitimize the history, conditions, and cultural development of their communities in the United States. Although the advent of small-format video technology increased the possibilities of representation, only a handful of emerging Puerto Rican makers have emerged on the scene. Frances Negrón-Muntaner, an island-trained anthropologist and Ph.D. candidate, collaborated with community activist Alba Martínez to create AIDS *in the Barrio* (1988), a documentary film about AIDS in the Puerto Rican community. She recently completed *Brincando el Charco: Portrait of a Puerto Rican* (1994), a semiautobiographical docudrama about Puerto Rican identity. Cuban-born Ela Troyano completed *Once Upon a Time in the Bronx* (1993), a nonlinear narrative about two Puerto Rican rap artists, and *Carmelita Tropicana: Your* Kunst *Is Your* Waffen (1993), a melodrama-musical about performance artist Carmelita Tropicana. Iris Morales, entertainment lawyer and former member of the Young Lords Party (quoted earlier), is collaborating with Pablo Figueroa on an examination of the legacy of the Young Lords, a militant political organization created during the political heyday of the 1960s. A few makers have opted to work in

other areas of the independent media field. Yvette Nieves-Cruz studied cinema studies at New York University and directed *L.E.A.R.*, a
videotape on the anti-imperialist artists league in Mexico. For several
years she worked as director of CineFestival in San Antonio, Texas,
a major venue for Latino film and video in the United States. Because
of the tenuous nature of the field, many have deserted it for more secure careers.

Puerto Rican cinema has grown from its infancy to toddlerhood
with little guidance and parental direction. It emerged during the tu-
multuous era of the documentary form, characterized by a sense of
urgency and expediency of the moment. The social and political revolution many clamored for demanded that films reflect the "truth"
and that they be finished by any means necessary. Puerto Rican filmmakers developed in spite of the structural obstacles inherent in denying "voice" within this society. Now, as more makers gain experience and mastery over the forms of their choosing, they will use the
medium with more precision, sophistication, flair, and experimentation. Although considerable time has elapsed since those early days,
there is still a striking need for Puerto Rican and Latino makers to
produce and direct films and videotapes about a multiplicity of issues
and concerns. Some of these concerns are directly linked to the status
and conditions of the Puerto Rican and Latino communities in the
United States, yet it would be a grave loss if the makers were to limit
themselves—or be limited by cultural institutions and their gatekeep-
ers—to just those themes. As we live in a complex and changing world,
our special place within the margins allows us to interpret American
culture and society in a unique way. We can contribute to the contemporary cultural discourse by producing filmic texts that present the
complexity and the innovative and myriad experiences of our survival
in an often hostile terrain. Our contributions can be used to deconstruct and reconstruct the assumptions of this society by presenting
other perspectives that are more dialectical in embracing the contradictory nature of life and its dynamic movement. We can present another sense of space, rhythm, and time that is multidimensional and
pollinated by a mélange of rich cultures and traditions that are always changing. To continue our process of growth as media makers
and as members of various communities, we require not only more
production and access to resources, but more Puerto Ricans actively
involved in the critique and study of formal issues of film and video.

And we need vehicles to allow more experienced filmmakers to pass on their knowledge about the subtleties of fund-raising, negotiating contracts with crews, producing, and so on, to less experienced makers. Although it is heartening that organizations like the Latino Collaborative in New York provide technical assistance to encourage and pave the way, production resources remain elusive.

The films and videotapes discussed in this essay grounded a generation of Puerto Ricans who had been nurtured with the dual and contradictory impulses of a colonized people with a passion to resist. We were "never meant to survive," as Audre Lord says in her poetry, and yet we survived, fought back, and created. These films and videotapes are our testament to survival. They forced us to look at ourselves, to step outside of our condition and objectify our reality, to deconstruct and then visually reconstruct it with a new vision and power extracted from that painful process. They allowed us to reflect on ourselves—the films were our passageway—and allowed us to move from objects to subjects. As makers, we were tormented by lack of opportunity, experience, and resources. As spectators, we liked what we saw, but sometimes we didn't. Many times we disagreed with the interpretation, but we could never deny that we were engaged in a life-death dialogue with images about our existence.

Those films and videotapes gave us strength. They fed us collectively. Nobody ever looked at us except as objects, and here we were looking at ourselves; sometimes we recognized ourselves—the fear, the hatred, the acquiescence, the strength, and, always, our contradictions. Those films and videotapes came out of a movement for voice. At this historical juncture, we have found our voice, but it is still new to us. Our communities are politically fractured and there is no cohesive nature to our relentlessly slow progress toward social and political equity. Film and video, therefore, reflect the need for us to dialogue about our condition. *Dolores* and AIDS *in the Barrio,* by the nature of their subjects, compel us to dialogue about the nature of racism, sexism, and homophobia within our culture and community. The new generation that has been raised within the United States has developed its cultural referents almost entirely from popular culture. We require films that celebrate our emerging cultural forms, born of a new *mestizaje* (mixture of culture, races, and cosmologies) of Caribbean, Central and Latin American, African American, and African Caribbean shared experiences. We require films that celebrate the new forms of resistance—the overt and covert forms that they take through song/rap, language, music, and other cultural forms and organizations. We need a media that represents the best of our *mestizaje*—a mélange of our human experience with all its complexity, beauty, and insight.

Notes

1. Bernardo Vega, *Memoirs of Bernardo Vega,* ed. César Andreu Iglesias (New York: Monthly Review Press, 1984), xii.
2. *El Pueblo Se Levanta,* 16mm documentary film distributed by Third World Newsreel.
3. Vega, *Memoirs of Bernardo Vega,* 203.
4. Ibid., 231. The articles are cited in *Memoirs of Bernardo Vega.*
5. Lillian Jiménez, "Puerto Rican Video Artist: Interview with Edin Vélez," *Jump Cut* 39 (June 1994): 99–104, 6.

Greater Cuba

Ana M. López

> I carry this marginality immune to all returns,
> too much of an *habanera* to be a new yorker
> too much a new yorker to be
> —even to go back to being—
> anything else.
>
> Lourdes Casal[1]

Exile has become a fashionable position from which to
"speak." Empowered by postmodern practices that proclaim the de-
centeredness of contemporary capitalist life and by postcolonial theories of discourse that privilege the hybridity and ambivalence of
exile (both inside and outside, belonging yet foreign) as a significant
site from which to challenge the oppressive hegemony of the "center" or the "national," the exilic experience—along with borders,
margins, and peripheries—has become a central metaphor of contemporary multicultural artistic and critical practices.

Defining what such a position means for cinematic practices is, however, a difficult task.[2] Certainly, in the case of the very rich "Chilean
exile cinema," we could argue that the sociohistorical experience of
political exile gave rise to a painfully postcolonial, often postmodern,
"national" cinema: self-reflexive, nostalgic, produced outside the borders of the nation-state (often even outside the continent itself).[3] But
speaking of other less clear-cut "exiled" cinemas in today's increasingly heterogeneous worlds filled with wandering artists and international coproductions is more complicated. And the task becomes even
more complex when we seek to find such a cinema within the United
States, even in Hollywood itself. Simply being a foreigner—the "outsider" looking in—is not enough. If we take the Chilean exile cinema
as a possible model, the principal prerequisite for an exile cinema
would seem to be a politically motivated diaspora; in other words, a
"forced" political exile without the possibility of return.

In the Chilean case, the tragedy of the diaspora had a special immediacy and political poignancy. Almost universally, cultural circles could respond negatively to Pinochet's regime of terror and sympathetically to the Chilean exiles and to their efforts to position themselves politically and culturally outside their nation. But the last thirty years or so have also witnessed the slow development of an exile cinema/video practice that has been neither as sympathetically received nor as homogeneously articulated. This "other" island, the films and videos of exiled Cubans, has often grated harshly against the sentiments of those for whom *the* island represented our only utopian hope in the Americas.

Certainly one cannot compare the 1973 Chilean debacle with the 1959 Cuban Revolution; if anything, the politics of these events were diametrically opposed and thus gave rise to very different exile populations. Nevertheless, the Cuban exile community is a significant one that cannot be dismissed. Despite Cuba's long history of exile (already marked by wars and displacements when it became "independent" in 1902, political and economic instabilities created mass exoduses in 1925–33 and 1952–58), no exodus has been as massive or prolonged as the one provoked by the 1959 revolution. By some (conservative) estimates, as much as 10 percent of the island's present population (ten and a half million, according to the 1987 census) lives in exile.[4] This significant part of the "nation" is deeply woven into the history of a "Cuba" that exceeds national boundaries. At the margins of the nation as such, this community functions both as mirror (sharing traditions, codes, symbols, discursive strategies) and as supplement. Furthermore, although a cursory (gringo) look might see the Cuban exile community as homogeneously allied with the far political right because of its continued opposition to the revolution, it is important to note not only its heterogeneity and its historical variances,[5] but also, more specifically, that the exiled filmmakers are not all necessarily typical of the more hysterical and anti-intellectual Miami/New York exile groups that still think of invasions and infiltration, hold fund-raisers, elect presidents and mayors in exile, and draw up elaborate postsocialism capitalist reconstruction plans for the island.

Of course, that the majority of Cuban exiles overwhelmingly sought refuge in the United States also had a determining influence on their politics (a reciprocal relationship) and their cinematic/video output.[6]

On the one hand, the politics of the Cuban exiles, especially their anti-Castroism, challenged the pro-Cuban Revolution feelings of most people involved in independent/alternative practices; on the other, as yet another exile/Hispanic minority group, they have had few opportunities to "make it" in the entertainment mainstream defined and controlled by Hollywood. Although buttressed by official U.S. policies and actions against Cuba since 1961, Cuban exile film- and video-makers have, paradoxically, had a difficult time articulating their arguments and being heard. Within artistic circles, their exile has, in general, not been a privileged position from which to speak. Their efforts to assemble a national identity within/out of exile—to reconstruct a national history—have often been seen as the marks of a strident ethnocentrism already compromised by their challenges to the island's utopia rather than as anguished cries of exilic loss, liminality, and deterritorialization coupled with the paradoxical need to build, to reterritorialize, themselves anew.

The exile of Cuban filmmakers must be traced back to Cuba itself and to specific events in the island that provoked it. Immediately after the 1959 revolution, the few established producers/filmmakers left Cuba for the United States, among them Manolo Alonso, the "czar" of Cuban film. After nationalization, his film "empire" (studios, etc.) provided the newly formed ICAIC (Instituto Cubano del Arte e Industria Cinematográficos) with a basic infrastructure. Nevertheless, the establishment of ICAIC and the revolutionary government's commitment to the cinema attracted and pleased almost all of the cinephiles, technicians, and amateur filmmakers that had been active in the various (political and apolitical) cine club movements of the 1950s. However, a survey of the first five years of *Cine Cubano* (1960–65) reveals that of the ten Cuban award-winning feature filmmakers mentioned, five subsequently chose exile: Eduardo Manet, Fausto Canel, Alberto Roldán, Roberto Fandiño, and Fernando Villaverde. Many others involved with ICAIC also chose exile: among them, cinematographers like Ramón Suárez, who photographed Tomás Gutiérrez Alea's films between *Las Doce Sillas* (The twelve chairs [1962]) and *Memorias del Subdesarrollo* (Memories of underdevelopment [1968]); actors like Eduardo Moure, who was the male lead in the first episode of *Lucía* (1968) and in *Historias de la Revolución* (1961); authors/scriptwriters like Edmundo Desnoes (*Memorias del Subdesarrollo*), Antonio Benítez-Rojo (*Los Sobrevivientes* [The survivors (1978)]; *Una Mujer, un Hombre, una Ciudad* [A woman, a man, a city (1978)]), and René Jordán (*Cuba 58* [1962]); and graphic designers like Antonio Reboiro, who was responsible for many of ICAIC's striking early film posters.[7] What prompted them to leave?

In print, several of the exiled filmmakers have traced their disaffection with the revolution to an event that provoked a national intellectual crisis: the *P.M.* affair.[8] In 1960, working independently of ICAIC, a group affiliated with the cultural magazine *Lunes de Revolución* (a supplement of the newspaper *Revolución* edited by Carlos Franqui) produced a short film for the magazine's weekly television program. A "free cinema"-style exploration of nightlife in the bars and cafés around the Havana waterfront, the film was called *P.M.* or Post Meridian and was directed by Sabá Cabrera Infante (the brother of novelist Guillermo) and Orlando Jiménez-Leal, a young cameraman who had worked for the newsreel production company Cineperiódico. Neither was affiliated with ICAIC. The film aired on television and received a favorable review from Nestor Almendros, who was then a critic in the influential mass-circulation weekly *Bohemia*. Almendros believed the film to be a "jewel of the experimental cinema" that "probed deeply into the reality of an aspect of popular life."[9] However, when the filmmakers applied to ICAIC for a theatrical exhibition license for the film, it was denied. ICAIC's decision was difficult for many to understand. Those associated with the film and/or with *Lunes* cried "censorship," while ICAIC maintained that the film was irresponsible to the revolution and that they had the right and authority to delay/prohibit its distribution. As Michael Chanan points out, this modest film about the somewhat seedy nighttime activities of marginal Havana types was perhaps only "mildly offensive,"[10] but the historical moment—only six weeks after the Bay of Pigs invasion and Castro's official declaration of the socialist character of the revolution—was tense and emotionally charged. The debate over *P.M.* reached such heights that Castro himself intervened in a famous speech known as "Words to the Intellectuals" that closed a series of meetings among intellectuals held at the National Library. His words were prophetic and have been often quoted: "Within the Revolution, everything; against it, nothing."[11]

Despite many claims that the *P.M.* affair was the decisive event that motivated filmmakers to seek exile, most did not leave Cuba until the late 1960s. The debate over *P.M.* revealed that there were various political positions among cultural workers and caused a restructuring of the noncinematic arts scene centered on the closing of *Lunes*, a change in the direction of Casa de las Américas, and the creation of UNEAC (Unión Nacional de Escritores y Artistas de Cuba [National Union of Writers and Artists of Cuba]) in 1961. However, because the cultural agenda suggested by Castro's "Words to the Intellectuals" was not in itself restrictive, it led to a period marked by a certain creative anarchy and a testing of the limits of what was possible under the definition "revolutionary." The tensions that surfaced in this period among artists (primarily writers) and between cultural circles and the revolutionary intelligentsia would not come to a head until 1968–71, when the polemic case of the writer Heberto Padilla caused an international furor that culminated in a formal "tightening up" of the definition of revolutionary art and culture.[12]

In any case, although Orlando Jiménez-Leal, Sabá Cabrera Infante, and Nestor Almendros (who lost his job in *Bohemia* after the *P.M.* affair) left in 1962–63, few of those working in ICAIC left Cuba before 1965. The bulk of departures of ICAIC personnel, in fact, occurred in the period 1965–68.[13] Thus, these departures—although perhaps traceable in spirit to the *P.M.* affair—were more closely linked to the series of events that began in 1965 with the formation of the Central Committee of the Communist Party and the internment in forced labor camps (called UMAPs: Unidades Militares de Ayuda a la Producción [Military Units to Aid Production]) of homosexuals and other "undesirables" and "deviants" (in 1965–67). Personally threatening some and morally threatening others, for many within the artistic communities this was "lo que le puso la tapa al pomo" (the last straw). (It is interesting to note that no active ICAIC creative personnel left the island during the last massive exodus, the Mariel boat lift of 1980. However, among the "Marielitos" were various former ICAIC workers, most notably Raúl Molina, a documentary director between 1961 and 1966 who was fired from ICAIC because of "ideological conflicts" and worked in "anonymous" nonskilled jobs—farm laborer, gas station attendant—until his departure.)[14]

Despite their scattered departures over more than a decade, many of the exiled Cuban filmmakers, together with others (too young when they left and considered "exiles" as a result of circumstances)[15] who became filmmakers while in exile, have sustained a specific "Cuban" identity: they identify themselves as Cubans, have most often worked with Cuban issues/themes, and, for the most part, maintain an anti-Castro political line. In different ways, their films and videos, especially those of the first and second generations of filmmakers, articulate and attempt to contain the traumas of exile by repeating and denouncing the actual experience (the history of departures) and by symbolically reconstructing the "lost" home (with)in a new imagined community. In fact, their films often participate in what may be called a "Cuban" political culture or political imaginary that exceeds the geographical boundaries of the island nation and that have been a constant feature of Cuban political life at least since the 1890s. Finally, the third generation of exiles, already less liminal and more assimilated, most often bypasses the explicit political discourses typical of the first and second generations, and is more interested in exploring that historically determining, but, in most cases, largely unknown, "Cuban" part of their self-definition as "Cuban Americans."

The First Generation

Of course, not all the exiled filmmakers have continued to make films. Francisco Villaverde, for example, who was part of the Rebel Army's Culture Unit in 1959 and worked at ICAIC between 1960 and 1963 as assistant and director of documentaries, was exiled in 1965, worked for the Associated Press news service in New York, and, since the mid-1970s, has been a literary critic for the *Miami Herald*. None of the authors/scriptwriters have continued to write for the cinema and have found "homes" in academia (Desnoes, Benítez-Rojo) or in journalism (René Jordán is the film critic for the *Miami Herald*).

Manolo Alonso, the "czar" of prerevolutionary Cuban film, settled in the New York-Miami axis and specializes in the production of stage and television musical shows. He and Spanish-language TV magnate René Anselmo were also involved in the establishment of Spanish-language TV channels 41 (New York) and 23 (Miami), and the network Univisión.[16] Alonso also seems to have directed the first postrevolutionary Cuban exile film in 1963: *La Cuba de Ayer* (Yesterday's Cuba), a two-hour film — primarily footage from prerevolutionary Cuba but also some testimonies and performances by recent exiles — that paints a nostalgic portrait of prerevolutionary life. In 1987 he completed a made-for-Spanish-TV movie, *El Milagro del Exodo* (The miracle of the exodus), which documents the achievements of Cuban exiles in the United States.

Many others have combined work in advertising or publishing with forays into filmmaking. Orlando Jiménez-Leal, probably one of the best known of the exile filmmakers, worked successfully in Spanish-language advertising in New York, was cinematographer for the Puerto Rican production *La criada malcriada* (The disobedient servant [1965]), and eventually set up his own production company, Guede Films, in the late 1970s. Guede Films produced *El Super* (1979), which was directed by Jiménez-Leal and his young brother-in-law León Ichaso and became the first Cuban exile fictional feature to be broadly distributed and exhibited in the United States and to win international awards.[17] (The "first" exile narrative feature shot in the United States was, according to all accounts, Camilo Vila's *Los Gusanos* [The worms, (1977)], a rarely seen low-budget feature shot in the Dominican Republic.)[18] Subsequently, Jiménez-Leal went on to direct *The Other Cuba* (1983), a feature-length documentary financed by Italian television (RAI) and, in collaboration with Nestor Almendros, the well-known, highly polemical documentary *Improper Conduct* (1984), produced by French television (Antenne 2) and the Films du Losange.[19] (Because of generational differences and his split with Jiménez-Leal after *El Super,* I have classified Ichaso as a "second generation" director and discuss his films later on.) In 1988, Nestor Almendros teamed up with another younger exile, Jorge Ulla, to produce *Nobody Listened,* a documentary denunciation of the treatment of prisoners in Cuban prisons. Most recently, two young Miami Dade Community College professors—Alex Antón and Jorge Cardona, both twenty-seven—filmed *Rompiendo el silencio* (Breaking the silence [1994]), a documentary about contemporary protest movements in Cuba that features interviews with Cuban dissidents in the island filmed by French journalist Bertrand de la Grange.[20]

It is this "political generation" that most clearly evidences the peculiarity of Cuban exile film, at once closely linked to the island's cultural and political history, but the most different—especially in style—from the island's (ICAIC's) cinema. These films articulate a contradictory, tragic discourse that mythologizes prerevolutionary Cuba in order to radically differentiate it from the revolutionary "present" of the island and link it to these filmmakers' exile. "First-generation" discourse is dependent upon explicit antirevolutionary politics and the documentary form and is, in fact, independent of the age of the exile and of the longevity of his/her diaspora: it is a position available to and used by Cuban exile filmmakers of all ages who still identify themselves primarily as Cuban *political* exiles.

In *The Other Cuba,* for example, Jiménez-Leal devotes over half of the film to a painstaking retelling of the events that led to the triumph of the revolution in 1959 and its early "glory years" (in fact, often using what looks like ICAIC footage) in order to set up its "betrayal" of the exiled ex-followers that he interviews extensively. Attempting to write an "other" history to contribute to the new community's social imaginary (challenging what for many exiles is the U.S. left's blindness to what really happened and also rehabilitating the political allegiances of now-exiled individuals like Carlos Franqui — author of *Family Portrait with Fidel* — who was once an ardent revolutionary and is thus rejected by the Miami exile community), Jiménez-Leal must filmically relive the experiences, positing the authenticity of the struggle against Batista in order provide a link between the island's history and the exiles' "Cuba."[21] Thus, by displacing nationalism from the nation itself, the film creates a space within which the fetishization of the lost "home" (and *patria*) can serve to lessen the trauma of exilic liminality and as a springboard toward a form of assimilation. In doing so, however, the film — and other exile productions — participates in what Nelson Valdés has identified as one of the central characteristics of the "Cuban" political imaginary, the invocation of the theme of betrayal. Valdés argues that in Cuba — before, after, and in exile from the revolution — "political differences . . . turn into charges of betrayal."[22] In other words, in "Cuban" political discourse, "betrayal" does not simply connote a move away from a given political program, but a breach of personal trust. For the exiles as well as for those on the island (as demonstrated by the late 1980s Ochoa case, where high-ranking officers were accused of drug trafficking), politics requires unconditional personal loyalty, and any wavering or political difference constitute betrayal. Thus the interviewees' insistent accusations that Castro betrayed his own ideals, his friends, his confidants, and finally the nation itself echo only too familiarly in Cuban ears.

Preceding the markedly different denunciation documentaries, Jiménez-Leal and Ichaso's independent feature *El Super* (based on a play by Iván Acosta) is solidly a film of exile longing and displacement. *El Super* tells the story of Roberto, a former apolitical bus driver who left Cuba in 1968 out of a generalized frustration with the system and ended up becoming the superintendent of a building in New York's Washington Heights. After a decade in New York, Roberto and his wife Aurelia are still struggling with assimilation: they cannot stand the winters, barely speak English, associate primarily with other Latinos, and are deeply disturbed by their teenage daughter's (Elizabeth Peña) increasingly visible Americanness. Roberto, in fact, is in the midst of a deep psychological crisis typical of the exilic condition: longing for a Cuba that never really was and unable to accommodate himself to the harsh realities of his adopted land. The film's solution to his angst—a move to Miami motivated by a job offer and dreams of sun-drenched palm trees and the sounds of Spanish—ends the story on a somewhat hollow triumphant note, for Roberto can never have what he longs for most: not to have left Cuba.

Unlike the denunciation documentaries that followed it, *El Super* displaces the explicitly political to address the experience of exile accommodation at a personal level. Thus, while we may consider the denunciation documentaries as part of the liminal phase of exile, this film that chronologically preceded them is, paradoxically, a film of assimilation that consciously celebrates an already existing new imaginary community.

The Second Generation

Besides these better-known Cuban exile directors, a "new" generation—born in Cuba but trained in the United States—has also emerged. Although there are marked slippages between the first and second generations, this group seems to cohere in in-between spaces: between the United States and Cuba, between the exiles and the North Americans. They are always attempting to "cross over," albeit in different directions. In his witty *Life on the Hyphen: The Cuban-American Way,* Gustavo Pérez-Firmat dubs this generation of Cubans in the United States the "one-and-a halfers," for they are *both* first and second generation: they live on the hyphen, may never feel entirely at ease in either U.S. or Cuban culture, but can avail "themselves of the resources—linguistic, artistic, commercial—that both cultures have to offer."[23] As Pérez Firmat goes on to argue, this is the group that has been responsible for the production of intercultural Cuban-American culture: in music, Gloria Estefan and Willie Chirino; in literature, Oscar Hijuelos, José Kozer, Cristina Garcia, and others. In cinema/ video, this hyphenated generation is more difficult to identify. Each individual seems to stand at a different point on the ethnic bicultural scale, varying from one-and-an-eighth all the way to one-and-seven-eights or even perhaps two. I locate León Ichaso, Ramón Menéndez, Jorge Ulla, Miñuca Villaverde, Iván Acosta, and Orestes Matacena in this group. Although their individual trajectories as filmmakers are quite varied, their partial assimilation has meant that they have often felt free to leave behind the explicit denunciations of the first generation in order to focus more and more on the nature of life as exiles; in other words, to wrest exilic nostalgia away from the tragic discourse of dispossession and to recuperate it as ethnic identity — Cuban-American, but also Latino.

Certainly, León Ichaso emblematizes the "crossover" phenomenon. After leaving Jiménez-Leal and teaming up with producer Manuel Arce (and his production company Max Mambru Films), Ichaso tried to build on the success of *El Super* to reach Hollywood. However, when their project to film a Cuban-American screwball comedy entitled *A Short Vacation* was shelved by Universal in 1982 (after spending two years in development, curiously, at the same time that *Scarface* was being planned by the studio), they independently produced their own allegory of failed crossovers, *Crossover Dreams*, in 1985. Starring the Panamanian singer-actor-politician and Harvard-educated lawyer Rubén Blades, the film tells the wry tale of a *salsero*'s struggle to "make it" in the New York City mainstream music scene. Like the tale it tells, *Crossover Dreams* is itself a crossover experience. It isn't simply Cuban-American, but rather a Latino film, deeply marked by the American ethnic experience and the values and narrative strategies of classic Hollywood cinema. Narratively, it tells a story about Latinos in the same terms that similar stories have been told about other ethnic groups' efforts to "make it" in the American mainstream. Visually, however, it offers us a complex map of the rich multicultural and multiethnic space of New York City's Loisaida.

Ichaso's most recent *Sugar Hill* (1993) continues this trajectory. The "Cubanness" is even more distant in this film about Harlem life, but what remains is an exquisite attention to place as it participates

Final scene from León Ichaso and Manuel Arce's *Crossover Dreams*.

in the production of social life in those areas of New York City that are normally invisible. In this incarnation, Ichaso has become, in the words of the *New York Times* reviewer, "a New Yorker at heart."[24]

In Ichaso's (and Ramón Menéndez's) films, the Cuban-American experience has been replaced by a more generalized focus that simultaneously reflects the realities of an assimilation that in many cases is already more than thirty years old as well as the commercial imperatives of "entertainment" films that aspire to mass audiences.

Jorge Ulla, another who was exiled quite young, has chosen a markedly different path. In 1978, he directed his first feature film, *Guaguasí,* in the Dominican Republic (not completed or released until 1982). Lushly photographed by Ramón Suárez (who won prizes for *Memories of Underdevelopment*), *Guaguasí* is a fictional tale about the effects of revolutionary policies on a "simple" man who stayed behind, a *guajiro* or peasant who joined the guerrillas accidentally and, after the revolution, became a harsh executioner of his own friends, a betrayer. The film has rarely been seen in the United States, although it was one of the three Latin American films (representing the Dominican Republic) selected in the prenominations for the best foreign

film Academy Award category. In 1980, Ulla directed *In Their Own* √
Words (with Lawrence Ott Jr.), a thirty-minute documentary about the
Mariel exodus sponsored by the U.S. Information Agency. Filmed as
the exiles were arriving at Key West, the film uses their testimonies
to attempt to explain this sudden massive exodus and highlights the
experience of leaving and the feelings of these new exiles. Perhaps
because of the experience of working on *In Their Own Words,* and
despite the fact that he claims a preference for fiction filmmaking,
Ulla went on to make documentaries with Orlando Jiménez-Leal (*The
Other Cuba*) and Nestor Almendros (*Nobody Listened*), thus joining
forces with the "first generation" of exile directors and their passionate politics.

Unlike Ichaso and Ulla, Miñuca Villaverde works in a very personal
and poetic style and is one of the most suggestive filmmakers of this
group. After working as an experimental filmmaker in New York (under the auspices of the Women's Interart Center) and directing the
award-winning shorts *A Girl in Love* and *Poor Cinderella, Still Iron-
ing Her Husband's Shirt,* she moved to Miami with her ex-filmmaker
husband Francisco and directed the documentaries *To My Father*
(1974) and *Tent City* (1984). *To My Father* is a record of a Cuban
American family's interactions at a time of crisis: waiting for the death
of the family patriarch, the filmmaker's own father. *Tent City,* however, assumes a more provocative public stance. Documenting the
experiences of those Mariel boat lift exiles who were hard to relocate
and had to live in army tents under an expressway in downtown Miami for several months, the film chronicles Villaverde's own fascination with their marginality and dogged persistence to assert their own
identities. Since *Tent City,* Villaverde seems to have given up filmmaking and is now a staff writer for the Spanish-language cultural supplement of the *Miami Herald.*

Although more difficult to place than Villaverde and Ulla, Acosta
and Matacena have also produced work dealing primarily with exilic
assimilation. For example, after writing the play that was adapted for
El Super, Acosta went on to make *Amigos* (Friends [1985]), a low- √
budget feature produced by Camilo Viva about the painful assimilation of Mariel exiles into the Miami community: Ramón, who has been
in jail for eighteen years, arrives through Mariel and is welcomed by
his childhood friend Pablo, but he must learn to deal with the prejudice of the Miami exile community and even the unspoken resentment

of his own friend. Although conventionally shot and sometimes halt-ingly narrated, the film does capture the contradictions of the history of the "waves" of Cuban exile with humor and sensitivity. If *El Super* was *the* film of exilic assimilation of the 1970s, *Amigos* fulfills the same role in the 1980s, taking us from Key West, through the various Cuban enclaves of Miami, all the way north to Union City, New Jersey.

The Third Generation

Yet a third group of Cuban exiles—what might be called the "Cuban American" (no hyphen) or "third" generation—has been making its presence felt in alternative and independent film and video circles. The individuals in this group are younger, less interested in commercial crossovers, more assimilated, yet still insistently—alter-natingly—"Cuban." For example, Enrique Oliver's *Photo Album* (1984) offers a campy yet acute look at the transculturation of exile with tidbits such as a history of the evolution of the Cuban virgin in exile and the exorcism of an overly Americanized teenager by a San-teria priest. Multimedia artist Tony Labat has produced a number of tapes dealing with exile and transculturation. Among them, his *ñ* (1982) is a fascinating and very experimental analysis of that letter's inscription of difference while *Kikiriki* (1983) explicitly addresses La-bat's own return to Cuba and generates a meditation on machismo, violence, and masculinity. Dinorah de Jesus Rodríguez's *Ochún Oricha: El Balance Guerreros (A Trilogy)* (1990) explores the African pres-ence in "Cuban" culture. Rafael Elortequi, a University of Miami film school graduate, has done a number of experimental films. Raúl Fer-rera-Balanquet, a University of Iowa film school graduate and multi-media artist, has produced a series of tapes—among them *Mérida Proscrita* (1990), *We Are Hablando* (1991), *No Me Olvides* (1992), and *Olufina Abuela Balanquet* (1994)—that offer poignant analyses of the difficulties and marginalization of gay Latino life in a North-South context.[25] Ela Troyano's filmic range spans from the Warhol-esque New York downtown avant-garde scene to *How to Kill Her* (1990) (in collaboration with Cuban American playwright Ana María Simo) and *Carmelita Tropicana* (1993), perhaps the most trenchant example of this generation's "Cuban American Way."[26]

Ana María García's work speaks from a different place and with a different voice. She grew up in Puerto Rico, and that island's own complex status coupled with her own long-term commitment to contemporary Cuba has led her to a documentary practice that is independent, political, and fraught with difficulties. Her first film, *La Operación* (1977–81), is a denunciation of the planned sterilization of women in Puerto Rico that fits solidly within the parameters of the New Latin American Cinema. Her most recent *Cocolos y Roqueros* (1993) is an incisive analysis of contemporary Puerto Rican identity through music.

Also coming from a different "place" is Andy García's *Cachao* (1992). After his career as a Hollywood actor was well established, García fulfilled his longtime dream of rescuing the brilliant Cuban bass player Israel López "Cachao" from the oblivion of exile by producing a large concert in Miami. This extraordinary show serves as the backbone for this sometimes touching, sometimes cloying documentary, which tracks Cachao and his group through the rehearsals for the show, traces his musical career, and includes interviews with other Cuban exile luminaries like Guillermo Cabrera Infante. Although García rearticulates a Cuban musical past for a Cuban present that does not seem to require the island at all, he cannot bypass the first-generation discourses that demand denunciation and repudiation of the island's present. García has simultaneously argued that with this film he is not searching for roots ("because I never lost them") but that he is also "reliving the Cuba that he never lived" through its music, "which crosses boundaries ... but has always been the link" to his Cuban heritage.[27]

Nevertheless, this last generation—the Cuban Americans—is perhaps the most distant from the exile experience as such. Overall, their work is not linked to the usual anti-Castro political Cuban-exile agenda. However, their general concern with biculturalism (and the related loss, marginality, and difference) is still couched in the terms of an explicit exilic positionality—a Cubanness slipping into Latinoness—that is unavoidable; and which, full circle, returns them to the mainstream of the contemporary art scene.

Although this generation is also the most distant from the island itself—some left as tiny children, others were born in the United States[28]—its work is, paradoxically, the most closely linked to the island's cinema. In Cuba, an aggressive group of young "amateur" filmmakers, loosely associated with the youth cultural organization Hermanos Sainz (and, in many cases, students at the Instituto Superior de Arte in Havana or the Escuela Internacional de Cine y Televisión in San Antonio de los Baños) and working independently of ICAIC, has begun to express similar cinematic concerns and experimental multimedia approaches. Films and video work such as *Un Pedazo de mí* (A part of me [Jorge Luis Sánchez, 1989]), *Empezar de Cero* (Starting at zero [Ibis Gómez García, 1991]), *Oscuros Rinocerontes Enjaulados (Muy a la Moda)* (Dark caged rhinoceros (very much in fashion [Juan Carlos Cremata, 1991]), and *Emma, la Mujer Marcada* (Emma, the marked woman [Camilo Hernández, 1991]) tackle topics that the national cinema has shied away from (respectively, marginality in contemporary Cuba, the excessive presence of Martí busts throughout Havana, Cuban irreverence, and notions of cultural identity) in a highly experimental and iconoclastic fashion.[29] For both sets of filmmakers, the expressly political — the revolution — is not a direct concern, but a decentered subtext that is subsumed within other categories of life and experience. Perhaps because of their youth, because of their comparatively similar exposure to different varieties of film and video work, or because of a generalized postmodernist climate that has reached into the island itself, the work of the third generation of Cuban American filmmakers and of the new generations emerging in Cuba share a common ground.[30]

In the long and complex history of Cuba and its diaspora, its film and video productions seem to have, partially, effected a graceful reencounter. There is now, it seems, a small "Cuba" that exceeds all national boundaries.

Postscript: The Special Period

When I wrote the first version of this essay a few years ago, that "graceful reencounter" seemed utopian, but not impossible. The Torricelli Act, despite tightening all restrictions on U.S. trade with Cuba, paradoxically liberated cultural exchanges and made the idea of a "Cuban" cinematic practice that exceeded national boundaries seem feasible. In fact, within the island itself, ICAIC's own cinema had begun to make gestures toward a rapprochement with the exile thematic and had undergone a kind of transnationalization that seemed to bypass the previously requisite repudiation of exiles. Whereas in its first thirty years ICAIC had only produced two feature films dealing explicitly with the diaspora and its consequences — *55 Hermanos*

(55 brothers) and *Lejanía* (Parting of the ways), both directed by Je- ✓
sús Díaz—two others were released in the early 1990s: *Mujer trans-* ✓
parente (Transparent woman [1990]), a compilation film with one
episode dealing with the trauma of return, and *Vidas Paralelas* (Par- ✓
allel lives [Pastor Vega, 1992]), a fictionalized comparison of life in
Union City, New Jersey, and in Havana. In video (coproduced by ICRT
[Cuban Radio-Television Institute] and Channel 4 [United Kingdom]),
Estela Bravo produced *Miami-Havana,* a documentary about the emotional traumas of exile focused on a group of Marielitos who were
imprisoned in the United States and subsequently returned to the island. Even Cuba's premier director, Tomás Gutiérrez Alea, received a
Guggenheim fellowship to work on a script for a sequel to *Memories
of Underdevelopment* in collaboration with longtime New Hamp-
shire resident Edmundo Desnoes. Furthermore, his *Strawberry and
Chocolate* (1994), an analysis of internal exile produced by official
homophobia, became the best-received and most widely seen Cuban
film in the United States and was even nominated for an Academy
Award.

But the effects of the crisis engendered by the collapse of the Soviet Union (and the withdrawal of all financial subsidies to the island), and the Cuban government's often contradictory, faltering moves
toward change, have rippled through the ranks of filmmakers and
have produced a different "generation" of exiles that problematizes
all chronological sequences. For example, Sergio Giral, a longtime
ICAIC director of important films such as *El Otro Francisco* (The other
Francisco [1976]) and, most recently, *María Antonia* (1990), now lives
in Miami and is on the lecture circuit. Mario Rodríguez Joya, a brilliant photographer and the cinematographer of a good percentage of
ICAIC's most successful films, recently moved to Los Angeles. Juan Carlos Cremata (director of *Oscuros Rinocerontes Enjaulados*) is in Mexico. Creative personnel from other media institutes have also left the
island permanently: José Luis Llánez, the director of award-winning
ICRT productions, is in Miami, along with Jorge Antonio Crespo and
visual artist Nicolas Guillén Landrían (director of *Coffea Arábiga* ✓
[1971], which many argue is the best documentary ever produced by
ICAIC).

Most recently, two film production students from the ISA (Instituto
Superior de Arte)—Carlos Zequeira and Luis Vladimir Ceballos—
arrived in Miami with potentially incendiary footage featuring inter-

views with Cuban *roqueros* (heavy metal fans) who nihilistically (politically?) contaminated themselves with the Human Immunodeficiency Virus and are currently interned in the "La Conchita" *sidatorio* (AIDS asylum). Although not even a documentary as such, the footage generated a minor journalistic storm, including coverage in the *Miami Herald* and a feature in the *New York Times Magazine.* Early in 1995, Tomás Gutiérrez Alea also made headlines when he became a Spanish citizen, although he declared his intention to continue living in Cuba and argued that the rationale for the citizenship change was to facilitate coproduction deals.

Although none of these filmmakers have yet to secure financing for film production in the United States—either for new projects or to complete existing ones—their presence here will undoubtedly produce a new "wave" of exile productions that will speak with yet another voice and will project yet another set of experiences and contradictions of exile, within exile, and for nationness.

That these and other images have been and continue to be extraordinarily powerful weapons in the struggles for definition of the "Cuban" nation was amply demonstrated in the debacle that followed the much-touted "Diálogo" conference held in Havana in April 1994. Officially entitled "La Nación y la Emigración" (the nation and immigration), the three-day conference was sponsored by the Cuban government to discuss Cuba's relation to its diaspora and featured a planeful of invited exiles from the United States and other countries. Although the conversations and debates held during the conference may or may have not have proved useful in opening up relations between the United States and Cuba, their significance was superseded by a twelve-minute video. Shot surreptitiously during a closing reception hosted by Fidel for the delegates, the tape was mysteriously (with or without official permission) sold to the international press two days later, before the delegates had returned to Miami. It featured a number of Cuban Americans paying their compliments to Fidel and vying for his attention. The "star" of the video was Miami-based attorney Magda Montiel, who had hoped to win a Florida congressional seat on the Democratic ticket. When her turn came to greet Fidel, she shook his hand, kissed and hugged him, and emotionally said, "Thank you for what you have done for my people. You have been a great teacher to me." Aired insistently on every Spanish-language news broadcast for two or three days, this video clip dashed not only Montiel's political career, but all hopes for a Cuba-U.S. dialogue. For the Miami media and the Miami community, the conference immediately became a "love fest" between Fidel and the treacherous exiles who had betrayed their "real" identity as Cubans. And, once again, the theme of betrayal asserted itself against all odds—and against all conference participants and future dealings between Cuba and the exile community.

Some months later, in the summer of 1994, the yet unresolved *balsero* crisis unleashed yet another set of complications for Cuban-U.S. relations, which further compromised the exile position. No longer smoothly generational and symmetrical (if it ever was), the panorama of Cuban exile has recently become a marked palimpsest of accommodation, assimilation, and transnationality; of comfort, work, and misery. And new work in film and video will undoubtedly reflect upon, engage with, and help generate new sites for the utterly unstable yet sometimes utterly privileged position of "Greater Cuba."

Notes

This essay is a revision and expansion of "The Other Island: Exiled Cuban Cinema," published in *Jump Cut* 38 (June 1993).

1. Lourdes Casal, "Para Ana Velford," in *Palabras Juntan Revolución* (Havana: Casa de las Américas, 1981), 61. Unless otherwise noted, all translations from Spanish-language sources are my own.

2. Hamid Naficy has begun this project in his "Exile Discourse and Televisual Fetishization," *Quarterly Review of Film and Video* 13.1–3 (1991): 85–116.

3. The literature on the Chilean exile cinema is quite extensive, but for a good summary see Zuzana Pick, "Chilean Cinema in Exile, 1973–1986," *Framework* 34 (1987): 40–57.

4. Peter Marshall, *Cuba Libre* (Boston: Faber and Faber, 1987), 248. Less conservative figures indicate the possibility that as much as 12 percent of the present Cuban population (or 1.2 million) lives abroad. See, for example, Ileana Fuentes-Pérez, "By Choice or by Circumstance: The Inevitable Exile of Artists," in *Outside Cuba/Fuera de Cuba* (New Brunswick, N.J., and Miami: Office of Hispanic Arts, Rutgers University and the Research Institute for Cuban Studies, University of Miami, 1988).

5. For example, the earliest exiles have been quite unforgiving of those who collaborated with Castro and the revolution and whose subsequent change of political opinion has not convinced them. Thus, Carlos Franqui, an ex-Castro ally, is not very welcomed in Miami circles (he lives in Italy): when he was introduced to the audience awaiting a screening of *The Other Cuba*

(based, partly, on his story) at the Miami Film Festival in 1985, the audience's resounding boos convinced him to remain in his seat rather than go up on the stage and face the crowds. See Enrique Fernández, "Miami's Autores," *Film Comment* 21.3 (May–June 1985): 46–48.

6. Various exiled film workers did *not* come to the United States immediately—most notably, Nestor Almendros, who left Cuba to become a world-famous cinematographer in France and only came to the United States when he began to work for Hollywood producers in the late 1970s. (Almendros died in Paris in 1992.) Humberto López Guerra, produced a documentary in Sweden entitled *Castro y Cuba.* Fausto Canel spent ten years in Spain and directed several films—*La Espera* (Power game), *La Espuela* (The spur), and *María la Santa* (María, the saint)—and a TV serial (*El Juglar y la Reina* [The Joker and the Queen]) before moving to the United States and directing *Campo Minado,* a feature-length documentary about the return of democracy to the Southern Cone. He is presently living in Hollywood and working on the screenplay adaptation of his novel *Ni tiempo para pedir auxilio* (Miami: Ediciones Universal, 1991).

7. Tracking the journeys of Cuban exiles involved with film and video is a difficult task, which has become even more complicated in the last few years. I have relied on personal knowledge, some accounts published in the Spanish-language press and in the *Miami Herald,* and María Eulalia Douglas's *Diccionario de Cineastas Cubanos, 1959–1987* (Havana/Mérida: Cinemateca de Cuba/Universidad de los Andes, 1989), which identifies past and present ICAIC personnel (including those that had left as of 1987). José Antonio Evora—former *Cine Cubano* editor and current Guggenheim fellow—has also been a most helpful informant.

8. See, for example, Nestor Almendros, "A los Dictadores les Gusta el Cine," *Noticias de Arte* (New York, September 1987): 10–12; and Guillermo Cabrera Infante, "Cuba's Shadow," *Film Comment* 21.3 (1985): 43–45.

9. Nestor Almendros, "*P.M.,*" *Bohemia* 53.21 (May 21, 1961); reprinted in Nestor Almendros, *Cinemanía* (Barcelona: Seix Barral, 1992), 172.

10. Michael Chanan, *The Cuban Image* (London: British Film Institute, 1985), 101.

11. For the complete text of Castro's speech, see "Palabras a los Intelectuales," *Política Cultural de la Revolución Cubana: Documentos* (Havana: Editorial de Ciencias Sociales, 1977), 5–47.

12. Padilla, an award-winning (UNEAC, 1968) yet disaffected poet, was arrested for dissidence in 1971. His subsequent public confession and apology, the ban on his books, and the government's refusal to allow him to travel (until his final departure via Spain in 1980) caused an international scandal that provoked the first split between Cuba and international intellectual circles. For an excellent assessment and compilation of important documents see, Lourdes Casal, ed., *El Caso Padilla: Literatura y Revolución en Cuba* (Miami: Ediciones Universal, n.d. [1972?]).

13. In fact, this chronology somewhat contradicts the sociological understanding of the nature of the various "waves" of Cuban exiles. According to

sociologists Amaro and Portes, for example, the first wave, 1959–62, consisted primarily of elites who already had well-established business/connections in the United States. The second wave, 1962–65, were the middle-class professionals who "escaped" for political and ideological reasons. The exiles of the third wave (1965–74) increasingly were "those who searched" for better economic opportunities. See Nelson Amaro and Alejandro Portes, "Una Sociología del Exilio: Situación de los Grupos Cubanos en los Estados Unidos," *Aportes* 23 (January 1972).

14. See Jorge Ulla, Lawrence Ott, and Miñuca Villaverde, *Dos Filmes del Mariel: El Exodo Cubano de 1980* (Madrid: Editorial Playor, 1986), 158. Molina, who wrote the preface to this publication of the scripts of Ulla's and Villaverde's films, now lives in New York and works in the Latin American Department of Associated Press.

15. In addition to those that accompanied their parents into exile, the Cuban diaspora also included a number of children and teenagers sent by their parents to the United States (between 1960 and 1963) in response to rumors that the government was about to impose child custody laws that would give the state absolute authority over all children. Over several years, fourteen thousand children were met by the Catholic Charities organization, which set up camps in Miami and later relocated the children to orphanages and foster homes throughout the United States.

16. See Rosendo Rosell, "¿Por Qué No Acordarnos Hoy de ... Manolo Alonso?" in *Vida y Milagros de la Farándula Cubana,* vol. 2 (Miami: Ediciones Universal, 1992), 226–28.

17. *El Super* won the grand prize at the Mannheim festival, a festival award at Biarritz, and was selected for a Mostra at the Venice festival in 1979.

18. I have been unable to view this film. However, all accounts indicate that it was produced on a shoestring budget and barely distributed within south Florida. The story was set in the late 1950s and focuses on five prisoners who undergo tests of emotional endurance and political conviction in between sessions with a sadistic interrogator in a revolutionary guerrilla group. It was based on a 1975 play by Eduardo Corbe, photographed by Ramón Suárez, produced by Camilo Vila and Danilo Bardisa, and starred, among others, Orestes Matacena.

19. For a detailed analysis of *Improper Conduct,* see the essay by Marvin D'Lugo in this volume.

20. *Rompiendo el silencio* aired on Miami Univision affiliate Channel 23 on October 1, 1994. It is also available on video from the producers.

21. I use "Cuba" to refer to the greater nation, beyond the geographical confines of the island, that includes the exiled communities.

22. Nelson Valdés, "Cuban Political Culture: Between Betrayal and Death," in Sandor Halebsky and John M. Kirk, eds., *Cuba in Transition* (Boulder, Colo.: Westview Press, 1992), 217.

23. Gustavo Pérez Firmat, *Life on the Hyphen: The Cuban-American Way* (Austin: University of Texas Press, 1994), 4–5.

24. David Gonzalez, "Harlem Was on Their Mind," *New York Times,* February 20, 1994, H11.

25. Ferrera-Balanquet's work is analyzed in more detail in the essays by Frances Negrón-Muntaner and Christopher Ortiz in this volume.

26. For detailed analyses of her work, see the essays by Frances Negrón-Muntaner and José Esteban Muñoz in this volume.

27. Rocío García, "Andy García debuta como director," *Aquí New Orleans* (January 1994): 16; Alex Abella, "The New Rhythm of Florida," *Los Angeles Times Magazine,* May 23, 1993, 38.

28. With the exception of Ferrera-Balanquet, who was over eighteen when he left Cuba during the Mariel exodus.

29. For more information, see Alejandro Ríos, "Otro Cine Cubano de Hoy," *Cine Cubano* 133 (November–December 1991): 53–57.

30. Perhaps it is also important that these young Cuban Americans have managed to make "pilgrimages" back to the island itself, not so much to exorcise the past, but to reencounter their Cubanness.

Drama Queens: Latino Gay and Lesbian Independent Film/Video

Frances Negrón-Muntaner

The 1980s and early 1990s were important years for the production and public discussion of U.S. gay and lesbian independent media. In some cases, attacks from the New Right brought unprecedented
attention to work by (mostly) gay men, including gay men of color.
With very few exceptions, however, the work of Latino gay and lesbian
cultural producers was not part of these national debates, despite the
fact that Latino gay and lesbian media has circulated since the early
1980s, and increased dramatically thereafter. Perhaps, as Chicano gay
performance artist Luis Alfaro once noted, to be censored one must
be heard first (Sadownick 1989). The disavowal of Latino gay and lesbian cultural production is also reproduced at the level of film scholarship, where queer theorists and feminists alike continue to ignore
its existence and specific representational strategies. Recent examples
of this situation include the four hundred-plus-page anthology *Queer
Looks* (1993), in which only one article addresses issues pertaining
to Latinos.[1]

This state of affairs is partly the result of several tendencies in U.S.
scholarship. The first (and historically more consistent) is the tendency to theorize the diversity of gay and lesbian community formations as a homogeneous block of "white" representations, subjectivities, and experiences. A second, and perhaps less obvious, but no less
problematic, tendency, is the frequent use of African American subjectivities as the sign of diversity and difference *itself*. As Robert Reid-
Pharr (1993) comments, "Its inclusion, no matter how trivial or simplistic helps fend off charges of elitism, Eurocentrism, xenophobia,
and racism" (60). Latino gay and lesbian cultural practices, even when
they are visually (albeit problematically) represented in films such as
Paris Is Burning (1991), also tend to be homogenized under a generic
"black and Latino" experience without critical attention to difference
and specificity. This last tendency in film and criticism is significantly

59

different, however, from the efforts of filmmakers of color to represent strategic affinities between Latinos, African Americans, and Native Americans (i.e., Raúl Ferrera-Balanquet, Osa Hidalgo de la Riva, and the House of Color Collective) within a general conceptualization of diaspora and/or native cultures.

First Act

This essay will attempt to map some of the historical, political, and aesthetic contexts of Latino gay and lesbian film and video production, emphasizing the consistent use of certain discourses and representational strategies in a selected number of works, such as *Susana* (1980) by Susana Muñoz, *Seams* (1992) by Karim Aïnouz, *¡Viva 16!* by Augie Robles and Valentín Aguirre (1994), *Mérida Proscrita* (1990) by Raúl Ferrera-Balanquet and Enrique Novelo-Cascante, *How to Kill Her* (1990) by Ana María Simo, and *Carmelita Tropicana: Your Kunst Is Your Waffen* (1993) by Ela Troyano. Through an active dialogue with these films and videos, I will outline specific strategies used by some Latino gay and lesbian filmmakers to subvert and transform Latino cultural forms and social constructs from within.

The minor public explosion of Latino gay and lesbian sexualities/textualities during the last fifteen years can be attributed to several factors. Without suggesting a strict causality, these elements have contributed to the opening of cultural spaces for this media to flourish, build an audience, and articulate Latino gay and lesbian identities. First, a number of gay and lesbian Latinos (mostly Chicanos and Puerto Ricans) were formed during and participated in the civil rights-inspired cultural and political movements of the 1970s. Despite the fact that many of these makers were/are not "out," they have participated in the creation of Latino and independent film/video infrastructures, and in critical debates around Latino cultural production. Thus, they laid the groundwork for the production and reception of more recent Latino queer films and videos, as media advocates and through visual experimentation, innovative approaches to formerly erased subjectivities (particularly women), and the proposal of alternative discourses about sexuality, family structures, and gender relations.

Second, the increased influence and critical canonization of the work of several openly gay or lesbian Latino and Latin American cultural producers such as Gloria Anzaldúa, Cherríe Moraga, Manuel Puig,

and Reinaldo Arenas facilitated the articulation of Latino queer subjectivities within the academy and in broader political/cultural movements and debates (for example, Third World feminisms, Marxist criticism) and within some gay and lesbian communities.

Third, and connected to the U.S. prominence of writers such as Arenas, is the 1980 Mariel boat lift and subsequent debates around the
Cuban state's antihomosexual policies. Films such as Nestor Almendros and Orlando Jiménez-Leal's *Improper Conduct* (1984) constructed
a sympathetic portrait of politically persecuted Cuban gay men and
lesbians as a metaphor for the "evils" of the Cuban Revolution. Despite the debatable premises of this film, the broad representation of
Cuban gay and lesbian subjects cannot be discounted in a schematic
account of Latino gay and lesbian political community formations in
the United States.[2] Not only have several Cuban gay and lesbian filmmakers discussed here actually sought exile through Mariel, but also
non-Cuban filmmakers such as Graciela Sánchez (*No porque Fidel
lo diga* [1987]) have proposed a Chicana lesbian perspective on the
Cuban situation, as part of a strategy to raise issues such as the "origins" of homophobia in Latino cultures. Furthermore, reports of ha-
rassment, torture, and incarceration of Cuban gay men and lesbians
divided many among Latino gays and lesbians (particularly those with
any connections to the left), foregrounding issues of queer visibility
among some Latino communities.

Fourth, and more immediately, the sharp increase of gay and lesbian work toward the end of the 1980s is linked to transformations
brought about by the AIDS epidemic. The AIDS crisis created a political and discursive need to address heterosexism and promote safer sex
practices in Latino communities across the country (including those
that did not self-identify as "gay" or "lesbian"). Responses to the
epidemic included films and videos by AIDS activists working within
the most radical sectors of the AIDS movement (i.e., the work of Ray
Navarro and video collectives such as House of Color), and by film/
videomakers working for Latino organizations or constituencies. This
media proliferation was partly made possible because same-sex sexuality, particularly among men, could be articulated within a health
crisis discourse (illness/danger) on behalf of the health and safety of
the general Latino community. In this sense, the AIDS video *Ojos que
no ven* (1987), produced by the Instituto Nacional de la Raza, inau-
gurated a different space for the representation of Latino gay sexual-

ity, this time mediated by melodramatic representational strategies framed by the *telenovela*.[3]

Fifth, despite the fact that most Latino gay and lesbian pioneers have been/are "closeted" and that early AIDS films cautiously sanitized gay male representations, *Susana* (1980), by Jewish Argentinian filmmaker Susana Muñoz, provides a point of departure for a discussion of Latino gay and lesbian independent film/video aesthetics and the establishment of one of its most significant modes: the personal, reflexive (staged) documentary.

Last, the popularity of drag in both commercial and independent film over the last decade (made by both queers and heterosexuals) has highlighted Latino and Latin American drag queens and transsexuals. Thus, one encounters representations of Latino and Latin American gay men in drag in such disparate films as Monika Treut's *My Father Is Coming*, Carlos Aparicio and Susan Aiken's *The Salt Mines, Mambo Mouth* featuring John Leguizamo, and María Novaro's *Danzón*. Although these films are often voyeuristic or exoticizing, they nonetheless contribute to a proliferation of Latino gay and lesbian representations.

Before fully engaging with the task at hand, a clarification of the two key terms of this essay is necessary. The first is, predictably, the category of "Latino" itself, since it does not articulate a racial, ethnic, national, or strictly linguistic specificity. "Latinos" are produced through a combination of effects produced by racism, Latin American colonialism, the contemporary civil rights discourse, class euphemism, political strategy, and crossing national or ethnic borders.[4] The films and videos discussed here have been produced by diverse groups of ethnic and national subjects (Argentinians, Chicanos, Cubans, Brazilians), of diverse social classes, gender, races, education, and migratory histories. However, given the porousness of these categories in relation to production ("ethnic" within a "nation") and distribution (transnational, panethnic), the term "Latino" is not altogether irrelevant because it refers to modes of representation, exhibition strategies, and imagined communities of producers and spectators of "Latino gay and lesbian films" in the United States.

The second set of difficulties in the study of Latino gay and lesbian media stems from the concept of identity itself, which both enables and problematicizes the discussion of desires in a nonnormative way. The use of "Latino gay and lesbian" as an identity marker to encompass such a diverse body of texts no doubt produces a homogenized subject that erases differences in sexual, historical, community, and symbolic practices. In this sense, the creation of a supposedly more complex "identity" (hyphenated to include markers for gender, sexuality, and ethnicity) threatens to persist as a sign of (unified) difference instead of a space for hybrid, fluid, and contradictory practices. Ironically, the very instability of a Latino gay and lesbian subjectivity is repeatedly performed in several of the discussed films and videos, resisting the discourse of a sovereign Latino queer identity.

Drama Queens: Family Trauma, Ambiguities, and Melodrama

Despite all identity disclaimers, two strong tendencies mark the films and videos discussed here: formally hybrid, reflexive, "staged" identity narratives and subverted melodramas framed by a musical genre (bolero, *ranchera*, tango). Given that these works were produced between 1980 and 1993, and that they consistently use specific representational strategies, Raymond Williams's (1977: 132) notion of "structure of feeling" to describe "a social experience which is still in process ... not yet recognized as social but taken to be private, idiosyncratic as social and even isolating" seems particularly fitting as a point of departure. Williams's formulation has already been used by self-identified queer theorists and filmmakers such as Greg Bordowitz (1993), who defines a specifically queer structure of feeling as the relationship between how heterosexist oppression attempts to "contain" queer sexualities and how queers fight oppression by forming communities. Bordowitz, however, identifies only one queer structure of feeling marked by masquerade. In this space, I would like to propose several Latino gay and lesbian structures of feeling that constitute diverse Latino queer subjectivities, communities, and sensibilities.

Appropriately, the first independently produced Latina lesbian film still in distribution — *Susana,* a black-and-white film short by Susana Muñoz (who later collaborated with Lourdes Portillo in two films: *Las Madres de la Plaza de Mayo* and *La Ofrenda: The Days of the Dead)* — is exemplary of one of these "structures of feelings." Also evidenced in Karim Aïnouz's *Seams* and Frances Negrón-Muntaner's *Brincando el charco: Portrait of a Puerto Rican* (1994), this structure of feeling has at least six basic elements: formal hybridity (mixing of diverse genres and modes of address), self-reflexivity, the construction of an artist persona often involved in a journey of discovery and confrontation, the representation of geographical dislocation, the contextualization of the subject's drama within the immediate and/or symbolic family, and the self-conscious use of media to construct an alternative reality for the speaking subject/subject of representation. Furthermore, these films have been made by native Spanish- or Portuguese-speaking filmmakers about "themselves" and their families for English-speaking audiences in order to reconstitute an imaginary community, not in the place of birth (the "homeland"), but in the United States. In this sense, the choice of language in these films suggests a desire to affirm an immigrant gay identity in U.S. terms to audiences constituted around gay or lesbian Latino, or gay/lesbian Latino, identities rather than to Latin American nationals. These films are not, however, exercises in nostalgia but texts of simultaneous healing and rupture, assimilation ("English") and affirmation of difference (accent), folded maps of journeys of no return that leave the speaking subject always wanting.

I will engage with the deployment of these strategies in *Susana* and *Seams*. A third text, *¡Viva 16!*, a video on Chicano gay and lesbian histories in San Francisco, will act as counterpoint to the trope of personal journeys, and will serve as a transition to the second, or melodramatic, "structure of feeling."

Despite *Susana*'s deceptive quality as a "straightforward" reflexive documentary, the film's strategy is that of staging identity as a family drama in which (unlike the AIDS films of the 1980s) the daughter confronts her family and puts them on trial (with the audience as witness) for their homophobia. Similar to the AIDS films, however, is the conflation of family and community (in this case the "motherland"). The voices of former lovers, siblings, and parents establish a dialogue with the structuring (empowered) and besieged (constructed) voice of Susana, who makes use of U.S. white lesbian-feminist discourses and styles of the late 1970s to continuously resist her family's/motherland's metanarrative of "normal" womanhood. The family's complicity with the construction of an immigrant lesbian location allows for reading the film as a staged "reconciliation" (Kotz 1993) in which Susana's sister Graciela embodies the possibility of acknowledging Susana's difference, marked by sexuality. However, this desire is often overshadowed by the more consistent strategy of equating the motherland with oppression and the pressure to conform evidenced by the construction of Graciela as the embodiment of the properly socialized Argentinian, middle-class, white, heterosexual subject. In this case, the family members' "broken" English acts as a reminder that this is a performance for another context, in the service of a new identity that, despite its oppositional staging, requires the complicity of all for its effectiveness.

Combining home movies, staged interviews, voice-overs from the filmmaker's persona's parents, family album photographs, provoked encounters (akin to Jean Rouch and Edgar Morin's *Chronicle of a Summer*), scripted interventions by Graciela (who is shown reading her lines), still photography, and archival footage, *Susana* produces a multilayered text with the self-described intention of defining the "true" self of the lesbian subject (in opposition to those constructed by family and homeland) through a practice of self-conscious image making (film and photography). As Kotz (1993) suggests, "What is at stake, from the outset, is who gets to represent Susana and how: what genres, narratives, and histories her life will be shaped and understood by.... Even though this is her film, it is clearly not her story only" (72). Yet, although never identified as problematic, Susana's image of herself with friends, and former and current lovers, suggests the transient nature of experience (only available through representation) and the fragility of self-representation as a sign of truth. As a Latina lesbian film text, *Susana* constructs a space for a Latina lesbian subject who chooses alliances with the white and/or Jewish community, but it does not examine the differences and tensions within these communities. Thus, it is not surprising that *Susana*'s only depiction of sexual interaction shows two identically dressed women with light skin and long hair tensely touching each other's bodies. A sequence ostensibly about the sexual pleasures between women, this is the film's least sensual moment, raising questions about the location of pleasure in this newfound identity and the strategies used to represent these pleasures beyond their opposition to traditional Argentine culture.

As in *Seams*, fleeing the homeland is constructed as the only viable way to reconstitute a space for gay and lesbian desires. In this sense, this is a "structure of feeling" of an immigrant cinema. In *Susana*, family antagonism makes the move necessary for the founding of a "speaking" lesbian subject. Susana's mother's voice-over stages her daughter's raison d'être by commenting: "I can't find any problem

From *Seams,* directed by Karim Aïnouz. (Photo courtesy of Frameline.)

about her.... Until she grew up and found out that Mendoza was too small for her and decided to leave home." And Susana, of course, says "Yes, mother," recontextualizing the mother's critique as the voice of patriarchal complacency rooted in the family, the media (through a rare campy use of a Disney cartoon), and the nation.

The voyage to subjectivity is represented through another opposition, that of Susana as artist. In fact, "being" a lesbian and a photographer/filmmaker is embedded in the same narrative of becoming: "At the same time I discovered my vocation for art and women." Still photography is thus used in multiple ways in the film: to introduce characters, as a tool for family therapy and, most important, as the only representation about herself that Susana trusts as truthful. In this sense, the album photographs are allied to a sexist "field of vision" of the parent who took them and only a practice of self-conscious lesbian representation will transform how lesbians are represented and read. The founding of lesbian subjectivity, then, coincides with a representational praxis that seeks a fixed notion of the subject, but nonetheless registers the contradictions of that quest.

Aïnouz's *Seams* shares the reflexive strategies enacted in *Susana,* yet configures a second structure of feeling based on the use of melodrama and romantic musical forms such as the bolero. A formally complex film, *Seams* combines archival footage, interviews, fictionalized fantasy, and home movies in a family drama that mediates between gay and women's survival strategies in patriarchal cultures. Whereas in *Susana* the spectator never "meets" the parents, in *Seams* one never "sees" the filmmaker persona. Thus, *Seams* uses hybrid and reflexive strategies for opposite purposes: to locate a language of resistance within the homeland culture even when the subject is geographically displaced and critical of certain aspects of his formation as a Brazilian male subject. *Seams* spans a twenty-six-year period (1966 to 1992) concurrent with the life of the filmmaker. As in *Susana,* the speaking subject is, literally, located in another place. The opening underlines the sense that all knowledge is a situated knowledge (Haraway 1991) as the voice-over contrasts the sexualization of Brazil in a travel-guide description with the patriarchal (national) definition of Brazil. To foreign interests (sexual and economic), Brazil is more desirable as sensual and female; to be penetrated. For a Brazilian male subject bent on maintaining heterosexual privilege, Brazil is a land of "machos." Yet, for a Brazilian gay male subject attempting to come to terms with a public political identity, Brazil is also the voices of his grandmother and great-aunts as they resist and negotiate the complex historical context within which they have lived.

Seams makes the use of English problematic, articulating a structure of feeling denied by *Susana,* Aïnouz's voice-over declares: "When I speak these names [of his great-aunts] in this language, it sounds odd; a bundle of meaningless syllables." *Seams* articulates the inability of the immigrant subject to share loss with the "original" audience. In this sense, this is a tale of loss unvoiced, a melodrama not unlike the story narrated by his great-aunts and visually represented as a series of fictional vignettes with a soft Brazilian ballad in the background: "a melodrama that reminded me of my mother's and grandmother's fate." The ritual telling of the melodrama — similar to the women's ill-fated relationships with men — acts as memory and fantasy, containment and contentment, where women's voices are constructed through patriarchal structures. As Aïnouz comments, describing how all men eventually abandon his household: "We became a patriarchy without men."

In its more radical moments, *Seams* suggests that immigrant Latino cinema is always an impossible exercise in translation. This practice of translation occurs at various levels and is never satisfactorily resolved: (1) the coding of the sexism and homophobia present in everyday language, (2) a tracing of the chain of associations implicit in specific words and their multiple meanings, (3) a literal translation of these words and analysis to English, and (4) perhaps even more complexly, Aïnouz's own appropriation of the great-aunt's stories. Thus, "macho means bofe which means tripe which means homen which means man," so that "man" becomes an empty category only traceable to performance and memory, yet with specific effects beyond the performance.

Just as translation is insufficient and "man" a symbolic structure, *Seams* uses several nonessentialist strategies to locate the speaking subject's desires as a gay man. These strategies include the self-conscious use of Aïnouz's great-aunts and grandmother's stories to construct the voice of a male subject, the seduction of a "feminine" sensibility (melodrama), and the recurring images of cotton in various stages of transformation, metaphorically suggesting a subject always in process: raw, cotton balls, thread, waste. Parting from a discourse of affinity rather than identity, *Seams* creates a fluid subject position unified only by the resistance to patriarchal power structures identified as heterosexist and homophobic and located in language. It is by reading the great-aunt's stories as resistance strategies that Aïnouz learns that "Machos weren't to be trusted," and that men's importance in relation to women's lives is purely pragmatic: "I got married to get my own house," says Joanita. More important, he learned from his grandmother that "those who learn to get over a man, one hundred years they'll live." Not unlike the bolero, this piece of wisdom can be appropriated by a gay man because of the gender indeterminacy of its speaking subject. At the same time, despite the fact that Aïnouz was able to flee his house underlines that even as a *gay* man, he is still a man with license to leave at will.

The melodramatic vignettes that (together with the interviews) structure the film tell the story of María, her loving husband, and how fate tore them apart. Within the film, melodrama acts both as a site of pleasure and as a resistance narrative for his great-aunts, who (according to Aïnouz) saw in the story the contradictions they had lived through. Thus, the melodrama genre in *Seams* is appropriated for contradictory desires and pleasures (pains). Yet, Aïnouz's (film persona) identification with the melodrama suggests that here too is an irrecuperable loss; that indeed Brazil is not only the lessons learned from the aunts in their resistance to patriarchy but the desire for Brazilian men that is carefully disavowed in the narrative. This is, perhaps,

Aïnouz's loss: to be away from Brazil not as a woman but as a gay man; to be a gay man only when away from Brazil, as his last reported conversation with his aunt Celia reveals. Aïnouz asks his unmarried aunt Celia if she has ever slept with a man. Celia pretends not to hear, then asks Aïnouz when he will get a girlfriend. He — approaching her resistance to the disclosure of potential pleasures — pretends in turn not to have heard her. In this way, *Seams* complicates *Susana*'s drama by pointing to the instability of the desiring subject as well as the insoluble contradictions of the exiled subject who must leave home to be gay or lesbian, seeking symbolic mediation to come to pleasures learned there.

Robles and Aguirre's video documentary short *¡Viva 16!* uses still photography, interviews, and drag shows to tell a tale not of an individual subject in a quest for identity, but of an assorted group of mostly Chicano gay men defining and re-creating their history through space (two Latino gay bars in San Francisco), political organizing, and memory. Although many of the subjects in *¡Viva 16!* are Mexican immigrants or Chicano migrants from other parts of the United States who moved to San Francisco in search of the social space to be queer, their sense of identity comes from the multiple interrelations of people and spaces (exemplified by 16th Street), and thus it is always socially defined. At the same time, identity is shown to be an elusive category for the individual subjects even as they attempt to define themselves in relation to others. Thus, two activists (man and woman) speak about deep-seated gender conflicts within the Chicano gay and lesbian movement, while a transsexual Chicana makes clear that she considers herself a Latina, not a transvestite (performer): "Not just because we look alike means we are." Perhaps even more poignant is one young man's story of being picked up by a man who turned out to be a "crossdresser" while he was doing drag at a bar. Despite the claim by several subjects that they found themselves as gay or lesbian on 16th Street, the juxtapositions of stories, migratory histories, desires, and gender performances suggest that when they speak about "themselves" they are often not referring to others who share that same space and have an identical claim.

Apart from the direct commentary and editing that highlight identity as a slippery construct, the frequent use of drag performance and imagery from a Cinco de Mayo parade suggests that, as Butler (1990) has written, identity is a performance, for a specific audience and for

often unpredictable effects. As one of the older men interviewed recalls, "[we] lived two and three lives": an impersonation for the family, a persona for the gay spaces, and an undisclosed identity for chance
encounters in dark alleys. Different from all other films/videos discussed
here, ¡Viva 16! alternates between Spanish and English without attempting to translate or provide subtitles. Thus, the video is addressed
to a spectator who must be bilingual (and fluent in Mexicanismos and
Chicanimos), interested not in the spectacle of the other but in collective dialogue.

Drama Queens: Recent Latino Gay and
Lesbian Film/Video

If *Susana* attempts to reconstitute a space for Latina lesbian
subjectivity by negating the homeland culture, a number of films from
1990 onward, including ¡Viva 16!, present a new set of strategies for
articulating Latino gay and lesbian subjectivities that use musical forms
as well as specific forms of melodrama. Although the drag queens in
¡Viva 16! are also represented dancing to disco music, the video suggests that memory is inscribed in the bolero or *ranchera,* and that this
poetics of love and loss coalesces in the melodrama.

In many Latino gay and lesbian films, bolero and other romantic
musical forms have been used to interpellate pan-American/Latino
audiences. Rooted in European traditions of *amor cortés,* romanticism,
and late nineteenth-century modernism, the bolero became a pan-Latin
American mass-media phenomenon in the twentieth century and one
of the most accessible ways for many Latin American subjects to fan-
tasize, imagine, and give free rein to their desires (Castillo 1990; Zavala 1991). Furthermore, the bolero constitutes a culturally specific
form for sharing with the world that which makes "lovers" (culturally understood as heterosexual) suffer. In this sense, the bolero is a
vehicle for making desire public, while the ambiguity of gender in the
writing, performance, and reception of the bolero makes it particularly susceptible to queer appropriation. Thus, a bolero written to a
woman from a presumably (ambiguous) masculine perspective, sung
by a female performer, can become a lesbian seduction; the same bolero,
sung by a drag queen at a gay bar, also transforms its referents. The
multiple possibilities of signification of the bolero construct a poetics
of the body and the play of presence/absence, where, to paraphrase a

popular Lacanian presence, desire is never where one thinks it is, but where it desires to be.

The bolero is analogous in its seductive effect to melodrama and camp, which also privilege performance (although camp, unlike melodrama, seduces through irony, not identification). The bolero seeks to seduce the listener not by virtue of its discursive truth but by its elusiveness: "For if an object can be simply dominated, the subject of desire, by contrast, has to be seduced" (Baudrillard 1979: 174). Perhaps this tendency toward seduction as subversive strategy explains a certain resistance to articulating Latino gay and lesbian subjectivities exclusively through discourses of identity (as, for example, *Tongues Untied* by Marlon Riggs).[5] Even in *Carmelita Tropicana,* which articulates a very distinct antisexist, pro-choice, antiracist, anticapitalist politics, identity is mostly a parodic performance.

Besides the affinity to strategies of seduction, the bolero is also consonant with Latino gay and lesbian structures of feeling because it "verifies" personal suffering and renders it culturally legitimate (or even sublime). The bolero performs the function of a mnemonic device for Latino gay and lesbian histories—it is a coded history for lived experiences, fantasies, and past loves. Although the bolero is a form relishing the "never," "always," and "forever," it is also continuously reinvested with new lovers (new histories), thus pointing to the arbitrariness of desire and the fluidity of historical narrative and signification. On this and other levels, the bolero is never free of contradictions and excess; it resists normalizing discourses such as those of marriage and family, and often attempts to give voice to an irrationality that the singing voice/subject cannot explain—"que por qué te estoy queriendo, no me pidas la razón, pues yo mismo no comprendo, ni mi pobre corazón" (do not ask why I love you, I do not even understand my own poor heart)—or have adequate words for. These last elements are extremely important for this discussion because, in a homophobic context, the acknowledgment of desire as irrational and beyond the homosexual's control can be a liberating premise for many gay and lesbian subjects.

The extensive use of the bolero by Latino gay and lesbian film- and videomakers suggests a simultaneous transgressive and recuperative impulse. It is transgressive to the extent that it subverts the preferred heterosexual readings of sexuality and desire in Latino cultures by appropriating a legitimized and dominant heterosexual cultural form, and recuperative to the extent that it leaves gender polarity intact. Perhaps more important, the use of the bolero is a strategy for symbolic integration—not marginalization—into the body social of an imagined Latino/pan-Latin American community. If nothing else, then, these films make ordinary gay and lesbian lives somewhat extraordinary in the dramatization of personal decisions that stand for an entire cultural configuration. The simultaneous symbolization and dramatization of everyday life is seductive to many gays and lesbians to the degree that resistance is located even in the most intimate (and secret) of acts. At the same time, because of its tendency to displace the social onto the personal theatrically, the melodrama is a flexible genre for imagining a new order of things.

Mérida Proscrita, directed by Ferrera-Balanquet and Novelo-Cascante, tells the story of two unlikely lovers in the city of Mérida, Mexico. The narrative begins with a bolero by Pedro Infante ("Historia de un amor"), supposedly playing on the radio (a significant detail because it was through radio technology that the bolero created its mass audience). The bolero is used ironically in this sequence, as indeed, for some audiences, this is an "unusual" love story: it is not, as most bolero listeners would expect, heterosexual. The bolerista's voice frames everyday images of the street, police, traffic, flag, and church as part of something extraordinary that will unfold—"es la historia de un amor como no hay otro igual" (it is the story of a unique love affair)—and as accomplice to the drama depicted: the ever-deferred kiss between the two main characters (named in the credits as the Lover and the Hustler). Thus, a seemingly trivial line by a radio announcer concerning a major "event" in the city comments ironically on a deferred intimate moment that is made impossible not by the individuals involved but by the repressive apparatuses (church, state, police). At the same time, the video is still anchored in a construction of romantic love as a transcendental narrative of redemption for the alienated subject (the Hustler).

As a melodrama, Mérida Proscrita is a hybrid form that incorporates the testimonio—where the Hustler, for example, tells the circumstances of his life (poverty, orphanhood, lack of education, alienation)—as well as the ironic distancing of camp. In one of the most deconstructive and pleasurable scenes, the melodramatic excess of an encounter between the Lover and the Hustler is undercut by the presence of another man blocking the spectator's gaze. This unnamed char-

acter, previously seen walking with the Lover in animated conversation, continues walking through an apartment building until he faces
an audience of neighbors looking at the action from a balcony. Once
in front of his audience, he folds the bedsheets he had been using as
a costume and, pretending to be a tenor singing the sound track's opera,
concludes Puccini's aria and receives a standing ovation. In this sequence, various structures are questioned without compromising the
audience's pleasure. Camp is used to ridicule melodrama conventions
even as melodrama serves to make "real" the Lover's pain and the
Hustler's frustration. The melodrama also "feminizes" the Hustler,
who now takes on the discourse of the Lover by asking for another
chance. This brief sequence combines melodrama, opera, drag, and
camp to bring the couple's dilemma into the public sphere. The ap-
plause, while ambiguous, allows for several readings, validating (1)
the singer for his deconstructive performance, (2) the Lover's "true"
love, or (3) the Hustler's request for another chance. In sum, the melodrama makes the love that dare not speak its name a pleasurable
spectacle.

How to Kill Her, a black-and-white film by Cuban playwright and
filmmaker Ana María Simo, uses similar narrative structures. As in
Mérida Proscrita, the main characters of How to Kill Her never speak
in synch and the language of feeling is, again, the bolero, but this film
is set on the Lower East Side and the language of communication is
English. How to Kill Her opens with a bolero by Beny Moré under a
New York landscape of sky, water, and bridge. A pan of a Lower
East Side park with Moré's lyrics ("Este tiempo sin tus besos, yo
sufro. Son mis horas de agonía sin ti. Oh, oh, vida, no te alejes ..."
[Life without your kisses makes me suffer. Hours of agony pass without you. Oh, oh, my love, don't leave me ...]) transforms the landscape
into a metaphor for loss (following a classic romantic premise) and into
a witness to extraordinary pain and suffering. The bolero also makes
suffering larger than life and hyperbolic, because, as the main character Mora herself later admits, she never even slept with Elsa, the
object of her obsessive desire. The bolero is thus not a descriptive language but a culturally specific way of managing suffering, a pan-Latino
structure of feeling.

As the narrator begins her tale once the bolerista concludes, we
are told that Mora has become suicidal. After waking up horrified that
she has slept in a park, Mora throws herself against an iron fence,

overtaken by frustration. As in many boleros, in *How to Kill Her* love is constructed as an illness. The narrator's voice (which, in a symbolic act of complicity, is often Mora's voice) is explicit: "People thought she was cured of Elsa. But Mora was still sick." This illness, as in melodrama, can lead to masochistic behavior in which the subject's frustration culminates in repeated acts of self-violation (Elsaesser 1991). Memories of happier times with the woman she desires continue to threaten her with madness, while the bolero confirms that these feelings were (are) legitimate. A desperate attempt to become "cured" takes Mora to her psychoanalyst, who fears for her patient and wants to prescribe medication. Mora, however, refuses: "I'm not taking any of that shit. I'm sane." Thus, a common American, middle-class solution to the excessive behavior of a Latina subject is ridiculed as inappropriate: Dr. Stern (irony is not lost) compulsively consults her two wristwatches while she muses whether Mora is psychotic. In this case, the bolero appears much less irrational than the respectable scientific practice of psychoanalysis. Dr. Stern's inability to understand the codes of the bolero as symbolic framing creates a ridiculous encounter between science and emotion, thought against emotion. Thus, Dr. Stern asks: "Why kill her? If you kill her, you'll be in pain for the rest of your life." In order for Mora to come to terms with a delegitimized absence, she makes sense of it dramatically: "I'm in pain for the rest of my life now. It'll be less painful to have a real motive. Right now the motive is ridiculous." Mora is, of course, not sick. She only wants what many boleros suggest is appropriate when one is abandoned by a lover: revenge. Mora knows what will make her "feel" better. "This is how I'll kill you. I'll beat you to a bloody pulp.... I'll tie you into chair until you see me and when you finally see me, I will shoot you." Despite the fact that Mora never "kills" Elsa, the film itself is a performance of that desire for revenge, couched between the pleasurable memory of love and the *despecho* (spite) of being abandoned.

Carmelita Tropicana is a short film narrative featuring Cuban performance "artiste" Carmelita Tropicana. The film combines a melodramatic plot (a group of members of the lesbian feminist organization "GIA" are arrested after defending a clinic against Christian activists) where Carmelita Tropicana runs into the woman who mugged her a few days before on her way home. Further coincidences produce affinity between the mugger Di and Carmelita as the former explains how she received nurturance and support from Puerto Rican women during a previous imprisonment. Through this and other strategies (shifts from singing a *ranchera* to Afro-American spirituals), the film destabilizes any sense of a universal lesbian and/or Latina subjectivity: some lesbians are white and butch and serving time in jail while others are Latina, activists, and afraid of bugs. Yet, a sense of family or affinity may be forged in difference. This affinity permits a form of cohesion between former antagonists, and a mistake (Carmelita's lawyer has four names on her list as authorized to leave the prison) solidifies a new order of things where Di becomes a "productive" citizen by establishing an extermination business. However, far from a happy (ironic) ending, Di also dies of AIDS. In this sense, the film uses the arbitrariness of the world according to melodramatic conventions to suggest that it is created by structures rather than individuals.

Carmelita Tropicana makes explicit quotations to the bolero as a form: in the opening sequences, for example, Carmelita wakes up in front of a poster of María Félix, queen of the Mexican melodrama and muse of bolero composer Agustín Lara. A cut to a sign that reads "Lower East Side" and returns to *la Doña* also suggests that "Mexico" is not too distant from Loisaida, reinforcing the premise that many of these films and videos use the bolero to imagine and seduce a pan-Latino imagine community and audience. The reference to melodrama and the bolero is also made explicit, and used critically, when in prison Carmelita recalls the story of her aunt Cukita (at twenty-nine an "old maid" or perhaps a lesbian), who was killed by a suitor who in turn killed himself. In a flashback, the bolero "Lágrimas de sangre" (Blood tears) is played while Cukita awaits her death unawares. The film noir quality of this melodramatic representation (black and white, jump cuts, acute angles) suggests that melodrama deployed acritically and within a masculinist vision of the world can also lead to death. The excessive (and drag) performances in this sequence both ridicule the more vulgar uses of melodrama (*cursilería*) and use the form to critique domestic violence.

Yet, perhaps *Carmelita Tropicana*'s most important difference from other melodramatic/bolero structures lies in its more extensive use of camp humor to create critical distance from the melodrama. This points to a need to avoid clustering all these diverse strategies—camp, *ranchera,* and melodrama—under the category of gay camp. Indeed, the pleasures associated with (implicitly bourgeois, white, male) camp— exaggeration, artifice, and extremity (Bergman 1993); incongruity, theatricality, and humor (Newton 1993); life as theater, the world in quotation marks (Sontag 1969); aestheticism, pleasure in the incongruous, and drag (Babuscio 1984)—can also be read into the *telenovela* and other forms of melodrama, making clear-cut distinctions difficult. However, in Latino gay and lesbian films, camp introduces an irony that is reflexive and theatrical in ways that exceed the structures and even the effects of melodrama. While melodrama privileges identification, camp functions through distancing; while melodrama can be campy in its unself-conscious excess, camp always entails active relationships between subject and object/situation. Thus, Carmelita's platform shoes, ruffles, and thick accent are excesses not possible within classic melodrama. Her campiness functions to call attention to the incongruous in U.S. reality without promoting full identification or sympathy (i.e., the antiabortion activists). Thus, camp serves as a distancing strategy through humor and facilitates a critical attitude when the melodramatic elements threaten to slide into complicity.

Finally, the performance of the Mexican *ranchera* tropicalizes the prison. The four women lip-synch dressed in a blurred code of fatigues and *rumbera* (in true drag fashion), destabilizing the meaning of being in or out, subtly critiquing domestic violence and the erasure of women's stories in official history. Thus, the *ranchera,* a typical space for the construction of "bad" and suffering women, becomes a feminist anthem where a unified "we" refers to women united against patriarchy and the silence around violence against women. The play of opposites ("el amor nos da calor y también un gran dolor" [love gives us great warmth and even greater pain]) and the secularization of religion ("haciendo de la liberación nuestra nueva religión" [making liberation our new religion]) also function as camp in that they constitute a shift of identification and gender performance different from the uses of the bolero found in all other films discussed here. Instead of mourning the loss of someone or attempting the seduction of another, the *ranchera*'s performance undermines the melodramatic "reality" by suggesting that "life is itself role and theater, appearance and impersonation" (Babuscio 1994: 44). In this sense, camp can be used to revalorize lives and the experiences of the "frivolous" at the same time that it critiques the logic that defines the serious and the frivolous. The return of the *ranchera* after Carmelita's last performance as a tribute to Di also constitutes a "nonserious"

intervention for a serious purpose (as eulogy). Camp allows the celebration of Di's life through humor, whereas classic melodrama would
have soaked it in tears.

In sum, these Latino gay and lesbian films/videos suggest that drama
queens continue to question and invent ways of representing the complexity of queer cultures and the contradictory pleasures of our "selves."
As a man receiving an award toward the end of ¡Viva 16! comments:
"I thought about Martin Luther King and 'I have a dream' ... but
you know, Martin was straight [laughter] and I'm gay. And, gays, we
dream, yes, but if you're a queen you have a fantasy. And I have a
fantasy that someday ... we'll make a commitment to ourselves ...
to love ourselves."

Notes

The revision of this paper owes much to a panel discussion organized by
Arnaldo Cruz for the 1994 Latin American Studies Conference in Atlanta ti-
tled "Performing Latino Homosexualities." I am particularly endebted to
José Quiroga's paper, "(Queer) Boleros on a Tropical Night."

1. *Queer Looks,* ed. Martha Gever, John Greyson, and Pratibha (New
York: Routledge, 1993).
2. For a more detailed overview of the divided responses to *Improper
Conduct,* see the essays by Ana M. López and Marvin D'Lugo in this volume.
3. For a general discussion on Latino AIDS media, see Navarro and Saalfield 1989.
4. For a diverse range of opinions on the definition and strategic use of
"Latino," see Chon A. Noriega, "El hilo latino: Representation, Identity and
National Culture," *Jump Cut* 38 (June 1993); Juan Flores and George Yúdice,
"Living Borders/Buscando América," *Social Text* 24 (1990); and Martha E.
Giménez, "Latinos, Hispanics ... What Next?" *Heresies* 7 (1993).
5. For further discussion on *Tongues Untied,* see "Watching Tongues Un-
tie(d) while Reading Zami: Mapping Boundaries in Black Gay and Lesbian
Narratives," in *Feminism, Multiculturalism and the Media,* ed. Angharad
Valdivia (forthcoming, Sage Press).

References

Babuscio, Jack. "Camp and the Gay Sensibility." In Richard Dyer, ed. *Gays
and Film.* New York: Zoetrope, 1984. 40–57.
Baudrillard, Jean. *Seduction.* New York: St. Martin's Press, 1979.
Bergman, David, ed. *Camp Grounds: Style and Homosexuality.* Amherst:
University of Massachusetts Press, 1993.

Bordowitz, Gregg. "The AIDS Crisis Is Ridiculous." In Martha Gever, John Greyson, and Pratibha Parmar, eds., *Queer Looks*. New York: Routledge, 1993. 209–24.

Butler, Judith. *Gender Trouble*. New York: Routledge, 1990.

✓ Castillo, Rafael. *Fenomenología del bolero*. México: Monte Avila Editores, 1990.

Elsaesser, Thomas. "Tales of Sound and Fury: Observations on the Family Melodrama." In Marcia Landy, ed., *Imitations of Life: A Reader on Film and Television Melodrama*. Detroit, Mich.: Wayne State University Press, 1991. 68–91.

Haraway, Donna. *Simians, Cyborgs and Women: The Reinvention of Nature*. New York: Routledge, 1991.

Kotz, Liz. "Unofficial Stories: Documentaries by Latinas and Latin American Women." *Centro Bulletin* 2.8 (spring 1990): 59–69.

———. "Anything but Idyllic: Lesbian Filmmaking in the 1980's and 1990's." In Arlene Stein, ed., *Sisters, Sexperts, Queers: Beyond the Lesbian Nation*. New York: Penguin Books, 1993. 67–80.

Navarro, Ray, and Catherine Saalfield. "Not Just Black and White." *Independent* (July 1989): 18–23.

Newton, Esther. "Roles Models." In David Bergman, ed., *Camp Grounds: Style and Homosexuality*. Amherst: University of Massachusetts Press, 1993. 39–53.

Reid-Pharr, Robert. "The Spectacle of Blackness." *Radical America* 24.4 (1993): 51–64.

Sadownick, Doug. "Two Different Worlds: Luis Alfaro Bridges the Gap between Gay Fantasies and Latino Reality." *L.A. Weekly* 11.29 (1989), 62–63.

Sontag, Susan. *Against Interpretation*. New York: Farrar, Straus and Giroux, 1969.

Williams, Raymond. *Marxism and Literature*. London: Oxford University Press, 1977.

✓ Zavala, Iris. *El bolero: Historia de un amor*. Madrid: Alianza Editorial, 1991.

Close Readings

Crossing Invisible Borders:
Ramón Menéndez's *Stand and Deliver* (1987)

Ilene S. Goldman

Early in *Stand and Deliver* (Ramón Menéndez, 1987) Jaime Escalante boosts his students' confidence in their math abilities with a brief history lesson: "Did you know," he says, "that neither the Greeks nor the Romans were capable of using the concept of zero? It was your ancestors, the Mayas, who first contemplated the concept of zero, the absence of value. True story. You *burros* have math in your blood." A few scenes later he tells the same roomful of students at Garfield High School in East Los Angeles, "You already have two strikes against you. There are some people in this world who will assume that you know less than you do because of your name and your complexion. But math is the great equalizer." *Stand and Deliver* thus establishes a tension between assimilation and maintaining an identity distinct from dominant culture. This tension finally erupts into conflict when the Educational Testing Service (ETS) suspects the students of cheating. Framing this suspicion as a flagrant case of institutional racism perpetrated by ETS, the film's narrative illustrates the difficult relationships between an ethnic minority, in this case Chicanos, and a system that serves the so-called white majority. It borrows from a generic tradition — neophyte teacher wins the respect of a group of delinquent kids and guides them to success — made popular by such films as *Blackboard Jungle* (Richard Brooks, 1955) and *To Sir, With Love* (James Clavell, 1966).

Like Mr. Thackery (Sidney Poitier) in *To Sir, With Love,* Jaime Escalante (Edward James Olmos) is not an experienced teacher. Thackery teaches because he cannot find an engineering job. The job is a temporary means of survival. By the end of the film, Thackery recognizes the satisfaction he derives from teaching and decides to stay. Escalante, in contrast, has left a higher-paying position specifically because he wants to teach high school. The challenges of Garfield High School threaten to break his resolve, but in the end he too renews

81

his commitment to teaching. Although Thackery and Escalante end up in classrooms for different reasons, both face students who dare them to teach. Thackery and Escalante stand apart from their colleagues because of racial and ethnic difference. Both challenge their colleagues' resigned approach to students disadvantaged by socioeconomics and ethnicity. *Stand and Deliver* emphasizes the students' and their teacher's Latino heritage. The school system sees this ethnicity as an obstacle to learning, an attitude epitomized by the math department chair, Raquel Ortega. For Escalante, ethnicity provides an entrée into the students' minds. By the end of the film, the students find strength in their Chicano identity and fight a system that would limit their opportunities because of that identity.

An independent film, *Stand and Deliver* was funded by a number of different organizations. The seed money came from *American Playhouse*, a Public Broadcasting program that has funded a number of Chicano films, including *The Ballad of Gregorio Cortez* and *El Norte*.[1] The rest of the funds were assembled from a variety of sources, in the artisanal fashion of much oppositional and independent cinema. Although *Stand and Deliver* subsequently became one of the four films that caused critics in the late eighties to foresee a "Hispanic Hollywood" (along with *La Bamba, Born in East L.A.,* and *Milagro Beanfield War*), few Chicano/Latino films have followed these box-office successes and none has continued *Stand and Deliver*'s particular narrative tradition. On the other hand, *Lean on Me* (John G. Avildsen, 1989) carries on the tradition of *Blackboard Jungle, To Sir, With Love,* and *Stand and Deliver,* telling the story of Joe Clark (Morgan Freeman), a principal who vows to transform a troubled New Jersey inner-city high school. In *Renaissance Man* (Penny Marshall, 1994), Bill Rago (Danny DeVito) is an unwilling civilian teacher who inspires a group of underachieving army privates with lessons about Shakespeare. In all of these films the students are racial minorities and/or economically underprivileged. The teachers come from the other side of town, literally and figuratively. In the process of proving that these students can rise to their expectations, each teacher learns something from the students as well. By the end of the films, teacher and students have arrived at a place of mutual respect and admiration. Thus, while *Stand and Deliver*'s message of cultural pride and the necessity of fighting for change is situated around a "Chicano" theme (and an independent mode of production), it is difficult to simply identify *Stand*

and Deliver as a Chicano film, precisely because this message may also be understood as the intended message of the Hollywood teacher film in general.

Still, Chicano film scholars have referred to *Stand and Deliver* as a Chicano film and as a Chicano/Latino film.[2] Its story of peaceful struggle against institutional racism resists mainstream representations of Chicanos, affirming achievements rather than perpetuating violent images and role models. Borrowing from Paul Willemen's interpretation of countercinema, we might maintain that Chicano cinema (and *Stand and Deliver*) emphasizes a politics of deconstruction rather than an aesthetics of deconstruction: "A politics of deconstruction insists on the need to oppose particular institutionally dominant regimes of making particular kinds of sense, excluding or marginalising others. . . . The politics of deconstruction, then, insists on the need to say something different; an aesthetics of deconstruction dissolves into endlessly repeated difference games."[3] Thus, if, as Rosa Linda Fregoso argues, "the project of Chicano cinema may succinctly be summed up as the documentation of social reality through oppositional forms of knowledge about Chicanos,"[4] then *Stand and Deliver* fits the bill.

However, if the definition of Chicano cinema depends on the film being by and about Chicanos, one must question where *Stand and Deliver* falls, both in terms of its ethnic representation and its ambivalent politics.[5] Directed by the Cuban-born Ramón Menéndez and starring the Chicano actor Edward James Olmos, *Stand and Deliver* recounts the efforts of Bolivian-born Los Angeles resident Jaime Escalante to teach Advanced Placement (A.P.) calculus to a predominantly Chicano group of students at East Los Angeles's Garfield High School. One of its young stars, Lou Diamond Phillips (who achieved box-office recognition playing Ritchie Valens in *La Bamba*), is Filipino American. Nonetheless, *Stand and Deliver* presents a countervision of youths in East Los Angeles, youths assumed to be Chicano based on the neighborhood in which they live and the particular slang with which they punctuate their English dialogue.[6] Politically, the film is ambivalent as well. Although *Stand and Deliver* exposes and seeks to unsettle institutional racism, its criticism unfolds within a conventional, even conservative, narrative pattern. Indeed, racism is tackled only once by name — in a heated discussion between Escalante and the two ETS investigators. The film subtly plants the idea and when the students "stand and deliver" a second time, their conquest over a biased system is implicit and complete. Thus, *Stand and Deliver* is less a political or social critique than a film about cultural pride, teaching, learning, and the power of education. In the final analysis, *Stand and Deliver*—with its combination of elements of Chicano cinema and a popular narrative approach—navigates a narrow path between an oppositional cinema and Hollywood (and their attendant politics).

Stand and Deliver begins with Escalante's first moments at Garfield High School. As Escalante walks into the office, small white lettering announces to the viewer that the film is "Based on a True Story." Chon A. Noriega writes, "Most Chicano feature films are based on true stories or historical events."[7] Stressing the importance of the re-lationship between fiction and history, Noriega asserts, "These films attempt to reclaim a forgotten past, but also choose to do so within the parameters of narrative—as opposed to documentary—cinema."[8] Unlike other Chicano feature films, *Stand and Deliver* retells contem-porary events, not decades-old history. It dramatizes recent history before it is lost—resisting mainstream representations of a violent gang-infested East Los Angeles and affirming the importance of educa-tion and Chicano pride. As an ethnic film, as Chicano cinema, *Stand and Deliver* counters mainstream perceptions of students in East Los Angeles with "truth" rather than with fiction. The "truth" in *Stand and Deliver*, however, is antithetical not only to most fiction represen-tations of Chicanos, but to most "factual" representations as well, such as news coverage. For some film reviewers, *Stand and Deliver* was a fairy tale and its basis in the "true story" of Jaime Escalante was difficult to believe when compared to the regular news coverage of the barrio, which focused solely on drugs and gang violence.[9] None-theless, being "based on a true story" lends the film a certain note of authenticity and self-analysis, which mainstream audiences seem to expect of ethnic films. Its historical relevance and cultural soul-search-ing allowed for the film's unexpected (though modest) crossover suc-cess.[10] The very elements that ally *Stand and Deliver* with Chicano cinema also complicate its classification as such.

Escalante hopes that A.P. calculus will prepare his students to enter a system that typically excludes Chicanos. Escalante's battle against the system begins upon his arrival at Garfield. He tells the secretary that he is the new computer science teacher. She responds that Garfield does not have computers. Raquel Ortega then introduces herself to

Scene from *Stand and Deliver*, directed by Ramón Menéndez.

Escalante and explains that he will be teaching basic math because the school has no money for computers. In the next scene a still-bewildered Escalante enters a classroom full of chatting students. The chalkboard is decorated with graffiti as are the bulletin boards that surround the room. There are more students than chairs. Escalante discovers that a number of his students speak no English. Curtailed funding, graffiti, and language barriers situate Garfield as a barrio school, troubled from within by gang problems and vandalism, forsaken from without by the larger public education system.

Escalante, the outsider, emerges as the force that reopens the path between the barrio and the larger world and that reestablishes communications between the students and the faculty. Escalante makes things happen because he is comfortable both in the barrio and in the system. The film highlights his ability to pass effortlessly between Chicano Los Angeles and a mixed, middle-class Los Angeles from the first moments: The title sequence begins with a full-screen image of moving water. As the camera pulls back the water appears to be a river and is finally revealed to be a duct in the middle of an urban area. A bridge crosses the duct, connecting two neighborhoods by allowing travel between them. Figuring Escalante's border crossing, the next shot shows him driving across the bridge, leaving downtown Los Angeles. For the remainder of the credit sequence, the camera alternates between shots of Escalante passing through East Los Angeles and the neighborhood that Escalante sees as he drives. Escalante's view from the car window establishes the ethnicity and socioeconomic status of the neighborhood—vendors selling fruit on the side of the road, calling out to cars in Spanish; store and truck signs in Spanish; a group of Latino men in T-shirts and jeans riding in the back of a pickup truck; Mariachi musicians carrying their instruments down the street; a store with piñatas covering its window.

Escalante watches his surroundings like a tourist. By crossing the bridge and driving through East Los Angeles he is positioned as a border-crosser. He is further framed as an outsider by his role as a new math teacher, hired to teach computer science but reassigned to basic math. Compared to Ortega, Escalante speaks English with a heavy Latin American accent. Among the faculty this accent marks his difference. However, in the classroom it facilitates his relationship with his students and provides a linguistic bridge. At home in his quiet middle-class neighborhood, Escalante talks to an Anglo neighbor who is polishing a boat in his driveway. The dialogue informs us that Escalante has left a high-paying job to teach high school. The mise-en-scène completes the image of Escalante as a middle-class family man supported in his decision by an adoring wife. Throughout the film Escalante easily moves between the two worlds of the high school and his ethnically mixed neighborhood.

Escalante's border crossing is subtle. The significant border in *Stand and Deliver* does not separate two geopolitical entities. Nor is it a tangible physical border. Rather, it is the divide between socioeconomic classes and ethnic groups. Most people, particularly those on the privileged side, avoid recognizing and discussing this border. A similar border is traversed daily by Thackery in *To Sir, With Love* and by Richard Dadier (Glenn Ford) in *Blackboard Jungle*. Racial and ethnic prejudice and cultural difference complicate travel across the border. *Stand and Deliver* shows how these problems are manifest within the barrio as well as in the larger scheme. For instance, at a faculty meeting the principal asks for suggestions for improving the math department. Ortega says that the teachers are doing all that they can. She argues that despite Garfield's tenuous accreditation situation they do not have the resources to teach more. She asks how they can be expected to "teach logarithms to illiterates." Ortega clearly expects very little from her students and thinks them incapable of surprising her. Escalante interjects, asserting that he could teach more. He tells the principal that the only resource he needs is *ganas*, desire.

Later, Escalante has to threaten to quit in order to teach calculus. Ortega bitterly remarks that Garfield students are not able to handle advanced math, much less to pass the Advanced Placement test. She argues that if they fail, he will have deprived them of the little self-confidence they have. If heeded, her objections would ultimately maintain the impassability of the divide by denying the students one set of tools for crossing. Escalante, in defiance, insists that any student will rise to the level of expectations. He faces additional opposition when he proposes teaching a preparatory course over the summer—the summer classrooms are reserved for remedial students. Finally, Escalante wins, even though he and his students sweat out their lessons in the locker room without air-conditioning. When the school year begins again, Escalante demands that his students and their parents sign a contract committing them to the work needed for calculus—two hours during the school day, an hour before and after school, and Saturdays. They grumble and complain, but each and every student returns with a signed contract. As Escalante promised Ortega, his students rise to his expectations.

Escalante gives his students the tools he believes they need to qualify to enter the system. He takes them on a field trip to connect the classroom lessons to the real world. With this trip, Escalante escorts his students on their first border crossing. It is from this experience that he gets the idea to teach calculus, to enable them to make the crossing on their own. Accompanying his students on a literal border crossing is integral to the success of the neophyte teacher. In *To Sir, With Love* Thackery wins his students' respect by arranging for a trip to a museum. Like Escalante's trip with his students, this outing connects what the students learn and discuss in the classroom with what they might encounter outside of school. In *Renaissance Man*, Rago takes his students to see a professional production of *Hamlet*. To get to the play the students and Rago make two crossings: first, they leave the army base, moving from a military to a civilian space; second, they drive across the United States border into Canada, literally crossing into another national territory. Border crossing, especially in *Stand and Deliver,* represents the ultimate achievement — learning to balance one's ethnic identity with the assimilation required to participate in the larger system.

The representation of Chicano youths in *Stand and Deliver* challenges their image seen in dominant film and television. Perhaps more important, *Stand and Deliver* provides a more hopeful image of Chicanos than many of the Chicano feature films of the late eighties (*La Bamba, Born in East L.A., Break of Dawn*) or the gang movies of the late seventies and the early nineties (*Boulevard Nights, Walk Proud;* and *American Me, Bound by Honor*). In the final scenes the viewer is reminded that this is a true story. After the students retest, Escalante impatiently awaits the new scores. The film ends with the principal receiving the grades over the phone and repeating them to Escalante. Escalante says he wants the original scores reinstated and leaves. He walks away from the camera, down a long hallway toward an open door flooded with white sunlight. As he exits he punches the air in a victory salute. Screen titles tell the viewer how many Garfield students passed the A.P. calculus exam from 1982 through 1987.

In order to complete the realistic image, narrative classroom scenes are intercut throughout the film with brief glimpses of some students' home lives. These sequences show the obstacles and pressures the students must overcome. They also further situate the narrative within a specifically Chicano context, as opposed to a generalized vision of U.S. Latinos. The brevity of these contextualizing scenes leads to a degree of stereotyping. For instance, dialogue in Spanish rarely contains narrative information. Rather, it functions as an ethnic marker, and relevant dialogue is spoken in English. The non-English-speaking students who appear in the first classroom scene quickly disappear. Spanish is thus relegated to a prop, an instrument that tells us something about the characters, in this case their Chicano heritage.

Stand and Deliver borrows from Hollywood's representations of Latino women and men. However, the characters in this film contradict the narrative expectations established by these stereotypes. Chicano cinema's resistance of the mainstream informs these cameo scenes. The narrative singles out three girls in the class: Lupe, the dutiful eldest daughter; Claudia, who represents wild, untamed sexuality; and Ana, the quiet, virginal girl. Each of these types derives from mainstream representations of Chicanas as virgin, whore, and sidekick or supportive wife.[11]

Lupe has long red hair and the plump figure attributed to the maternal Latina. Her flip attitude in the classroom promptly vanishes, revealing a good sense of humor. At home Lupe performs the traditional duties of the eldest daughter, fixing her father's meal for his night shift and putting the other children to sleep. Finished with her chores, she settles down to study. Her mother comes in from her day shift and asks Lupe to turn off the light, ending Lupe's studying for the evening. Although Lupe is clearly devastated when the students are accused of cheating on the A.P. exam, she remains strong, calming her boyfriend Pancho and helping him through the crisis. She is the nurturing, maternal character who sacrifices herself to enable her lover's or her family's happiness. But Lupe is a fighter. She is the first to note the racism implicit in the accusation, the first to call ETS to schedule the second test, and consistently the best student in the class.

Claudia has dark curly hair, light skin, and a slim figure. She usually wears fashionable, sexy clothing. In an early scene she leaves an afterschool chat with Lupe, Pancho, and Tito to join a Ray-Banned date driving a black BMW. Lupe remarks, "She thinks she is so cool because she dates *gabachos*."[12] Frequent references are made to Claudia's active social life, culminating in Escalante's comment that Claudia needs to stop fooling around over the weekend and do more work from her shoulders up. In direct opposition to type, Claudia urges her mother to sign the calculus contract. Her mom, wearing a hair-tinting cap and squirting highlights onto wisps of hair, warns Claudia that boys will not like her if she is too smart. Claudia responds that she does not want to be dependent on "some dumb guy" all her life. Her peers may perceive her as the class sexpot, but Claudia has different plans.

The most ethnic-looking of these three girls, Ana is slight and dark-skinned with chin-length dark hair. She is the quietest girl in the class. Her father pulls her out of school in the middle of the year so that she can work in the family restaurant. He tells Escalante that there is no reason for Ana to go to college, despite her dreams of becoming a doctor. He believes that shy, quiet Ana would not finish college because she would get pregnant and drop out. Eventually Ana returns to school and, by the end of the film, wins a scholarship to the University of Southern California. Her reenrollment indicates her father's willingness to accept that she is not just another no-good girl, that she has the potential to break away from his and society's expectations of her underachievements.

Only two of the boys are seen at home—Pancho and Angel. Pancho appears briefly, on his back working under his car. His grandfather bothers him by holding a live chicken by its legs and letting it peck at Pancho. Later Pancho helps Lupe watch her younger siblings, participating in a water fight in her backyard. Pancho believes that he is the dumbest student in the class. In desperation he offers to quit, reasoning that the class will do better without him. He is the Chicano already defeated, who feels safe staying in his own neighborhood. Eventually Pancho takes the exam and, like his classmates, passes it twice. He may not end up in college, but he learns that he can face a challenge.

Garfield High School suffered from severe gang problems in the seventies.[13] In adapting Escalante's real-life story to the big screen, Menéndez continued the gang problems into the early eighties. This choice strongly connects *Stand and Deliver* to those earlier classroom dramas focused on the unseasoned teacher's ability to transform delinquent, hopeless students. It also obscures the historical context that made way for the depicted events:[14] the difficulties at Garfield in the 1970s—low grade averages and high dropout rates along with the gang problems—followed on the heels of student walkouts in East Los Angeles in 1968. The 1968 student strikes are considered by many to be the starting point of the Chicano civil rights movement. By collapsing much of Garfield's history and eliding other parts, *Stand and Deliver* fails to engage the Chicano movement and its accompanying political and cultural issues.

In the neophyte teacher films there is typically one student in the classroom who resists the teacher more than the others. This student's awakening signals the teacher's success. In *Blackboard Jungle* the holdout is Gregory Miller. Portrayed as a black gang leader, Miller turns out to be a sensitive student who encourages the other students to support Dadier. The biggest holdout in Escalante's class is Angel, a gang member who does not want his "homies" to know that he is interested in learning. Angel's clothing and posture connect him to the stereotypical Chicano gang member—he wears a hair net, dark sunglasses, and Chino pants that fit like those of 1940s zoot suits. He walks with a well-rehearsed, disaffected slump in his shoulders. Standing still, Angel strikes a defiant pose, daring anyone to mess with him.

Early in the film, Angel leaves the classroom in the middle of a quiz because his gang leader, Finger Man, beckons him from the doorway. He later approaches Escalante to admit that this was a mistake. However, he needs the *profe* to cut him a deal so the homies won't see him carrying his books. Escalante agrees and gives Angel three textbooks, one for his home, one for his locker and one for the classroom. Angel promises in return "*protección,* protection." *Stand and Deliver* shows Angel studying at home with his grandmother coughing in the next room. He covers her with a blanket, grabs a cigarette and a jacket and spends the rest of the night cruising with his buddies. After a whole night of driving, throwing bottles at random storefronts, and generally raising a ruckus, Angel arrives at school, late and unkempt. As the film progresses, Angel moves further away from his gang and closer to the classroom. The next time he is late it is because he has taken his grandmother to a medical clinic. He breaks the mold by exhibiting *ganas* and achieving academic success.

Escalante and his students reach their goal on the day of the first A.P. exam. His quick switches from father/friend to stern teacher to tough guy keep the students on their toes and command their attention. Like his predecessors, Mr. Thackery and Richard Dadier, Escalante may be new to teaching, but he understands how to motivate these students. The students love Escalante because he believes in them, because he refuses to let them be beaten by the system. The ensuing ETS investigation completes *Stand and Deliver* by raising the stakes for Escalante and his students. The Garfield students are suspected of cheating because they made too few mistakes on the exam. Escalante asserts that the scores would never have been questioned "if my kids did not have Spanish surnames and come from barrio schools." They must prove themselves not just to ETS, an organization that represents the gates to higher education and passage across the border, but also to Garfield's faculty and the Chicano community. Given the option to retest or forfeit their scores, the students and Escalante recognize that retesting might appear to be an admission of guilt. But standing their ground on principle might be equally costly. They retest. They all pass, clearing their names and reaffirming their achievements. Their decision and their success belong not just to the students and their teacher, but to Garfield High School and to the community. They affirmed their Chicano pride and they proved (twice) that they are qualified to cross the border.

After the real students passed the exam a second time, Jaime Escalante was honored by the Reagan White House for his excellence in teaching. The film's conservative criticism of institutional racism not-withstanding, *Stand and Deliver* became a Reagan-era allegory for the role of education in the assimilation of diverse ethnic groups. Jaime Escalante and the film based on his story supported the mythology of the Reagan administration's esteem for teachers, despite the fact that the administration was cutting education funding and limiting salary raises in the public school system. The significance of this allegory to conservative forces in the United States is perhaps demonstrated by the fact that *Stand and Deliver,* originally planned as a made-for-television movie, was distributed by Warner Brothers and achieved unexpected box-office success.

Yet, despite *Stand and Deliver*'s conservative approach and appeal, the film's narrative challenges mainstream representations of violent Chicano youth. The film itself challenged Hollywood's whiteness. *Stand and Deliver* is an oppositional film because it says something differ-ent, participating in a politics of deconstruction. To communicate its message beyond its Chicano audience, the film uses a traditional generic pattern and Hollywood distribution mechanisms. Like Esca-lante's students, *Stand and Deliver* strikes a balance between affirm-ing and maintaining Chicano identity and participating in a larger dominant culture.

Notes

1. For a production and marketing history of *Stand and Deliver, The Ballad of Gregorio Cortez,* and *El Norte,* see David Rosen, *Off-Hollywood: The Making and Marketing of Independent Film* (New York: Grove Weiden-feld, 1990); and "Crossover: Hispanic Specialty Films in the U.S. Marketplace," in *Chicanos and Film: Representation and Resistance,* ed. Chon A. Noriega (Minneapolis: University of Minnesota Press, 1992), 241–60. See also Aljean Harmetz, "Math Stars in a Movie," *New York Times,* March 20, 1988, sec. 2, 21.

2. *Stand and Deliver* has been mentioned briefly in a number of essays, particularly in connection with the predicted "Hispanic Hollywood." See, for instance, Rosa Linda Fregoso, *The Bronze Screen: Chicana and Chicano Film Culture* (Minneapolis: University of Minnesota Press, 1993), 39. Kathleen Newman discusses the film in her essay "Latino Sacrifice in the Discourse of Citizenship: Acting against the 'Mainstream' 1985–1988," in Noriega, ed., *Chicanos and Film.*

3. Paul Willemen, "The Third Cinema Question: Notes and Reflections," in *Questions of Third Cinema,* ed. Jim Pines and Paul Willemen (London: British Film Institute, 1989), 7–8. Willemen is interpreting Peter Wollen's defi-

nition of countercinema as part of his introduction to Third Cinema. This definition allows for less aesthetically experimental films to be understood as countering a dominant culture even as they use its narrative tools.

4. Fregoso, *The Bronze Screen*, xv.

5. The definition of Chicano cinema as "by and about" Chicanos comes from Chicano filmmakers themselves. Chon A. Noriega comments that "The word 'by' is taken to mean that the writer, producer, or director is Chicano." He further notes that this definition "grounds the debate in questions of production (or participation) as well as of signification" (in Noriega, ed., *Chicanos and Film*, xviii). The notion that Chicano cinema is "by and about" Chicanos results in an understanding of "Chicano" as both an ethnic and a political construct. For a further discussion, see Fregoso, *The Bronze Screen*, xv–xvii.

6. Carlos E. Cortés notes the difficulty of determining which U.S. Latino group a character belongs to. His essay "Who is María? What is Juan? Dilemmas of Analyzing the Chicano Image in U.S. Feature Films" (in Noriega, ed., *Chicanos and Film*, 83–104) offers guidelines for differentiating between groups, asserting that "precision in content analysis requires a categorical rigor in separating Americans of different but closely related ethnic backgrounds" (86). The suggestions include careful scrutiny of language and understanding regional differences.

7. Chon A. Noriega, "Between a Weapon and a Formula: Chicano Film and Its Contexts," in Noriega, ed., *Chicanos and Film*, 153. See also Kathleen Newman, " 'Based on a True Story': Reaffirming Chicano History," *Tonantzin* 7.1 (January–February 1990): 16, 19.

8. Noriega, ed., *Chicanos and Film*, 153.

9. Mainstream representations, from news reporting to stereotypes in Hollywood movies and daytime soap operas, claim their own version of truth about Chicanos and Latinos. For an insightful reading of the press criticism of *Stand and Deliver*, including the reception of its "truth," see Chon A. Noriega, "Chicano Cinema and the Horizon of Expectations: A Discursive Analysis of Film Reviews in the Mainstream, Alternative, and Hispanic Press, 1987–1988," *Aztlán: A Journal of Chicano Studies* 19.2 (fall 1988–90): 1–32.

10. According to figures compiled by David Rosen and Nancy Sher, *Stand and Deliver* grossed more than $14 million in theatrical ticket sales. See Rosen and Sher, *Independent Features: Supporting and Promoting Narrative Films*, Benton Foundation Bulletin 4 (1990), 2; and Rosen, *Off-Hollywood*, 220. An article in the *Los Angeles Times* reported *Stand and Deliver*'s "fast start at the box office": "It averaged a healthy $13,730 per screen in 30 theaters its first weekend in mid-March. After its third weekend, the film was still averaging a respectable $8,000 per screen in 60 theaters" (Victor Valle, "The Latino Wave: More Show Biz Doors Are Opening since *La Bamba*," *Los Angeles Times*, April 2, 1988, sec. 6, 1).

11. See Fregoso, *The Bronze Screen*, 93–94, for a brief explanation of these stereotypes in other Chicano films of the 1980s. For earlier accounts, see the articles by Carlos Cortés, Cordelia Candelaria, Linda Williams, and

Sylvia Morales in *Chicano Cinema: Research, Reviews, Resources,* ed. Gary D. Keller (Binghamton, N.Y.: Bilingual Review/Press, 1985).

12. In Mexico, *gabacho* is a derogatory term for Spaniards. In Chicano slang, it refers to someone who is not a member of the community, an outsider.

13. See Victor Valle, "Real-Life Flashback to 'Stand, Deliver,' " *Los Angeles Times,* March 17, 1988, sec. 6, 1; Aljean Harmetz, "Math Stars in a Movie," *Los Angeles Times,* March 20, 1988, sec. 2, 1. In Valle's interviews, one of the students involved in the original ETS investigation objected to the portrayal of Angel, the *cholo* tough, commenting that " 'There was really no one in our class who was like that.' He said his classmates were college-bound students who didn't identify with the image of the *cholo* or *barrio* tough."

14. I would like to thank Chon A. Noriega for pointing out this aspect of *Stand and Deliver*'s portrayal of Garfield's truth and history.

Reterritorialization in Recent Chicano Cinema: Edward James Olmos's *American Me* (1992)

Kathleen Newman

Some thirty years of activism by those involved with the Chicano political and cultural movement and with latina feminism has had its impact. Against the odds, a small number of Chicano directors, producers, and writers have created an impressive body of work in all film and video formats (fiction feature films and shorts, film and video documentaries, experimental films, video art installations, broadcast and cable television programs, etc.), which, like the work of African American, Asian American, Native American, and other latino filmmakers and videomakers, is now beginning to receive the critical attention in film and television studies it deserves. Like these cinemas, Chicano cinema also has made a significant contribution to the improvement of the national political system. Here I am not speaking of the immediately perceptible surface of our national politics — such as elections or governmental institutions or programs. I am referring to the daily political practices by which we, as an aggregate of citizens, structure our nation. In film criticism in general, Chicano cinema has been evaluated for its various aesthetics and for the ways in which it has contributed to political struggles, to identity politics, to the transformation of race and class relations in the United States — and it is appropriate that film criticism consider these aspects of Chicano cinema. Cinema also can serve, however, as historical evidence of periodic shifts in the slow processes of State transformation. Recent work on State theory in the humanities suggests that small discursive fluctuations at the microlevel of film image and sound can have an impact on the structuration of a national collectivity, akin to the impact of the more macrodiscursive formations traversing the formerly analytically separable political, economic, and ideological spheres.

Chicano film and video have contributed, in fact, to the reterritorialization of our nation-state. Reterritorialization is not a common political term and, indeed, it does not refer to specific physical territory at

95

all. Derived from the abstract analyses of State theory, it is, however, a term of crucial importance to any discussion of national social formations because it refers to the practices by which — *on an ongoing basis* — State violence against citizens, or deterritorialization, is averted and equality among citizens is made possible. In national societies constituted and structured by profound inequalities dividing the socius along lines of class, race, gender, sexuality, religion, or ethnicity, the potential for violence is part and parcel of the state formation itself. Reterritorialization would include all those practices that make possible equality among citizens in an internally divisive national social formation. How the images and sounds of Chicano cinema have contributed to the reterritorialization in the United States is the theoretical focus of this article.

First, however, as a way of recalling nearly two decades of Chicano feature film production, while at the same time taking into consideration current debates in the Chicano filmmaking community, let me begin with two quotations that concern relatively recent projects of directors Edward James Olmos and Luis Valdez. At the time of the release of his directorial debut, *American Me,* in March 1992, Olmos was asked about the possibilities for Chicano directors in Hollywood:

> With the critical acceptance of Joseph Vasquez's "Hanging with the Homeboys" and the completion of "American Me," Olmos would love to say we're on the verge of a Hispanic renaissance in film. He'd be lying if he did. "We're not there yet. Maybe this is the beginning. I was hoping 'Zoot Suit' would do it, and it didn't. I was hoping 'Gregorio Cortez' would do it, and that didn't happen. Then 'La Bamba' came along and I thought that would kick (the industry) into reality because it was the most commercial and well-viewed Chicano film ever (grossing $100 million worldwide). But you know what? They didn't take it as an ethnic movie, even though it was directed by Luis Valdez."[1]

A few months later, Luis Valdez also addressed the difficulty of making fiction feature films as a latino in Hollywood. Commenting on the well-publicized latino protests against his decision to cast a non-latina in his planned film on Frida Kahlo (one of several projects on her life in the planning stages at the time), which caused his production to be postponed, Valdez spoke of his dealings with potential producers:

> Now when we were finally sitting down to the issue, bear in mind that this has all taken several months and that it's still a development deal

and there are no guarantees. They told me we can't do this picture with a Latina actress. I said, "Why not?" "Because she won't have the box office power in order to pull this off." ... I'll tell you this, I've had a lot of moments where I've stood up to Hollywood in back rooms and refused to do the bidding of producers and I have walked out of projects. That never makes it to the press, because I'm there practically alone, with a few Chicanos who are trying to get their movies financed. I fight these battles practically in silence.[2]

These quotations reveal four key points about current Chicano film production. First, more than a decade of noteworthy latino feature films had not made possible easier access to financing for Chicano filmmakers. Second, current industry distribution strategies, which favor genre and star discourse rather than the name recognition of directors, function to the detriment of Chicano directors whose names do evoke a complex and rich history of cultural struggles and who would draw a significant public. Third, "bankability" is a source of racism, excluding a priori sectors of actors: the Catch-22 of casting latinos in starring roles seems to be that they cannot be cast now because they have not been cast previously. Fourth, a Chicano feature-film director answers to at least two groups: (1) the industry, which, on the whole, seems to be ignorant of the extent to which the United States is historically latino, and which defines the viewing public as box office, and (2) the latino film community, whose expectations regarding participation in production and on-screen self-representation have not been realized. Indeed, in the film and television industry there has not been an increase of latinos in proportion to the nation's demographic profile and the representation of latinos on screen has barely improved over the last decade.[3]

Keeping in mind this historical trajectory, let me now turn to the question of Chicano cinema's contribution to reterritorialization and let me employ Edward James Olmos's directorial debut film *American Me* as an example of the ways in which film in general can contribute to reterritorialization. I have chosen this example because of the film's extremely problematic politics. Rosa Linda Fregoso has argued persuasively that although the film does not celebrate a Chicano nationalism, in opposition to previous Chicano films, it does participate in a recognizably long-standing patriarchal politics of gender.[4] In what follows, I would like to examine, first, how the linkage of gender and violence in the film is articulated at the level of state formation and, second, how the film works against, rather than promotes, deterritorialization.

The film, which treats the life of Santana, a fictional leader of the Mexican Mafia in the California prison system from his adolescence to his death, has been criticized for its excessive violence and its negative portrayal of Chicano culture. Although both epic and melodramatic, the film does deploy its violence purposefully. The two crosscut anal rapes in the film, which have received particular attention in popular and academic film criticism (two of a total of four rapes in the film), in fact narratively structure the entire film. These two rapes — Santana's anal rape of Julie, his first and only girlfriend once he leaves prison as an adult (also his first sexual experience with a female), and the gang rape in prison by members of Santana's Mexican Mafia of the son of the rival traditional Mafia in the drug trade, which ends with the latter's death by anal knifing — serve as the reference for the male and female voice-overs that open the film. Santana's and Julie's voice-overs anticipate the didactic conclusion that the violence that is the way of life for Santana and his *clica* serve neither the individual nor the community. However, they also anticipate the unexpected reterritorialization in which the film participates.

On the surface, the rape of Julie would appear, by paradigmatic substitution with the rape-murder of the gang rival's son, to be an extension of one of the most prevalent of the warrior-citizen tropes in current U.S. cinema (deriving from the Vietnam War feature film's transformations of the tropes of World War II films), which requires male-male bonding to be founded not merely on the exclusion of females but on a violent eradication of that gender.[5] In fact, the film is structured so that, in the concluding scenes, the character of Julie is the only one who survives male-to-male eradication.[6] There are two formal elements in this newer trope of female survival. The first concerns the status of rape in the film. The first rape is the gang rape of Santana's *pachuca* mother by Anglo sailors during the Zoot Suit riots of the forties, which resulted in Santana's birth and in his rejection on an emotional level by his mother's husband. The second rape is that of Santana by another teenager at knifepoint when he was an adolescent in juvenile prison for the first time; Santana's murder of his assailant results in his transfer to Folsom and his subsequent gang leadership. Both rapes are meant in the film to serve as metaphors for the treatment of Chicanos by an oppressive Anglo society. The subsequent two rapes, however, are perpetrated by Chicanos, and while they could be considered to represent Chicano internalization of Anglo oppression, all four of the rapes must also be read against the basic emotional triangle of the film, the three boys who originate the *clica*: Santana, Mundo (both Chicanos), and J.D., an Anglo raised in the barrio, who self-identifies as Chicano. It is J.D.'s concern that Santana, upon his return to prison, has lost his ability to lead and is weak (debilitated by female influences) that precipitates Mundo's and J.D.'s decision to have Santana killed and to assume leadership of the Mafia. Here, the film carefully constructs a male-male bond between Santana and J.D., wherein their love is homoerotic. Thus, Santana's rape of Julie is narrated as a betrayal of his own values and his connection to J.D. *at the same time as* it is an act of aggression against a woman and his own community, because, as a matriarch, Julie stands for the community and its survival. The status of rape in the film changes, then, from metaphor to actant as the presence of characters who are rape victims structures the development of the film narrative.

The second formal element regarding female survival concerns the crosscutting of Santana's murder in prison with three occurrences outside of prison: (1) Puppet's murder, on orders from J.D., of his beloved cousin Little Puppet, who was the cause of Santana's return to prison; (2) Julie's decision to seek an education and her personal refusal of the Saint Dismas medal Santana has sent her from prison (and his comparison of her to "a door to another life where my seed might have been affirmed"); and (3) the final scene of the drive-by shooting of a rival gang by a very young member of the next generation of the *clica*. These scenes read formally, by reason of the similar editing, against the earlier crosscut rapes. Santana's murder, then, is not a syntagmatic extension of the three other scenes but rather a paradigmatic substitution for all of them. His murder encapsulates the injustice of the gang system, the hope for the Chicano community within the system, and the current hopelessness of the barrio youth. By creating a structural equivalence between the rapes and the murders, the film is able to accomplish the very odd transference of status of Santana as villain to Santana as hero, and, through his structural appropriation of Julie's position at the end of the film, his substitution as a masculine Cassandra for the Chicano barrio. Rape victim and murder victim as actants have moved the narrative to a conclusion wherein gender is disconnected from character and redeployed in the service of epic.

As adults, Santana (Edward James Olmos), Mundo (Pepe Serna), and J.D. (William Forsythe). (Photo courtesy of Universal City Studios.)

Santana is finally female in relation to J.D. and female as oracle in the place of Julie. From the position of a nonmale, it is his/her Saint Dismas medal—finally transferred to Santana's younger brother—that is both the hope and the interminable curse of the barrio.

However, homosociality returns to strengthen the male-male bonding trope in the film's conclusion. The rapes and murders in the film are figured overall as aspects of a long-standing system of male honor. J.D. interprets all actions as having to do with gaining or losing respect and class. Santana counters J.D., arguing, to paraphrase, that all that they had didn't have to be taken away, they themselves had given it away. In this sexualized dialogue, here comparing the result of his and J.D.'s actions as equivalent to being a victim of rape, Santana is speaking of rape in an outdated way in which the victim is considered to be complicitous in the rape, to have surrendered sexually. So central is the gendered sexuality of the film to its political interpretation that ultimately it is the male Anglo-Chicano sexual relations that bear the film's analytic conclusions. Not only does the character of Julie escape patriarchy by handing away the Saint Dismas medal, and not only does the figure of the female survive the male-male bonding of warrior-citizens, but, in the final sequence of the film, rape and patriarchy are nullified to reinforce the fact that her survival allows for the potential survival of homosexuality as an accepted normative practice.

This nullification of the rape and patriarchy is achieved through metonymy. In the final shot, when the barrel of the gun fired by the child in the drive-by shooting is framed in close-up from the audience's POV, the audience witnesses *as victim* the male-male rupture on the order of the schism between Santana and J.D. First, the generational loss signaled by the extreme youth of the shooter associates the viewing public with the older generation of the *clica* whose demise it has just witnessed. Second, the violence is random, for the shooter has not aimed at anyone in particular — not at a rival gang but at people in the barrio.[7] At the highest narrative level, the film ends with an *implied* return of Santana's and J.D.'s love, which in the past would have *made the system function*. One female matriarch (Julie) and one potentially gay, interracial couple (Santana and J.D.) are affirmed metonymically in the film as the only social actors with a chance in hell of improving the lives of this Chicano community. One suspects that, at the level of the script, the concluding scenes are Olmos's rather intuitive response to latina feminism. Yet the very fact that females are not sacrificed to male-male bonding registers an interesting discursive shift at the level of the nation-state. As we will see, the deployment of gendered violence in *American Me* does not ultimately resolve itself in favor of individual or sectoral eradication.

In our national society, at this historical conjuncture, because of the social divisions that continue to exist, the self-representation of latinos in film and on television necessarily always must have an impact on social structuration. More than an increase in political visibility for a community or a constituency within the nation, the audiovisual self-representation of latinos nationally serves to begin to transform the unjust divisory lines of race and class: it portends the day in which such unjust divisions will not exist *at the same time as* it reveals the way in which our current democracy is *tenuous*. We all know that, in order to endure, a democracy must be based on and structured by equality among its citizens. This common political knowledge also reveals a fact of great concern to State theory: the social divisions that erode equality — which lessen the participation of any sector of our national society in our political processes — do not merely create tensions in the socius, they also potentially destabilize the State.

Here it is important to remember that, because most theories of the State were developed in the social sciences, few of these theories find decentered subjectivity to be a structuring principle of the State. To give an example, sociologist John A. Hall and political scientist G. John Ikenberry, when arguing in an introductory text, *The State,* that social scientists are in general agreement regarding the definition of the State, do not take subjectivity to be a part of that definition:

> A composite definition would include three elements. First, the state is a set of institutions; these are manned by the state's own personnel. The state's most important institution is that of the means of violence and coercion. Second, these institutions are at the centre of a geographically-bounded territory, usually referred to a society. Crucially, the state looks inwards to its national society and outwards to larger societies in which it must make its way; its behavior in one area can often only be explained by its activities in another. Third, the state monopolizes rule making within its territory. This tends towards the creation of a common political culture shared by all citizens.[8]

Hall and Ikenberry stress government as the central aspect of the State and partially overlay this basic definition of the State with the collateral but separate concepts of nation and national society. In this formulation, "a common political culture" remains a monolithic concept, which is ultimately reductive of the nature of social formations. The social formation is seen to contain or be contained by government and national political culture rather than being constitutive of both. This is particularly evident in the way in which violence and coercion are defined as institutional practices wherein institutions are not understood to be expressions of social relations between Subjects or to interpellate specific multiple subjectivities. This contrasts sharply with common definitions of the State in Latin American political science, where theoretical work on the authoritarian State has produced a more nuanced understanding of the State as a social relation. Guillermo O'Donnell, the Argentine political scientist who first developed the concept of the bureaucratic-authoritarian State in response to State crises in his homeland, defined the State in general as follows:

> The state is fundamentally a social relationship of domination or, more precisely, one aspect—as such comprehensible only analytically—of the social relations of domination. The state supports and organizes these relations of domination through institutions that usually enjoy a monopoly of the means of coercion within a defined territory and that

generally are viewed as having a legitimate right to guarantee the system of social domination. As such, the state should be understood *from and within* civil society, though in its objective, institutional form it appears to be, and proclaims itself to stand, above society.[9]

The idea that the State permeates civil society as a social relation while manifesting itself as "above society" leads to the paradigms of decentered subjectivity developed in the theoretical debates in the humanities in the same period, that is, the late seventies. In these debates, government, if viewed as a statutory group (in the Sartrean and Foucauldian senses), that is, one that does not mediate sovereignty of citizens, may well function in the concrete sense suggested by Hall and Ikenberry, while the State, which does indeed mediate sovereignty as the ultimate third party in all intersubjective relations, as an ensemble remains "above society" in O'Donnell's sense. As an ensemble coterminous with the social formation and "imagined" (as Benedict Anderson has skillfully described) to be geographically coextensive with the national territory, the State is the abstract nexus of the socius though which social divisions, such as the major divisions of race, gender, and class in the United States, are consolidated (as a temporal praxis) as structuration of the national society, and through which competing decentered subjectivities constitutive of other institutional ensembles create the dynamic, conflictive socius as a whole.

Of these many discursive formations, it is perhaps the gender system that, in terms of violence, most immediately keeps pace with the State as institutional ensemble.[10] More often than not, the tropes of violence in the culture as a whole, in the arts, and in the entertainment industry gender the representation of violence. The social actors who actually mobilize the means of violence for governments as statutory groups, that is, the armed services and police organizations, are enabled and positioned by a complex semiotics in which variations on the trope of the superior warrior-citizen (superior to ordinary citizens, that is) flourish. Herein is where State violence and gender violence may simultaneously register the process known as deterritorialization. As mentioned earlier, deterritorialization is that moment in which the State abstractly authorizes the eradication of members or sectors of its own constitutive populace. The State as the guarantor of social relations *fails* as protector and mediator between Subjects and allows for the extirpation from the national territory (i.e., death) of some of its own citizens. Nicos Poulantzas referred to this process as homogenization, a term equally descriptive of the Holocaust in Europe or State terror in Latin America. In the case of the United States, given its central position in the current world economy, deterritorialization has yet in its history to reach those full magnitudes of expression, but the threat is there and the signs of its potentiality have been on the increase since the decade of the 1980s.

As we saw earlier, the discourses of gender and the State, given their mutuality of violence, manifested themselves in the activist politics of Chicano film in unexpected ways. The confused sexual politics and gender politics of the film *American Me* register the strange fact that at this specific conjuncture — 1992 — female survival was espoused over and against male survival based on the exclusive male-male bond of warrior-citizens. Although the surface messages of the film are disturbing and politically questionable, the underlying discourses are indicative of an incipient reterritorialization. *In the film, gender and sexuality are denied as appropriate criteria for the exclusion of anyone from the neutral status of citizenship and the nation as an ensemble is affirmed.* Furthermore, that nation in which all would belong is represented, at all narrative levels of the film, as multiracial and multilingual. The film, in spite of its evident narrative goal of serving as a local morality tale and its extremely belabored style, reterritorializes the State — and the United States as a nation — as a neutral site of equality and justice for all citizens.

Oddly enough, the scandal around Luis Valdez's decision to cast Laura San Giancomo in his film on Frida Kahlo had much the same discursive effect as did *American Me*. In the press, the actress Evelina Fernández, who played Julie in *American Me,* was seen as the leader of the protests against Valdez's decision. This was in part because of actions taken by Valdez himself, who canceled the San Francisco theatrical production of *Bandidos* reportedly because it would have involved his continuing to work with Fernández's husband. Likewise, the actress Rose Portillo was singled out because of her previous work with Valdez on *Zoot Suit*. What surfaced in the discourses on gender and citizenship, however, was not so much the politics of Valdez or his critics, or the female mediation of protest, but rather the nature of Frida Kahlo as a referent in our national society. It was clear that Valdez did not anticipate that a number of people would find it unthinkable that a non-latina play Frida: he did not recognize the iconic status of the Mexican artist for women, latinas in particular, in the United States. Tangentially, then, the protests revealed the same discursive conjuncture as did the film previously discussed: the female figure of Frida at the time registered an antiauthoritarian and antipatriarchal trend in our society, and a level of resistance to extirpation, symbolic or otherwise.

In conclusion, the fates would have it, for it is their perverse nature, that these two very brief examples of discourses of reterritorialization in Chicano film culture during the calendar year 1992 themselves were to be conflated with another trope, one not quite so neutral as it might have seemed on the surface: "a place called Hope." The inclusive slogan of the Clinton presidential campaign, however, was ultimately gendered as masculinist as the year progressed, because of a backlash against feminism and any politics of equality led by the political right (as best exemplified, perhaps, by some of the speeches given the first two nights of the Republican convention). By the end of 1992, social equality had no gender-neutral site in presidential politics. Thus, I find I am obliged to close this sketch of the relation of Chicano cinema to the State by observing that although one finds it very nearly impossible in the late twentieth century to believe in a neutral place called hope, one can remain hopeful that the ongoing work of Chicano and Chicana filmmakers will continue to register advances in the struggle of equality for all citizens.

Notes

1. Glenn Lovell, "Stand Out and Deliver: Edward James Olmos Commits Himself to a Tough Look at Life's Imprisonment," *San Jose Mercury News,* March 13, 1992, Eye Weekly Entertainment Guide, 12.

2. Jesse "Chuy" Varela, "Luis Valdez — the Frida Fracaso" (interview), *Cine Acción News* 9.3 (September 1992): 8.

3. For an overview of these developments, see Chon A. Noriega, ed., *Chicanos and Film: Representation and Resistance* (Minneapolis: University of Minnesota Press, 1992), and Rosa Linda Fregoso, *The Bronze Screen: Chicana and Chicano Film Culture* (Minneapolis: University of Minnesota Press, 1993). See also Chon A. Noriega, "The Numbers Game," *Jump Cut* 39 (June 1994): 107–11.

4. In *The Bronze Screen.* See also the articles by Carmen Huaco Nuzum on *American Me* in *Jump Cut* 38 (June 1993): 92–94, and by Sergio de la Mora, " 'Giving It Away': *American Me* and the Defilement of Chicano Manhood," in the *Cine Estudiantil '95* program (San Diego: Centro Cultural de la Raza, March 7–11, 1995): 14.

5. For a more extensive description of this phenomenon, see my "Latino Sacrifice in the Discourse of Citizenship," in Noriega, ed., *Chicanos and Film.* See also Susan Jeffords, *The Remasculinization of America: Gender and the Vietnam War* (Bloomington: Indiana University Press, 1989), and *Hard Bodies: Hollywood Maculinity in the Reagan Era* (New Brunswick, N.J.: Rutgers University Press, 1994).

6. Fregoso highlights the revelation of Julie's former gang membership as an important aspect of the trope of female survival. See *The Bronze Screen,* 133–34.

7. An interesting contrast to this narrative deployment of the drive-by shooting can be found in *Mi vida loca* (Allison Anders, 1994).

8. John A. Hall and G. John Ikenberry, *The State* (Minneapolis: University of Minnesota Press, 1989), 1–2.

9. Guillermo O'Donnell, "Tensions in the Bureaucratic-Authoritarian State and the Question of Democracy," in *The New Authoritarianism in Latin America,* ed. David Collier (Princeton, N.J.: Princeton University Press, 1979), 286–87; emphasis mine.

10. See, for example, Carole Pateman's *The Sexual Contract* (Stanford, Calif.: Stanford University Press, 1988), Jean Franco's *Plotting Women: Gender and Representation in Mexico* (New York: Columbia University Press, 1988), and my own *La violencia del discurso: el estado autoritario y la novela política argentina* (Buenos Aires: Catálogos Editora, 1991).

Ethnic Ingenuity and Mainstream Cinema: Robert Rodríguez's *Bedhead* (1990) and *El Mariachi* (1993)

Charles Ramírez Berg

Columbia Pictures' distribution of Robert Rodríguez's low-budget independent first feature, *El Mariachi* (1993), shortly after signing him to a lucrative two-picture contract, marks a significant break with two decades of Chicano cinema. This New Wave is much more mainstream than earlier Chicano filmmaking and far less overtly political; its appearance raises some interesting issues for Chicano cinema.[1] Is it possible for ethnic or otherwise marginalized filmmakers to enter mainstream media institutions and maintain their ethnic identity? Or is co-optation inevitable? As I have argued elsewhere,[2] although mainstream filmmaking typically resists changes—much less challenges—to dominant norms and forms, film history has demonstrated that impressive interrogations of the status quo are possible from within.

Nevertheless, Hollywood remains an especially risky place for minority filmmakers. In their quest for the broadest possible appeal, producers typically eliminate ethnicity. On an early visit to Hollywood, one Disney producer urged Rodríguez to direct an English-language remake of *El Mariachi*. Revise the script to make his protagonist "less ethnic," he was advised, and change the hero from a Mexican singer into an Anglo rock guitarist.[3] One way to counter such attitudes is to slip progressive politics into mass-mediated genre formulas, as Cheech Marin once put it, "so that they [viewers, but, presumably, producers as well] don't taste it, but, they get the effect."[4] It's not a bad tactic. As Armand White has noted, speaking of recent African American cinema, there is much to be said for films that choose not to "objectify their politics as an issue," but opt instead to make their subversive statements "inherent in the very presentation of character and setting, and in the manipulation of images."[5]

107

These sorts of manipulations will require the employment of a so-phisticated filmmaking aesthetic by Chicano cineastes, and knowing readings by us. Chicano critics' primary job, it seems to me, is to dis-cern to what degree — if at all — New Wave Chicano filmmakers have stirred the tangy zest of ethnicity into their films. This is the question I now ask of Robert Rodríguez's award-winning student film, *Bed-head* (1990), and of his low-budget mainstream hit, *El Mariachi*.[6]

Bedhead: Coming-of-Age Genre Meets Mexican Myth

Bedhead, a family comedy narrated by an adolescent Chi-cana, Rebecca (Rebecca Rodríguez), is a Mexican American version of the familiar preteen subgenre. A variant of the teen coming-of-age films, the preteen flick most often tells a childhood empowerment narrative that transforms a victimized and/or powerless child into a self-actualizing, self-sufficient agent.

Typically in these films, children confront adulthood and are chas-tened by it (*My Girl* [1991]), or are contaminated/*adult*erated by it (*To Kill a Mockingbird* [1961]; *A High Wind in Jamaica* [1965]; *Empire of the Sun* [1987]). Sometimes the youths actually manage to defeat it (*Night of the Hunter* [1957]; *Home Alone* [1990]; *Home Alone II* [1992]; *Dennis the Menace* [1992]; *Free Willy* [1993]) or at least hold it at bay (*E.T.* [1982]). Stephen King has often utilized this narra-tive trope, and interesting variations occur in several films based on his works: *Children of the Corn* (1984) and its sequel (1993), *Stand by Me* (1986), and two made-for-TV movies, *It* (1990) and *Stephen King's Sometimes They Come Back* (1991). In King's hands, the ado-lescent liminality narratives become horrific tales about the power-lessness of childhood that have two outcomes. In one formula (*Stand by Me, It,* and *Stephen King's Sometimes They Come Back*), adult corrup-tion is a deadly force. In the reverse, revenge variation (*Children of the Corn*), the children viciously strike back at the grown-up world at large.

Like the teen coming-of-age movies, ideologically most of these preteen films negotiate between childhood idealism and adulthood compromise, between, that is, innocence and hypocrisy. The critique that this ostensibly oppositional genre assembles is effectively contained, though, when biology overcomes the kids' burgeoning counterideology: the children grow into adults and eventually assimilate into the mainstream. The similar endings of *Rebel without a Cause* (1957) and *Home Alone* (1990), in which children and parents embrace despite unresolved differences, illustrate how the genre as a whole manages, in the final analysis, to preserve the status quo's conservative agenda by domesticating the children and incorporating them into the system. The formulaic happy ending occurs despite ample evidence that adults have forsaken their ideals and made the mainstream a moral wasteland.

Bedhead cuts against the generic grain in a likable, lighthearted way. True to formula, Rebecca is terrorized by her big brother, David (David Rodríguez), who knocks her down and causes an injury to her head. Mysteriously, though, the blow endows her with supernatural powers. Now she turns the tables on him, and gets him to kiss her feet, literally. But when she overplays her hand, ties him to her bike, and begins dragging him around the neighborhood, she falls and is injured again. Recovering in her hospital bed, she reflects on the day's experiences, realizes that she has received a precious gift, and resolves to exercise it discreetly — except when it concerns David. To keep him perpetually off balance, she displays her power one more time when he comes to visit. Spooked, he rushes out of the hospital room in a panic. In a final close-up, Rebecca smiles into the camera and the film ends.

Some of Rodríguez's critique of the system is obvious. For instance, he takes potshots at the nutritionally poor American breakfast. The kids eat "Little Dog's Big Cacotas" cereal (the translated name would be "Little Dog's Big *Big* Shits"), a breakfast food that, according to the sunburst blurb on the box cover, contains all of "1 essential vitamin." But, beyond such easy targets, Rodríguez's interventions modify the genre considerably and alter its conservative tendencies. The most prominent change, of course, is his choice of a Chicana protagonist. That alone transforms it into a progressive story of the raising of a young girl's consciousness in reaction to her brother's sprouting machismo. Enlightened and liberated, she playfully — but effectively — exercises her newfound sorcery, tests its limits, comes to terms with it, and learns how to deploy it strategically. In doing this, Rodríguez not only creates a counterhegemonic Chicano variation of a well-known Hollywood subgenre, he also revises the culture-specific myth of La Llorona.

As I discussed in *Cinema of Solitude*, one way to think of the narrative of *mexicanas* who buck the patriarchal system is to see it as a variation of the age-old Mexican myth of La Llorona.[7] Probably a mixture of European and Aztec tales, the Llorona myth is the narrative of a woman betrayed by a macho. In some versions, her lover takes their son away from her. In others, she kills the child in retaliation for being abandoned. In either case, she returns to haunt the male order either as a ghost or as a madwoman. What I detected in the Mexican films that I analyzed was a series of women descendants of La Llorona who challenged patriarchy and consequently threatened the system. Rodríguez continues the tradition of cinematic Lloronas by placing the myth in a contemporary, middle-class Chicano context.

David is a Mexican American macho-in-training who torments Rebecca endlessly. The last straw is his ruining the one doll—this Llorona's child—she had salvaged from his wholesale destruction. David has stripped off the doll's clothes and combed its hair straight up in a stiff "bedhead" hairdo. ("Bedhead" refers to the unruly look of one's hair when rising in the morning. David is so lazy that not only does he spend the whole day with a bedhead, he has developed it into a style.) Significantly, he has disfigured the doll by painting swastikas (what else?) on its face.

After she begins to notice "the awesome surge" of her antipatriarchal powers, she realizes that the reach of her ability is unlimited. "I could bring peace to the Middle East," she muses, "or become the first Mexican American female president of the United States." But first, playing Llorona-Delilah to David's macho Samson, she must get rid of David's bedhead and deflate his oppressive masculinity. Washing (cleansing?) him with a blast from a water hose, she douses his bedhead. When that fails to flatten his stiff hairdo, she "loses it," and becomes "a complete de-mento."

What's clear from *Bedhead'*s ending is that adulthood will not rob Rebecca of her powers because what she has acquired—in narrative terms, magic; in symbolic terms, a raised consciousness—is beyond the reach of ideology. *Bedhead*'s coming-to-consciousness narrative overwhelms the genre's assimilationist coming-of-age formula and instead of ending up a co-opted adolescent, Rebecca becomes a spy within the system—patriarchy's, machismo's, and David's worst nightmare. Read in this way, a couple of things are worth noting. First, because there is so much cultural layering in *Bedhead,* it's a good bet that only a Chicano filmmaker could have made it. Second, the more a viewer is aware of the interplay among Mexican, Mexican American, and American cultural elements in *Bedhead,* the more the film's progressiveness reveals itself.

El Mariachi: Hybrid Exploitation Film

For his first feature-length film, Rodríguez devised a taut, economical plot. A wandering minstrel dressed in black (Carlos Gallardo) arrives at a small Mexican border town. Carrying only his guitar in its case, the mariachi hopes to find a job singing in one of the local cantinas. Instead, he is mistaken for a hit man, Azul (Reinol Martínez), who also wears black, uses a similar guitar case to carry his weapons, and is in the midst of a bloody battle with the local drug racketeer, a North American called Moco (Peter Marquardt). The more the mariachi tries to stay out of harm's way, the more trouble finds him. Only Domino (Consuelo Gómez), the manager of a bar owned by Moco, befriends him. After both Azul and Domino have been killed by Moco, the mariachi trades in his guitar for one of Azul's pistols, and confronts Moco and his gangsters in a final showdown.

Analyzing *El Mariachi* is a more complex task because of its mixed genre heritage. It's a *mezcla* of two exploitation genres, the Mexican

Writer, director, producer, and cameraman Robert Rodríguez gives direction to Carlos Gallardo in *El Mariachi,* a Columbia Pictures release. (Photo courtesy of Columbia Pictures.)

Moco (Peter Marquardt) swears bloody vengeance in *El Mariachi*. (Photo courtesy of Columbia Pictures.)

narcotraficante film and the transnational action genre I call the warrior adventure film. Rodríguez adopted the mode of production from the first and adapted the narrative strategies and highly charged kinetic style of the second. Because he intended his film for the Spanish-language video market, and because Mexico's *cine fronterizo* (border film) provided a model for Rodríguez's frugal moviemaking strategy, it's appropriate to first discuss the influence of that Mexican film cycle on Rodríguez and his production of *El Mariachi*.

El Mariachi and *cine fronterizo* Mode of Production

Border films have flourished on the lowest end of the economic and aesthetic Mexican moviemaking scale for decades. The *narcotraficante* film, a Mexican police genre, is the most popular type of *cine fronterizo*. *Narcotraficante* films boomed from 1979 to 1989, when at least forty were made.[8] Arriving at a precise number is difficult because of their ephemeral mode of production (most were made by small, independent production companies, which sprang up overnight), their choice of media (some were shot on film, others on video), and, for some, their nontraditional distribution pattern (many bypassed theatrical exhibition, opting instead for release to Spanish-language home video markets in Mexico, Latin America, and the United States).[9]

This type of cinema was spawned by political, economic, and industrial conditions of the 1970s. It was then that, for all intents and purposes, the state took control of Mexican film production and forced independent producers out. Some of them found a highly profitable alternative by making low-cost films along the U.S.-Mexico border. They created close-knit enterprises that cut expenses by relying on family members for their labor pool, eschewing studio sets in favor of location shooting on ranches owned by relatives, and using whatever props were at hand. Initially, these productions were shot in the United States in order to avoid the expense of hiring union workers. A further cost-saving measure was the housing of cast and crew on the same ranches where the films were being shot. To trim costs still more, producers sometimes filmed two movies simultaneously. Each film typically took three to four weeks to shoot at a cost of fifty to eighty-five thousand dollars.[10]

It takes nothing away from Rodríguez to acknowledge his streamlining of this lean, superefficient production system to its cost-effective essence. As has been widely publicized, he was his own one-person film company, performing the creative duties (writer, director, director of photography, sound recordist, and editor) as well as the more labor-intensive ones (grip, gaffer, property master, and coproducer). He made *El Mariachi* for just over seven thousand dollars, shot it (on film) in fourteen days, and edited it on video. Not surprisingly, the U.S. press praised Rodríguez for his provident production ethic but failed to acknowledge his adherence to a well-established, low-overhead Mexican filmmaking tradition. And even in relation to that modest industrial practice, what Rodríguez did is still astounding: he made a quality feature film for one-tenth the budget generally regarded as appropriate only for inferior quality films.

El Mariachi as Warrior Adventure

Narratively, *El Mariachi* is in the tradition of a species of the transnational adventure film—the warrior adventure genre—rooted in the Hollywood western, which has blossomed because of a series of cinematic cross-pollinations between Asia and Hollywood. Principally, the genre includes Hong Kong martial arts adventures, low-budget U.S. variations on Hong Kong's kung fu themes, and Hollywood blockbuster actioners. As one martial arts critic has put it, their common defining feature is a protagonist who possesses and displays his fighting capability.[11]

One tracing of this genre's lineage would begin with Hollywood westerns, which influenced — and were influenced by — Japanese samurai films. Both of these in turn influenced the Hong Kong martial arts films produced by Run Run Shaw in the early 1970s. An international market for such films was clearly identified with the U.S. success of films like Bruce Lee's *Enter the Dragon* (1973), which grossed more than $100 million here.[12] After that, Hong Kong and U.S. martial arts action films boomed.

The stage was set by the martial arts set pieces in the James Bond films (for example, *Goldfinger* [1964] and *Diamonds Are Forever* [1971]). Hits like *Billy Jack* (1971), *Cleopatra Jones* (1973), and *Cleopatra Jones and the Casino of Gold* (1975) featured heroes expert in *hapkido*. They paved the way for Chuck Norris, who starred with Bruce Lee in *Return of the Dragon* (1973) and began his own series of low-budget, independently made warrior adventures in the late 1970s. Other martial arts stars such as Steven Seagal and Jean-Claude van Damme followed in the same vein. The high-rent, Hollywood blockbuster side of the genre includes such films as *First Blood* (1982), *Rambo: First Blood Part II* (1985), *Lethal Weapon* (1987), *Die Hard* (1988), and *Total Recall* (1989). In Hong Kong, two recent variants have evolved: John Woo's hyperviolent gangster movies and Jackie Chan's kung fu comedies.

The Warrior Adventure Narrative

Although this transnational genre has proliferated to the point that it exists in numerous story variants, from crime dramas to police thrillers to war adventures, it is possible to distill a basic narrative, and identify its essential elements:[13]

1. The genre centers on a *lone male protagonist* who possesses *special physical skills*. In the Hong Kong kung fu films and the Norris-Seagal-Van Damme spinoffs, this is the mastery of martial arts. Sometimes this is combined with police/commando/military training, in

everything from Jackie Chan's *Police Story* (also known as *Police Force* and *Jackie Chan's Police Force* [1986]) to all of Seagal's films, *Lethal Weapon*, and *Die Hard*.

2. Like many a movie hero, *this genre hero adheres to a personal code of justice and morality, which he directs toward altruistic ends.*[14] "As a policeman, I fight crime for justice," says Jackie Chan's guileless hero in *Police Story*, a principle to which all warrior adventure heroes subscribe. The society that the hero rescues can be local, regional, or global. In *Above the Law* (1988) and *Hard to Kill* (1990), Steven Seagal contains threats posed by urban gangs; in *Die Hard*, Bruce Willis saves the executives of a Japanese company held hostage by international terrorists in a Los Angeles skyscraper; in *Under Siege* (1992), Steven Seagal saves the world from nuclear destruction.

3. *The protagonist undergoes a severe test, involving a loss.* Often this comes in the form of an assault that nearly kills him, or kills a loved one, or both. In *Hard to Kill* (1990), hit men murder police detective's Seagal's wife and leave him for dead.

4. *Revenge motivates his physical rehabilitation,* wherein he regains the special abilities he once commanded. Steven Seagal awakes from a seven-year-long coma in *Hard to Kill,* and puts himself through a strenuous rehab regimen. Secret agent Mike Locken (James Caan) in Sam Peckinpah's *The Killer Elite* (1975) is similarly rigorous in his comeback training.

5. He is also *spiritually rehabilitated,* converting to or reaffirming his belief in some strain of Taoism, Buddhism, and/or Confucianism that promotes the sacredness of all life and underpins his martial arts prowess.[15] Sometimes an older male serves as philosophical mentor and martial arts coach; sometimes the hero goes it alone. In Bruce Lee's *The Chinese Connection* (1972), several elements are combined as the hero avenges the death of his fighting teacher.

6. After recovering, *the hero confronts and defeats the ruthless villain (usually a drug lord) in a violent and spectacular duel to the death.* An important distinguishing feature of these films that separates them from adventures like, say, the Indiana Jones movies, is the climactic showdown. In the climax of the Indiana Jones action adventures, Jones triumphs by enduring a test and withstanding a powerful spiritual force that eliminates the bad guys. In the warrior adventures, the hero always fights to vanquish the villain and a host of his

goons. The fight is a protracted, graphically violent, highly ritualized, and carefully choreographed set piece.

Genre as Systems of Viewer Expectation

That the narrative I have sketched out may be applied to a wide variety of films ranging from Bruce Lee's *Fists of Fury* (1971), and Sam Peckinpah's *The Killer Elite,* to several of Steven Seagal's films, *Lethal Weapon,* and *Total Recall* points to several possible classificatory stumbling blocks I'd like to address. First of all, is this a genre at all, or merely a familiar revenge narrative?

To answer, we need a working definition of genre. I'd suggest one that posits genre as not simply a body of similar films but, as Steve Neal argues, also — and equally —

> specific systems of expectation and hypothesis which spectators bring with them to the cinema, and which interact with films themselves during the course of the viewing process. These systems provide spectators with means of recognition and understanding. They help render films, and the elements within them, intelligible and therefore explicable. They offer a way of working out the significance of what is happening on the screen: a way of working out why particular events and actions are taking place, why the characters are dressed the way they are, why they look, speak and behave the way they do, and so on.... These systems also offer grounds for further anticipation.[16]

The films of the warrior adventure genre share an array of narrative elements, not only the revenge plot. And while one or another of them may be present in westerns, war films, detective films, and films noir, most if not all of them are present in this genre. Furthermore, the manner that the elements are combined by the warrior adventure activates a set of specific audience understandings, expectations, and anticipations that are satisfied exclusively by this genre.

A second issue is the amount of narrative overlap between this genre and the others I've mentioned. Since this is an international genre, a certain amount of blurring is to be expected. Moreover, overlap is only a problem if one considers genres to be separate and discrete categories, which I don't. The case of warrior adventures only serves to point out that genres are seldom if ever absolute categories, only patterned narrative responses to a cluster of interconnected social and ideological dilemmas. I agree with Robin Wood, who stresses the interrelatedness of genres and opposes regarding them as discrete and fully autonomous categories.[17]

Third, if this is a distinct genre, does *El Mariachi* belong to it? Yes, for several reasons. Its narrative contains most — perhaps all — of the genre's distinguishing elements: the loner hero who is alienated when he encounters a hostile, corrupt society, and who becomes a warrior as a result of this confrontation; the loss, albeit at the very end, of Domino and of the use of his hand because of a bullet wound; the reliance upon a cultural tradition as his spiritual guide; and finally, the climactic showdown with Moco. (The revenge element may also be present. It could be what motivates his transformation into a warrior at the very end, but we'll have to wait for the sequel to be sure.)

Additionally, the presence of several motifs and iconographic indicators supports the inclusion of *El Mariachi* in the warrior adventure genre. For instance, there is the hero in black, the color traditionally worn by martial arts warriors (made explicit by the title of Chuck Norris's *Good Guys Wear Black* [1979]). There is the wandering protagonist, a characteristic trope that harks back to the beginnings of the genre, in both Eastern (*Yojimbo* [1961] and *Sanjuro* [1962]) and Western (*Shane* [1953]) incarnations. There is a subtle reference, at one point, to martial arts weaponry. Trapped in his hotel room, the mariachi pulls a morning star (a spiked ball on a chain) from a decorative set of medieval arms on the wall and swings the ball around as if he might use it as a *nunchaku*, the hinged weapon used by martial arts fighters. (Typical of the film's continual cutting against the generic grain, the mariachi never uses it as a weapon, but as a hook to slide down the wire and onto a speeding bus.) Finally, there is the de rigueur heightening of fighting noises on the sound track. (There were more hints in *Bedhead* that Rodríguez was an aficionado of martial arts cinema: the exaggerated SNAP! on the sound track when Rebecca commands the garden hose into her hands; the fighting position Rebecca assumes as she experiences the surge of her awesome powers.)

At this point a table of key narrative elements might help to summarize the genre's distinctive features, distinguish it from other, similar genres, and explain why I included *El Mariachi* in the warrior adven-

Warrior adventure genre—key narrative elements

Genre or film	Wandering, alienated loner hero	Loss	Revenge narrative	Spirituality	Weak/ corrupt society	Duel to death
Warrior adventure (martial arts)	X	X	X	X	X	X
Action adventure (Indiana Jones)	Wandering, not alienated			Judeo-Christian; not invoked by Jones		
Detective (*Maltese Falcon*)	Alienated, not wandering	Partner's murder hardly affects him	Loyalty more than revenge		X	
Film noir (*Postman*)	X					
Western	X	Sometimes Anthony	(e.g., Mann's)			X
War				Patriotism		X
First Blood; Rambo	X	X	X		X	X
El Mariachi	X	X	Perhaps at end	Ethnicity as cultural memory	X	X

Note: Films referred to are *The Maltese Falcon* (1941); *The Postman Always Rings Twice* (1946; 1981); *First Blood* (1982); *Rambo: First Blood Part II* (1985); and *El Mariachi* (1993).

ture genre. In this graphic form, it can be seen how closely *El Mariachi* resembles the warrior adventure narrative. And, among other things, the genre comparisons reveal why some films, like the Indiana Jones action adventures, don't belong to the warrior genre, though others, like *First Blood* and *Rambo: First Blood Part II* do.

Genre as Industrial Formula

In identifying and defining the genre, we should not lose sight of the industrial understandings that coincide with an audience's; for, I would argue, it is precisely when narrative formula, audience famil-iarity, and industrial practice merge that a genre's existence is confirmed.[18] As evidence for the existence of the warrior action genre as an industrial formula, let me return to the Hollywood producer who told Rodríguez that his protagonist was "too ethnic." Remember, this was in the spring of 1992, after Rodríguez had signed with the powerful ICM (International Creative Management) agency but before he had committed to any studio, and about a year before the release of *El Mariachi*. The producer was one of various studio executives courting Rodríguez. At that point *El Mariachi* was deemed stunning but unmarketable because it was in Spanish. For Hollywood, films in foreign languages exist only as source material for potential American films. Hence French hits like *Three Men and a Cradle* (1985) and *La Femme Nikita* (1990) become *Three Men and a Baby* (1987) and *Point of No Return* (1993). By such ethnocentric, imperialistic reasoning, a Hollywood remake—in English—of *El Mariachi* should obviously be Rodríguez's first project. Besides wanting to "de-ethnicize" Rodríguez's hero, the producer suggested a revised plot. When a drug deal turns sour, the Anglo hero, a rock guitarist, is beaten to a pulp and left in the desert to die. Fortunately, he is found and nursed back to health by an aged Native American medicine man, who imparts the wisdom of his warrior ancestors to the recovering protagonist, and trains him to fight. The hero tracks, finds, and destroys the drug-peddling bad guys.[19]

Beyond the insensitivity of the "too ethnic" remark—which, purely as market-savvy advice, may have been dead accurate—what's interesting about the producer's proposed story line is how closely it resembles the genre narrative I just outlined. This genre obviously existed in the executive's mind as a distinct narrative with an established, well-understood pattern of understandings, expectations, and anticipations. Moreover, this pattern offered a way to gauge the marketability of Rodríguez's film. From this producer's perspective, the main plot problem with *El Mariachi* was that it varied too much from genre conventions, which would frustrate viewer expectations and likely result in a box-office dud.

Let me conclude this section by returning to Neale, who believes that genres are "best understood as *processes*" characterized by repetition and variation, stasis and change. This "process-like nature of genres manifests itself as an interaction between three levels: the level of expectation, the level of the generic corpus, and the level of the 'rules' or 'norms' that govern both."[20] What's so interesting about *El*

Mariachi are the ways it plays with all three levels. But before I discuss that, let me briefly set out the ideological dynamics of the genre.

Warrior Adventures: From Narrative to Ideology

A celebration of untrammeled male power, the warrior adventure genre negotiates between the solitary exercise of sanctioned violence on the one hand and the common good on the other. When, the genre asks, can an individual act violently and autonomously? Answer: when society is seriously threatened. In order that the hero's unrestrained vigilante justice not endanger the community it is supposed to preserve and protect, the genre presents a desperate situation. The evil is potent and menacing; society is either so weak it can't defend itself, or so corrupt that it's part of the problem.

Any genre, be it a western, a film noir, or a kung fu adventure, that has as its starting point a disintegrating society and the hero's reliance on an idiosyncratic code of behavior—as opposed to shared mores—implies a social structure whose moral center has not held. What's made of that ideologically varies from genre to genre. In film noir, for example, corruption is the dark side effect of capitalism; society is a collection of alienated individuals given over to instant gratification. In this genre, however, the weak society supplies the justification for vigilante violence. With the Visigoths at the gates, authorities—and audiences—have little choice but to dispense with civil liberties and allow the hero to trample on individual rights so that he can save society. "I'll give you every dope deal," says detective Gino (Steven Seagal) in *Out for Justice* (1990) as he bargains with his supervisor for permission to embark on a personal, police-subsidized vendetta, "just give me a shotgun and an unmarked."

Naturally, the genre's sanctioned vigilantism makes it disturbingly conservative.[21] Because of the reductive way the genre frames the lawlessness versus order issue, there is a pressing need for a champion. And not just any hero will do—this is no time for amateurs. What's called for is a contemporary Hercules. Thus the regressivity of the narrative is underscored by the casting. In both Hong Kong and Hollywood varieties, the actor who plays the hero is physically exceptional. In the martial arts films, he is a highly trained athlete who has made his body into a lethal weapon. In the Hollywood variant, actors like

Sylvester Stallone and Arnold Schwarzenegger are, literally, supermen. Why not, these films ask again and again, turn things over to the likes of them?

El Mariachi's Oppositional Genre Variations

El Mariachi makes some fascinating contestational responses to this inherent conservatism. Let's look at some of the ways that Rodríguez's film cuts against the generic grain.

1. *Protagonist* — The fact that the hero is a Mexican is a crucial difference. Any hero presents a locus for viewer identification and empathy. Given the lopsided number of Anglo male action heroes in film history, simply providing audiences someone other than a white male focus for their rooting interest is necessarily positive (the same is true for the Hong Kong films). Beyond that, though, there is the ordinariness of Rodríguez's hero, and of the actor who plays him.

The way the genre works, even if the character has no special physical skills, we know that the actor does, and that it will only be a matter of time before the narrative devises an excuse for him to display them. This is what was so intriguing about the variation *Die Hard* almost presented — Bruce Willis's hero wasn't another martial arts hard body, he was just an average Joe. Except, of course, that he wasn't — he was an experienced and very resourceful cop. In *El Mariachi*, though, the guitar player (and Carlos Gallardo) really doesn't have any special physical powers. He is truly what *Die Hard*'s hero nearly was — a man thoroughly unprepared for the mayhem that comes his way.

Clearly not a man of action, the guitar player's unpreparedness undercuts one element of the genre's veiled fascism — that is, the notion that only a superhero can successfully handle the evil that threatens. Rather, the mariachi's skills are art, culture, and morality, and, in this film, they are enough to overwhelm Moco.

2. *Masculinity/Machismo* — *El Mariachi* redefines heroism and masculinity in sharp contrast with the genre's established norms of manhood. A hero need not have the physical capabilities of a Mr. Universe or a martial arts master, nor be looking to save the world (and prove his masculinity); he can simply be a balladeer looking for a receptive audience. How often do we get to see a hero who lives for his art? How

many action heroes could say, as the mariachi announces proudly to Domino when he first meets her, "My voice is my life"?

But he's faced with an uncaring world. No one wants a mariachi, and the first bartender he encounters shows him why—he already has a one-man techno band. The bar musician, wearing a sequined sombrero as his sole cultural marker and banging out noises on his electronic keyboard, is a sad remnant of a rich musical heritage that includes Agustín Lara, Jorge Negrete, and Pedro Infante.

Of course, the other, oppressive side of that illustrious Mexican movie tradition was its accompanying machismo. But *El Mariaichi*'s antimacho hero effectively counters that. He neither drinks nor smokes, and the film is knowing enough to make a running gag out of it. The bartender has to look long and hard to find the mariachi a soft drink in his cooler overflowing with beer, and even Domino shoots the mariachi a questioning glance when he requests a soda. What sort of macho doesn't drink or smoke? In relation to reigning norms of masculinity in the United States, Mexico, and in the genre, the mariachi is unique: a male who does not depend on external signs—the pumped-up body, the hard-drinking lifestyle, the phallic weaponry—to confirm his masculinity.

But just as the town does not welcome a singer, it does not comprehend a man who does not exhibit conventional markers of manhood. In fact, it's the naturalized dominance of such signifiers of masculinity, and the mariachi's lack of them, that gets him into trouble. No one is prepared to believe that he is a male without any traditional indicator of masculine power—that he is a different kind of male. Therefore, the mariachi's guitar case is misread as his masculine sign, assumed to be Azul's trademark arsenal, and he is mistaken for the hit man. Being an antimacho in a macho universe is a very risky proposition.

3. *Spirituality*—One of the warrior adventure genre's more troubling aspects is its depiction of Eastern mysticism. The hero's spiritualism endows him with inner tranquillity, but all too often it is debased and simplified into a motivational linchpin that rationalizes his wreaking havoc and maiming foes. Tao is his license to kill.

El Mariachi is more reverential and less manipulative with the guitar player's spiritualism—his devotion to his cultural roots. Because he's not looking for a license to kill, his belief system can be more than facile motivation. For the mariachi, culture, memory, and tradition connect him to his familial past (the tradition of singing in his family that stretches back to his father and grandfather) and with his Mexican musical heritage. Additionally, they provide him with a co-herent credo and a moral basis for his explicit critique of global cap-italism.

4. *Weak/Corrupt Society*—In keeping with genre conventions, *El Mariachi*'s border society is thoroughly corrupt. Everybody is on the take: the cops, the bartender, the hotel clerk—even Domino is beholden to Moco. After the first sequence, law enforcement is absent. Bodies pile up, but the police never appear. However, *El Mariachi* posits a specific source of the social depravity, namely the United States and high-tech "progress." "Technology," the mariachi ruminates at one point, "has crushed us, robbed us of our culture, turned us into machines."

Thus the locale in *El Mariachi* is not just another sleazy border town. It's a town that's sleazy *because* it borders on the United States, whose relentless technology and ruthless market system have combined to destroy Mexican culture. Again, the scene that best exemplifies this is the musical "performance" by the one-man band. It's played for laughs, but beneath the comedy lurks the tragedy of the First World erasure of the Third.

5. *Criminal milieu*—The most corrupt and treacherous figures in the compromised world of this genre are the drug-peddling villain and his gang of thugs. *El Mariachi* conforms to the convention and never whitewashes the drug racketeering so prevalent along the U.S.-Mexico border. But it's clear about where to fix the blame for it. Here again the critique is specific and directed—the drug-running kingpin, Moco (does he know his nickname means "snot"?), is a gringo. Thus, in *El Mariachi,* drug trafficking is the logical extension of corporate America's international expansionism and exploitation. Drugs and technology are two sides of the same global market-driven, cultural-imperialistic coin.

It's interesting to note, for instance, how the structure of Moco's drug operation, where a gringo owner oversees Mexican laborers, mirrors that of *maquiladoras,* the assembly plants that (mainly) U.S. industries own and operate along the Mexican side of the border. Promoted in the mid-1960s as a boon to U.S. industry and a helping hand to unemployed Mexican workers, they quickly boiled down to institutionalized exploitation. Mexican workers were typically paid salaries that, with peso devaluation factored in, were one-twelfth the

U.S. minimum wage; in the late 1980s this amounted to about $3.30 per day.[22] Moco's borderland gangster is, like all movie gangsters, the shadow of a successful capitalist businessman. In this context, it's fascinating that the action in *El Mariachi* is in effect triggered by a worker's revolt over a salary dispute: Azul comes to get the money that Moco failed to pay him.

If Rodríguez bent the familiar genre formula nearly to the break-ing point, and overturned a number of its more regressive elements as he did so, the question that's begged is how and why the film was released by a major Hollywood studio. Had the film languished on some producer's shelf, there's a good chance it never would have been released. But Columbia Pictures decided to enter the film in selected festivals in the fall of 1992, and it became a favorite with audiences at Toronto and Telluride, and won the Audience Award at the Sun-dance Film Festival. Hoping that the film's unqualified festival suc-cesses would translate into healthy box-office revenues, the studio released *El Mariachi* as Rodríguez made it.

The numerous press stories that covered the festivals and the film suggest two reasons why those early audiences were so taken by the film. First, its low cost — the fact that the film was made for seven thousand dollars raised interest and curiosity, and, perhaps more im-portant, engendered audience sympathy. The second reason was the film's engaging, highly energetic style. Filmmaking on a shoestring may have initially drawn audiences, but it was the accomplished and compelling film that viewers actually saw that won them over. Let me conclude, then, by analyzing Rodríguez's formal style in *El Mari-achi* and speculating on its generic and ideological implications.

Rodríguez's Aesthetic: Creating from Constraints

Recognizing cinema's fundamental link with motion, the war-rior genre makes movement its subject. Its style is a combination of acrobatic bodies in motion and a camera eagerly moving to capture them. Films of this genre offer the same pleasures as the films of Harold Lloyd, Douglas Fairbanks, and Buster Keaton, where carefully choreographed gags were combined with fluid camera movements.

Based on the sort of spectacle they (can afford to) mount, warrior adventure films may be divided into two classes, the dozens made at the bargain-basement level and the relatively few Hollywood blockbusters. Because of their lower budgets and meager resources, the cheaper films rely on basic cinematic techniques, and this has had a liberating effect. A style that requires only a movie camera, an active imagination, and a keen cinematic sensibility, that relies mostly on what the camera lens can record and the body can do, rather than on the endless artifice technology can concoct, is a brand of cinema that has divorced quality from money. As Rodríguez puts it:

> Money has nothing to do with making a good movie or telling a good story. . . . You have problems on the set when you make a movie all the time. You can solve them one of two ways: real quick, with money, or creatively. Which makes your movie better? . . . a movie . . . is a creative endeavor. So sometimes you can actually be forced to be more creative when you have no money. And that can only make your movie better. You end up being more creative than you even intended. And we did that a lot here [with *El Mariachi*].[23]

One advantage of coming from the margins is that living there prepares minority filmmakers to be adept at creating from the materials at hand rather than from cash. For *El Mariachi,* Rodríguez tailored his script to what was available: a bulldog and a turtle, a school bus and a black motorcycle, two bars and the exterior of a brothel, a ranch, a swimming pool, and a freestanding porcelain bathtub.

Even though Gallardo is a game performer, he is not the equal of a Fairbanks, a Keaton, or a Jackie Chan. But Rodríguez more than compensates for that with his kinetic cinematic style. It is characterized by short takes (most shots are only a few seconds long) edited together in rapid-fire succession. His furious tempo is reminiscent of Sergei Eisenstein's staccato montage and the jump-cutting brashness of the French New Wave. Combining that with Rodríguez's shot selection (which favors close-ups and extreme close-ups), his playfully moving camera, and his use of speeded-up action for comic effect yields a formal style somewhere between Mack Sennett's herky-jerky slapstick and Sam Peckinpah's elegiac lyricism. Rodríguez approximates the cinematic frenzy of the Bruce Lee-Jackie Chan tradition via his indefatigable style.

When the best of the Hong Kong and low-budget American films like *El Mariachi* are contrasted with the Hollywood blockbuster variations, the cinematic difference is dramatic. It's a battle between ethnic ingenuity and high-dollar tricks. The blockbuster's heavy reliance on costly state-of-the-art special effects is, in a sense, one more conservative element. The sorts of effects associated with Hollywood warrior movies — computerized image enhancements and dazzling pyrotechnics — shift the emphasis away from human dexterity and toward technological expertise; that is, away from physical stunts people perform with their bodies and toward technological effects only Hollywood can provide — and afford. Expensive effects thereby reinforce the ideological thrust of the genre, illustrating the ideological message that we can't do it ourselves — "it" being everything from solving social problems to making movies. Someone better financed, more experienced, and more powerful should be in charge of that.

Ultimately, *El Mariachi*'s most progressive element and its greatest achievement may well be the effective and entertaining way it says no to all that. What Rodríguez championed with his making of *El Mariachi* is creativity over wealth. What his film bemoans is the loss of cultural memory in the name of progress. What it calls into question are dominant notions of masculinity, heroism, the U.S.-Mexico border, and, finally, cinema. You can hardly be more provocative or more subversive than that.

Notes

1. I have delineated the various stages of Chicano filmmaking and criticism in detail in two papers: "The Last Paper on Border Crossings: Toward Multicultural Criticism," Latino Media Arts: Theory and Culture Conference, Whitney Museum of American Art, November 15, 1992; and "From ¡Ya Basta! to ¡Al Fin!: The Evolution of Chicano/a Cinema and Criticism, 1969–1994," British Film Institute, London, May 20, 1994.

2. Charles Ramírez Berg, "*Ya Basta con* the Hollywood Paradigm! — Strategies for Latino Screenwriters," *Jump Cut* 38 (June 1993): 96–104.

3. Personal interview with Robert Rodríguez, March 10, 1992, Austin, Texas. Rodríguez also told this story on *Late Night with David Letterman*, NBC, February 26, 1993.

4. Quoted in Chon Noriega, "Café Orale: Narrative Structure in *Born in East L.A.*," *Tonantzin* 8.1 (February 1991): 17.

5. Armand White, "The New Players: Hollywood's Black Filmmakers Observe the Rules of the Game," *Emerge* (August 1992): 42.

6. Both films are available on the *El Mariachi* video and laser disc, distributed by Columbia/TriStar Home Video, 3400 Riverside Drive, Burbank, CA 91505; (818) 972-8686.

7. Charles Ramírez Berg, *Cinema of Solitude: A Critical Study of Mexican Film, 1967–1983* (Austin: University of Texas Press, 1992); see chapter 5, "Women's Images, Part II: The Feminine Revolt — From La Malinche to La Llorona to Frida," especially 77–96.

8. See Norma Iglesias, *Entre yerba, polvo y plomo: Lo fronterizo visto por el cine mexicano* (Tijuana, Baja California: El Colegio de la Frontera Norte, 1991), 48, 55. See also David R. Maciel, *El Norte: The U.S.-Mexican Border in Contemporary Cinema* (San Diego: Institute for Regional Studies of the Californias, 1990), 45–51.

9. In terms of identifying these films, Moisés Viñas, in his comprehensive index of nearly a century's worth of Mexican film, *Indice Cronológico del Cine Mexicano, 1896–1992* (México: Dirección General de Actividades Cinematográficas, Universidad Nacional Autónoma de México, 1992), does note the "type of production," that is, video or film, for this recent type of film. Where he indicates video as a category, however, it is unclear whether he means that these recent films were initially released on video (whether shot on film or video), or that they were initially shot on video. Furthermore, he gives this information on a film-by-film basis and does not provide any comprehensive tally of the number of such video films.

10. This information is summarized from Iglesias, *Entre yerba, polvo y plomo*, 42–88, and Maciel, *El Norte*, 3–6.

11. Marilyn D. Mintz, *The Martial Arts Films* (Rutland, Vt., and Tokyo: Charles E. Tuttle and Company, 1983), 219.

12. John Lent, *The Asian Film Industry* (Austin: University of Texas Press, 1990), 100. See also brief mentions of Hong Kong's martial arts cinema in Chiao Hsiung-Ping's "The Distinct Taiwanese and Hong Kong Cinemas" and Jenny Kwok Wah Lau's "A Critical Interpretation of the Popular Cinema of China and Hong Kong," both in Chris Berry, ed., *Perspectives on Chinese Cinema* (London: British Film Institute, 1991), 155–65 and 166–74, respectively.

13. From another perspective, John J. Donohue has isolated some different narrative elements, such as type of warrior, what he fights for and against, and what resolution is arrived at. See his *Warrior Dreams: The Martial Arts and the American Imagination* (Westport, Conn.: Bergin and Garvey, 1994), especially 53–69.

14. David J. Graper, "The Kung Fu Movie Genre: A Functionalist Perspective" in Sari Thomas, ed., *Culture and Communication: Methodology, Behavior, Artifacts, and Institutions* (Norwood, N.J.: ABLEX Publishing Company, 1987), 154.

15. Mintz, *The Martial Arts Films*, 69–73. See also Donohue, *Warrior Dreams*, 50–51.

16. Steve Neale, "Questions of Genre," *Screen* 31.1 (spring 1990): 46.

17. Robin Wood, "*Rancho Notorious*: A *Noir* Western in Colour," *CineAction!* (summer 1988): 84. See also Wood's "Ideology, Genre, Auteur" in his *Hitchcock's Films Revisited* (New York: Columbia University Press, 1989), 288–302, especially 292, where Wood states that the attempt to treat genres as discrete "is one of the greatest obstacles to any fruitful theory of genre."

18. See Neale, "Questions of Genre"; see also Steve Neale, *Genre* (London: British Film Institute, 1980), and Thomas Schatz, *Hollywood Genres: Formulas, Filmmaking and the Studio System* (New York: Random House, 1981).

19. Personal interview with Robert Rodríguez, March 10, 1992, Austin, Texas; Rodríguez on *Late Night with David Letterman,* February 26, 1993.

20. Neale, "Questions of Genre," 56.

21. Graper also sees the Hong Kong kung fu martial arts genre as conservative, though for a slightly different reason. In an analysis of how these films are received by lower-class American audiences, Graper concludes that they "function to keep this [lower-class] audience member in his socially-defined position and help to maintain the existing social class structure" (*The Kung Fu Movie Genre,* 157).

22. Judith Adler Hellman, *Mexico in Crisis,* 2d ed. (New York: Holmes and Meier, 1983), 112–15. See also Debbie Nathan, *Women and Other Aliens: Essays from the U.S.-Mexico Border* (El Paso, Texas: Cinco Puntos Press, 1991), 20. Both authors point out that the majority of the *maquiladora* workers are women.

23. Robert Rodríguez on the *Today Show,* NBC, February 26, 1993.

Flaming Latinas:
Ela Troyano's *Carmelita Tropicana:*
Your Kunst *Is Your* Waffen (1993)

José Esteban Muñoz

The heuristic impulse that propels this essay is concerned with a distinctly lesbian and Latina camp sensibility. There is some question as to whether or not "camp" is camp when it happens outside of its usual cultural parameters. The discourse on camp has been, at least since Susan Sontag's infamous notes from the 1960s, a discourse of middle- to upper-class white gay male sensibilities.[1] The notion of camp I will be mining in this essay is one in which "camp" is understood not only as a strategy of representation but also as mode of enacting self against the pressures of dominant culture's identity-denying protocols. *Carmelita Tropicana: Your* Kunst *Is Your* Waffen (1993), a short film by Ela Troyano, clearly articulates an ironic system of signs that, while still being very campy, is decidedly not employing the same referents as white male camp. The humor that *Carmelita Tropicana* produces represents a life world that we can understand, according to the film's eponymous performance artist star, as "Loisaida."[2] The Lower East Side of *Carmelita Tropicana* is a queer and Latina life world where dominant culture makes only one appearance in the form of over-the-top send-ups of abortion rights counterprotesters. Beyond that, the queer life world that the film depicts is one of Latinas and lesbians, political activists and performance artists.

Before I delve into my reading of *Carmelita Tropicana* and the specificities of *cubana* lesbian camp, I want to mention the one piece of cultural studies writing that has in some way loosely interrogated the issues of Latino kitsch: Celeste Olalquiaga's *Megalopolis: Contemporary Cultural Sensibilities.*[3] Olalquiaga's book delineates three degrees of kitsch sensibility in New York and its relation to Latino religious objects. The first degree constitutes a fascination with these objects because they represent a model of spirituality that is not avail-

129

able to the aficionado. They are representations of powerful emotion that help this first-degree kitsch follower grasp these higher emotions. Second-degree kitsch is the untangling of the icon from its religious/ emotional context. Its representation is dislodged from its cultural referent, the empty icon or gaudy bauble that can be found at Little Ricky's on the Lower East Side.[4] Finally, the third degree of kitsch is a true postmodern hybrid, the recycling of a past cultural construct for a present tense. Here Olalquiaga's primary example is the *altares* produced by Chicano, Nuyorican, and some white artists. In this final degree of kitsch, the kitsch object is recycled and recontextualized in a high-art setting. This recycling is, I will argue, central to any understanding of *Carmelita Tropicana*. The importance of this pioneering study is indicated in the film as the actual book appears at Carmelita's bedside in her own very kitschy bedroom. Interestingly enough, the book itself, within this frame and recontextualization, becomes a bit of "Loisaida" kitsch.

What Olalquiaga's book fails to do, however, is factor the unique relation of sexual minorities to the kitsch object. We might also tease out her use of the word *kitsch* instead of *camp,* a word that resonates as the way in which a minority culture reappropriates dominant culture. I want to suggest that Olalquiaga's word choice underplays and potentially erases the roles of queers in the production and consumption of kitsch objects and/or sensibilities. One of the difficulties of writing about kitsch and camp is that the two words oftentimes are confused with one another. This interchangeability is, of course, wrong, because both words have ontological lives distinct (though not entirely separate) from each other. Andrew Ross makes a distinction between the two by describing kitsch as having more "high"-art pretensions and a higher degree of self-seriousness, whereas camp seems to be slightly more ironic and playful.[5] Eve Kosofsky Sedgwick defines camp as being more spacious and "out" than kitsch.[6] Indeed, the word *camp* is integral to what Esther Newton calls the "gay world" of homosexuality, whereas kitsch's usage seems to be less tied to any one specific group.[7] In more recent accounts of aesthetics that relish the "tacky" or the "awful," the word *camp* seems to be dominating the discourse — prime examples of this are the works of Sontag, Newton, Ross, and Sedgwick. This itself is not a rule, as the example of Sedgwick, in *The Epistemology of the Closet,* deliminating the binary of art/kitsch makes evident. Kitsch is most definitely on the queer side of the binary in that text. But in *Megalopolis*, kitsch is not a survivalist mode of identity enactment within a phobic public sphere. Instead it is a nostalgic postmodern aesthetic that is basically a longing for a lost emotional intensity. I, like Olalquiaga, identify a certain mode of cross-generational, cross-cultural recycling in U.S. Latino culture, but unlike her I name it "camp" since I am interested in considering its convergences, alignments, and reverberations with the camp produced by sexual minorities. My reading will suggest that *Carmelita Tropicana* and its star's performance disrupt the stability of the camp = queer/kitsch = ethnic protocol.

Beyond the synthesis of the Latino and the campy, *Carmelita Tropicana* articulates a distinctly lesbian camp. Although there is no doubt that camp has overwhelmingly been associated with gay male subculture, the work of some lesbian and feminist theorists has begun to suggest a powerful tradition of female and lesbian camp. Pamela Robertson, for example, has undertaken a project to "de-essentialize" the link between gay men and camp, a link that, in Robertson's estimation, "reifies both camp and gay male taste."[8] Robertson suggests that

> camp as a structural activity has an affinity with feminist discussions of gender construction, performance, and enactment; and that, as such, we can examine a form of camp as a feminist practice. In taking on camp for women, I reclaim a form of female aestheticism, related to female masquerade, that articulates and subverts the image- and culture-making process to which women have traditionally been given access.[9]

Following Robertson's intervention, I see Troyano's film and its star's performance producing a mode of camp that subverts dominant image- and culture-making apparatuses (especially Hollywood film) that have rendered lesbians, Latinas, and especially Latina lesbians as either invisible or grossly caricaturized. An important byproduct of this mode of camp is the dislodging of the discourse of camp from male dominance.

But if the discourse of camp has been male-dominated, the social and aesthetic history itself suggests more complex and complicated dynamics. Although Ela Troyano's first film, *Bubble People* (1982), has not been widely seen, it both situates and comments on her work in relationship to that of Jack Smith. *Village Voice* journalist C. Carr provides a valuable account of an interaction between the director and her famous star Jack Smith:

> There is a scene in *Bubble People* where the spectral Jack Smith, look-
> ing like a drag queen biker, has a little encounter with the filmmaker Ela
> Troyano. "I am the Bubble Goddess" he intones, then pauses. "Tell
> me the truth. Has the camera started?" Close-up on his beads and
> beard and wraparound orange shades. "We can get better results if
> we're honest with each other, and you tell me the camera has started.
> Depicting what a great actor I must be."[10]

Within the campy moment one sees a serious instant where filmmaker and performer check in with each other, collaborating as equals;
it is ultimately an instant where, in the tradition of the North American avant-garde of the 1960s, the film's artifice is stripped away. This
was one of many collaborations between Smith and Troyano. According to Carr, Troyano began taking pictures because she wanted to
work with Smith, a performer she had admired, and he needed someone to take the photographs for his slide shows.[11] It is my belief that
reading Troyano's recent film as also influenced by Smith makes avali-
able a more comprehensive understanding of her production.

Smith, the now legendary avant-garde filmmaker and performance
artist who died of AIDS complications in 1989, pioneered an image of
hilarious and hyperactive gay male subjectivity that had not only not
existed before him, but was essentially unimaginable to queer spectators. Smith's project in his various underground acting jobs during
the 1960s, his own films, which included the censored underground
classic *Flaming Creatures* (1963), and his various stage performances
during the almost three decades that his career spanned were described by Michael Moon as "a fiercely unsentimental project of reclaiming his own and other people's queer energies (all kinds of queer
people, including gay ones) from the myriad forms of human wreck-
age into which our society has tended to channel it [*sic*]."[12] In the
same way that Olalquiaga's third degree of kitsch recaptures a lost
presence, Smith's performances and film reclaim lost queer energies.

Carmelita Tropicana features four very different versions of the
Latina: Carmelita, Orchidia, Sophia, and Dee. The film's star, Carmelita
Tropicana, is the alter ego/stage name of Alina Troyano, the filmmaker's
sister. In the film, the Carmelita character is a Loisaida performance
artist and lesbian activist. Her sidekick and constant companion is
the flaky Orchidia, also a member of the fictional direct-action group
GIA and a practitioner of postmodern dance, holistic medicine, and
the Afro-Cuban religion of Santeria. These women differ from each

Livia Daza Paris, Anne Iobst, Sophia Ramos, and Carmelita Tropicana in *Carmelita Tropicana: Your* Kunst *Is Your* Waffen. (Photo by Paula Court. Courtesy of Ela Troyano.)

other in their varying levels of spaciness and neurosis, but Carmelita's sister Sophia is nothing like the other Latina women in the film. Sophia is desperately trying to make it in the corporate business world and tries her best to dress for success. The film suggests that Sophia, despite her aspirations to be a conservative and upwardly mobile Latina, is often embroiled in Carmelita's life. Dee, a woman who first mugs Carmelita on her way home from a performance and later meets up with her victim in jail after the other women are arrested in a demonstration, is an "hermana sanguineda" (blood sister). Of all these women, Dee is perhaps the greatest challenge to dominant culture's understanding of just what constitutes a Latina. Dee is, by ancestry, a North American Anglo, but she was inducted into a Puerto Rican woman's gang in prison. Dee's identification as Latina undermines the misconception of Latinos as a racially homogeneous group. Dee's place in the film serves to destabilize any reductive understanding of Latina/o status. Dee's HIV-positive status also offers a representation of the ways in which the virus does not discriminate and affects women (especially women of color) with equal brutality.

The film's very first scene, in which the lesbian performance artist emerges from a backdrop of flashy colored curtains and proceeds to

feign a thick Cuban accent as she launches into her opening monologue, establishes the film's narrative space. During that monologue
Carmelita speaks of the mixing of cultures in the Loisaida:

> Loisaida is the place to be. That's right. It's multicultural, multigenera-
> tional, mucho multi, multilingual. And like myself you gotta be multi-
> lingual. I am very good with the tongue. As a matter of fact the first
> language I learned when I got to New York was Jewish. I learn from
> my girlfriend Sharon. She is Jewish. She teach me and I write poem for
> her in Jewish. Title of the poem is "Oy-Vay Number One:" Oy-Vay/I
> schlep and schelp/I hurt my tuchas/I feel meshuga/Oy-Vay. Thank you
> very much.

In this scene Cuban identity is recycled and remade. Carmelita's thick
accent during this monologue is obviously fake. The artist's name
harkens back to the famous nightclub that signified the excessive op-
ulence of prerevolution Cuba. The garish sparkling red dress that she
wears signifies a lost notion of glamour that is associated with the
Cuba of the 1950s. There is also a campification of the present that
occurs when Carmelita describes the Lower East Side as "multicultural, multigenerational, mucho multi, multilingual." This last reference to the multilingual sets Carmelita up to purr "I am very good
with the tongue," a double entendre quip that is reminiscent of Mae
West. Carmelita's Yiddish joke also aligns her with an earlier tradition of ethnic comics who were Jewish. All of what transpires in this
scene is a recycling that I want to identify as the film's camp practice.
The recycling encompasses a distant Cuban past (the Club Tropicana
of the 1950s, Ricky Ricardo's exaggerated accent, a showgirl's sparkly
red dress), an American past (the very history of stand-up comedy
and the formidable influence of Jews in this North American tradition), and the recent U.S. past (in the form of a reference to the already exhausted wars over multiculturalism in the academy and popular culture).

Carr has explained that "if Jack Smith has been her [Troyano's]
greatest influence as a filmmaker—along with Jacques Rivette and
Russ Meyer—she's been informed just as much by Smith's performance."[13] The centrality of performance art to Troyano's work is apparent in *Carmelita Tropicana*. Carmelita Tropicana's performance—
the very fact that she is clearly performing during the film's opening
scene—connotes the importance of performance within both the film
and the mode of cultural enactment that I am calling *cubana* dyke

camp. As the film's narrative proceeds from this space of performative enunciation, the spectator is left with the residual understanding that this narrative is not only about a performance artist but also about performance itself—particularly performance that is campy in its negotiations between Latina identity practices, queer/lesbian humor, and dominant culture.

After Carmelita describes the Lower East Side world as "the place to be," the film's next two scenes depict a different version of Loisaida. Walking home from her performance, Carmelita is mugged by a female assailant who later turns out to be Dee. The sequence depicts the reality of urban crime and violence that many U.S. Latinas cope with on a day-to-day basis. Nonetheless, the film's camp valence takes the edge off this incident when it is revealed that the mugger's only weapon is a pen. Here Troyano's film both achieves a realist representation and then, with its last twist, spins into absurdist dimensions first explored by Smith and other sixties filmmakers such as Ron Rice and Ken Jacobs. An establishing shot of a street sign that reads "Ave C" and "Loisaida" concretely locates the film's setting.

A tracking shot moves from the street sign to a large movie poster in Carmelita's bedroom. The poster is for a Latin American melodrama titled *La Estrella Vacía*, a phrase that can be translated as "The empty star." The poster, and other aspects of the mise-en-scène, demarcate Carmelita's personal space as being as thoroughly campy as her performance. Carmelita's bedcover is decorated with extravagant roses. Her bed itself is draped with a white mesh netting that gives it an almost Victorian look. The room's walls are painted a bright pink. The aforementioned copy of *Megalopolis* is strewn on Carmelita's bed. Her phone is an old black dial phone that looks as though it is out of a forties film noir. Carmelita is awakened from her slumber by the ringing phone. The Dictator orders the star to rendezvous with other members of GIA at Tompkins Square Park. As the Dictator barks her orders the call-waiting signal clicks on the phone line. Carmelita puts the Dictator on hold as she answers a call from her long-lost father on the other line. As she code-switches from English to Spanish, the brief conversation with her father reveals that she has a seven-year-old brother, Pepito, and her father is having his prostate operated on.[14] She switches back to the now-enraged Dictator, who quotes World Health Organization statistics on HIV infection in women and children. She follows this statement with a command to "never put me on hold." The phone conversation, like Carmelita's room, depicts the mixing of cultures and historical moments. The room's deco ambiance is offset by the postmodern theory book that is casually tossed on the bed. The old-fashioned phone has the ultramodern feature of call waiting. Her conversation with her lesbian activist mentor is cut up with a conversation with her Cuban father. Troyano employs this mixing across time and cultures to achieve a radical camp effect that reveals, in exaggerated terms, the *mestizaje* of contemporary U.S. Latino culture and politics.

Although Orchidia and Carmelita are space cadets in the eyes of the over-the-top butch character the Dictator, they work, within the film's comedic frame, as important social actors. Their trendy apparel— Carmelita's ridiculously high-heeled tennis shoes and Orchidia's multicolored beanie hat, and the standard issue New York activist leather jackets that both women wear—both lampoons and represents the lifestyle of the "Loisaida" dyke activist.

Fashion is important elsewhere in the film. Sophia, Carmelita's darker-skinned sister, is in "dressed for success Hispanic corporate woman" garb. The camera surveys Sophia piece by piece as she reads a magazine article that explains the various "don'ts" for Latinas in the corporate machine. Sophia, with steak-tartare lipstick, fuschia nail polish, excessively high heels, and gold door knocker earrings embodies all of these "don'ts" that the article warns against. In the next scene she appears in, Sophia's whole body fills the screen, displaying her amalgamation of fashion "mistakes." In this scene she is harassed by a bodega clerk who, through the lens of the usual racist assumptions of what a Latina looks like, presumes Sophia is a monolingual African American. Sophia snaps back sharply that "Latinas come in all colors, *nena.*" This scene is significant insofar as it humorously challenges racist depictions of Latinas within and outside of the Latina/o community.

To get what is powerful and potentially socially destabilizing about the *cubana* dyke camp I am describing, one must have some access to the queer life world that is being signified on. The fact that most of the film is set in a women's prison needs to be understood as a campy metacommentary on one of Hollywood's most common depictions of Latinas as tough bull dykes in the B movie "women in prison" genre. Part of the camp effect is the biting commentary about the treatment of Latina bodies within Hollywood's proscribed operating procedures. What is also relevant about the recycling of this site is the juxtaposition of seeing these particular Latinas, characters who are quirkier and more complicated than any image that Hollywood has been able to invent when trying to represent Latinas, within this standardized backdrop. Jean Carlomusto's video *L Is for the Way You Look* (1991) is another experimentation with the uses of lesbian camp. In that project an actual clip from a women's prison movie is shown, dubbed over with lines from lesbian theorists Monique Wittig and Audre Lorde. The scene concludes with the prisoners rallying together and chanting "let's get Zsa Zsa," a reference to Zsa Zsa Gabor's insistence that she could not go to jail for slapping a Beverly Hills police officer because she was afraid of the lesbians. Moments like these in Troyano's and Carlomusto's films take back the negative image and resuscitate it with the powerful charge of dyke camp.

In *Carmelita Tropicana,* Troyano uses the prison scene for a movie-within-a-movie through a flashback sequence that depicts the story that Carmelita tells her sister Sophia about the tragedy of their great-aunt Cukita. Whereas the prison scene itself mimics the B movie, the flashback is shot as a black-and-white silent film with musical accompaniment and subtitles. Great-aunt Cukita's husband is a refined *habanero* electrical engineer. After killing the woman whom he blindly fell in love with, he commits suicide by ingesting poison. The widowed aunt is then seduced by a lowly delivery boy who, presumably knowing that he can never really have Cukita, kills her after dancing a passionate tango with her. The black-and-white sequence recasts the entire film in terms of prerevolution Cuba and assigns two of the characters (the butch players in the main narrative) the roles of men. This female drag is in a way akin to a tradition of campy male drag that we might associate with venues like Jack Smith's performances or Charles Ludlum's Ridiculous Theatrical Company. Carmelita's transformation into the "ugly man," a rough, pockmarked, and unshaven proletarian deliveryman (and her new character, Pingalito, in her recent stage show *Milk of Amnesia*) is a campy reappropriation of the drag used in the rich tradition of North American avant-garde theater and drag revues. The male character in this sequence is supposed to register both outside of and inside of the erotics of "butch/femme." This depiction of a lost exilic homeland—with its politics replaced by a drag performance of an ill-fated heterosexual, class-defined romance—enables an opulent scene of cross-identification that is, in one manner

Carmelita Tropicana as the ugly man. (Photo by Mara Catalan. Courtesy of Ela Troyano.)

of speaking, *queer.* Cross-identifications, as Sedgwick and others have forcefully argued, are standard operating procedures for queers. Sedgwick has recently explained that queer is a moment of perpetual flux, a movement that is eddying and turbulent. The word *queer* itself means "across"; the concept itself can only be understood as connoting a mode of identification that is as relational as it is oblique.[15] I am suggesting that there is something distinctly queer about the lesbian cross-dressing in *Carmelita Tropicana,* that it reproduces various identifications across a range of experiences—cultural, racial, political, sexual.

The flashback posits a historical condition—"always the same story ... *violencia y amor*"—that unites the four women across their differences. It is at this point that the women-in-prison sequence transmutes into a send-up of a Hollywood musical. All the prison cells automatically click open and the four female protagonists emerge in *rumbera* outfits made out of what appears to be military fatigues. The musical number that ensues is a Mexican *ranchera* titled "Prisioneras del Amor." The choice of a Mexican *ranchera* is indicative of Latina camp's ability to index and reclaim clichéd and sentimental moments and tropes across *latinidad*. East Coast Latinas performing a West Coast musical genre with a Mexican song comments on the ways in which Hollywood cinema, along with other aspects of dominant culture such as census taking, collapses the diversity of the U.S. Latino community into one set of shallow cultural stereotypes. Troyano's film, in this instance, plays with this dominant mode of storytelling. The lyrics themselves, "Prisioneras del amor/prisioneras de la vida," could be the title of a Mexican melodrama. The song speaks in lavish terms of how love offers both great warmth and a grand pain ("el amor nos da calor y también un gran dolor"). The song unites the four women who had previously been squabbling with each other in the cell. The women speak of their commonality as prisoners of love and life. It calls for the throwing off of habits of incarcerated nuns and making liberation their new religion.[16] Although this musical number is extravagant and brilliantly over the top, it should not simply be dismissed as nothing more than campy fun. The metaphor of Latinas as prisoners is a poignant one when discussing the status of the Latina and lesbian image within representation. The idea of liberation that is invoked in this song is also a more serious and political call for liberation from a dominant culture that reduces such identities to hollowed-out stereotypes. Troyano's strategic use of camp allows her film and its characters to reinhabit these stereotypes, both calling attention to the inaccuracy of these representations and "fixing" such representation from the inside by filling in these representational husks with complicated, antiessentialist, emotionally compelling characters.

Carmelita Tropicana is a film that refigures camp and rescues it from a position as fetishized white queer sensibility. Camp is a form of artificial respiration; it breathes new life into old situations. Camp is,

then, more than a worldview; it a strategic response to the breakdown of representation that occurs when a queer, ethnically marked,
or other subject encounters her inability to fit within the majoritar-
ian representational regime. It is a measured response to the forced
evacuation from dominant culture that the minority subject experiences. Camp is a practice of suturing different lives, of reanimating,
through repetition with a difference, a lost country or moment that
is relished and loved. Although not innately politically valenced, it is
a strategy that can do positive identity- and community-affirming work.
Carmelita Tropicana represents *cubana* camp and at the same time
returns to the island itself with a highly melodramatic story, a story
that has been lost for the two sisters (the scene I described earlier).

Such a deployment of camp styles and practices is, at its core, a
performative move. Reiteration and citation are the most easily identifiable characteristics of this mode of camp performativity. According to Judith Butler, a performative provisionally succeeds if its action
echoes prior actions, and accumulates the force of authority through
the repetition or citation of a prior, authoritative set of practices. For
Butler, a performative draws on and covers over the constitutive conventions by which it is mobilized.[17] Butler's book is concerned specifically with the performative charge of queerness, and it is my contention that this theory is also applicable to the workings of various
minority groups. The repetition of the quotidian is precisely what the
cubana kitsch and Lower East Side lesbian style in *Carmelita Tropicana* is enacting.

The repetition that Butler outlines, like the reclaiming in Jack Smith's
work that Michael Moon outlines and the recycling that Olalquiaga
discusses, can all contribute to a potential understanding of the camp
project that is *Carmelita Tropicana*. The larger than life (i.e., Hollywood icon) takes on aspects of the everyday; the exotic is "de-exoti-
cized" and brought into the subject's sphere of the ordinary; artifacts
from the past that have been discarded as "trashy" (the word *kitsch*
comes from a German word loosely meaning "street rubbish") are
recuperated and become a different, "new" thing. With this in mind,
I want to argue that lesbian camp and also *cubana* camp are materi-
alized in *Carmelita Tropicana,* where its star works as the ultimate
campy dyke, and whose filmmaker and star bridge lost countries with
contemporary urban life, queer politics with Latina aesthetics, and in
general, elevates the trashy to blissful heights.

Notes

1. This is not to suggest that Sontag theorized a specifically gay male sensibility; she was, in fact, interested in explaining how camp was or at least could be more than just a homosexual phenomenon. This universalizing gesture elided the issue of how other minority communities might enact a camp discourse in favor of how (white) heterosexuals could develop a camp sensibility. See Susan Sontag, "Notes on Camp," *Against Interpretation* (New York: Delta, 1979). For a critique of Sontag's urbane homophobia see D. A. Miller, "Sontag's Urbanity," *October* 49 (1989): 91–101.

2. The term "Loisaida" is one that has been used to describe a neighborhood in the Lower East Side of New York City where *el barrio* meets bohemia.

3. Celeste Olalquiaga, *Megalopolis: Contemporary Cultural Sensibilities* (Minneapolis: University of Minnesota Press, 1992).

4. The store's name, not insignificantly, signifies upon one of the very first Latino characters that made it into the popular American imagination. The hybrid child of Ricky Ricardo (Desi Arnaz) and Lucy (MacGillicuddy) Ricardo (Lucille Ball) embodied the mixing and literal miscegenation that occurs when cultures collide or otherwise meet. Interestingly, the birth of Little Ricky on *I Love Lucy* became a national event in which fiction and real life coincided.

5. Andrew Ross, *No Respect: Intellectuals and Popular Culture* (New York: Routledge, 1989), 145. Ross goes on to explain that "kitsch has serious pretensions to artistic taste, and, in fact, contains a range of references to high or legitimate culture, which it apes in order to flatter the consumer. Kitsch's seriousness about art, and its aesthetic chutzpah, are usually associated with the class aspirations of and upper mobility of a middlebrow audience, insufficient in cultural capital to guarantee access to legitimate culture."

6. Eve Kosofsky Sedgwick, *The Epistemology of the Closet* (Berkeley and Los Angeles: University of California Press, 1990), 156. For a keen gloss on Sedgwick's reading of kitsch and camp as a binarism, see James Creech, *Closet Writing/Gay Reading: The Case of Melville's Pierre* (Chicago: University of Chicago Press, 1993), 45–51.

7. Esther Newton, *Mother Camp: Female Impersonators in America* (Chicago: University of Chicago Press, 1972), 105.

8. Pamela Robertson, " 'The Kinda Comedy That Imitates Me': Mae West's Identification with the Feminist Camp," *Cinema Journal* 32.2 (winter 1993): 57.

9. Ibid.

10. C. Carr, *On Edge: Performance at the End of the Twentieth Century* (Hanover, N.H.: Wesleyan University Press, 1993), 78.

11. Ibid., 83.

12. Michael Moon, "Flaming Closets," *October* 51 (winter 1989): 37. Moon's essay is the best account of the politics of Smith's queer performance and filmic production. Other useful accounts include Richard Dyer, *Now You See It: Studies on Lesbian and Gay Film* (New York: Routledge, 1990),

145–49; Carel Rowe, *The Baudelairean Cinema: A Trend within the American Avant-Garde* (Ann Arbor: UMI Research Press, 1982), 39–40; and David James, *Allegories of Cinema: American Film in the Sixties* (Princeton, N.J.: Princeton University Press, 1989), 119–27.

13. Carr, *On Edge*, 82.

14. Pepito, when he is shown at the film's end, is revealed to be Asian. This is significant insofar as the three siblings are all of different races yet all Cuban and Latina/o. This fact confounds U.S. popular understandings of just what a Latino might look like. It also depicts the three largest racial groups on the island of Cuba.

15. Eve Kosofsky Sedgwick, *Tendencies* (Durham, N.C.: Duke University Press, 1993), 5–9.

16. Interestingly, Ela Troyano portrays the object of a nun's desire in Su Friedrich's *Damned if You Don't*.

17. Judith Butler, *Bodies That Matter: The Discursive Limits of Sex* (Routledge: New York, 1993), 226.

Docudrag, or "Realness" as a Documentary Strategy: Felix Rodriguez's *One Moment in Time* (1992)

Marcos Becquer and Alisa Lebow

Video Realness: Harlem versus Paris

Writing about a video that treats the Harlem drag balls and its participants almost inevitably involves referencing the film that made the balls famous. In some ways *One Moment in Time* (Felix Rodriguez, 1992) picks up where *Paris Is Burning* (Jennie Livingston, 1991) left off.[1] If, as bell hooks points out, *Paris Is Burning* featured the drag balls as the center of its characters' lives, and the balls' spectacularity as the centerpiece of its cinematic narrative, in *One Moment in Time* these provide merely a backdrop, a significant but not definitive cultural point of reference for the lives it portrays.[2] Documenting the affair between voguer Hector Xtravaganza and Raymond, the straight man for whom Hector literally becomes a woman named Tiffany, *One Moment in Time* presents its subject in the complexities of everyday life. Unlike *Paris Is Burning,* it insists that there is more to a ball child's existence than the passionate desire for consumer culture and the glory of the drag-ball runway. We see Hector/Tiffany in the midst of profound, if tenuous, family ties, meeting the demands of an active social life, even having contemplative moments. We also witness h/er emotional and sexual involvement in the ultimately murderous love affair that motivates h/er bodily transformation.

In this way, *One Moment in Time* assumes the insider's relation to ball culture and life beyond it from which *Paris Is Burning,* with its specific observational ethnographic strategies, distances itself.[3] Through its use, for instance, of glossary terms to translate the "street jargon" used by the ball children, *Paris Is Burning* implicitly posits its audience as a group that would have no cause to be informed about the culture "under study." *One Moment in Time,* on the other hand, not only forgoes such translation but entirely does away with the impres-

143

sion that any translation is needed in order to decipher or decode the life it depicts, though Tiffany's world may nonetheless appear entirely esoteric to the uninitiated spectator. *One Moment in Time* thus implicitly posits an audience that would at least be familiar, if not intimate, with Tiffany's milieu, though, of course, she and her world do not suddenly become "transparent" as a result.

Made by an East Harlem-born Nuyorican filmmaker, *One Moment in Time* concerns itself almost exclusively with this audience "in the know" most specifically through its use of first-person voice-over narration performed entirely in "authentic" Latino-Black-gay street talk. The use of first-person voice-over to narrate visual sequences, a popular documentary strategy, enhances the audience's sense of proximity to the events shown, as it creates the impression that the camera was a witness to Hector/Tiffany's life-transforming events.[4] In addition, *One Moment in Time* uses "legendary" Hector Xtravaganza's real name and features "archival" footage of Hector in his life and in the media since he has actually garnered some public acclaim.[5] With this complex use of archival footage, the video relies on its audience's presumed familiarity with its subject in order to problematize the conventional status of such footage, which in documentary usually functions as a reference to the historically real. The footage here, while taken from Hector's actual life, is meant to reference the life of the fictional character Hector/Tiffany Xtravaganza. The intended audience of this video no doubt would be cognizant of this extratextual information and enjoy its intertextual resonances. Formally, *One Moment in Time* deploys—or imitates—these, among other, codes of realist documentary, only fully revealing itself as fiction with the credit sequence at the end (though admittedly there are clues throughout, even for those who would not recognize Hector).[6]

If we began by discussing *One Moment in Time* in relation to *Paris Is Burning*, this was not simply for the creation of a gratuitous descriptive counterpoint. *One Moment in Time* itself prompts the comparison. Its very first images, a montage of ball and vogueing footage that helps to introduce Hector and to situate him culturally and sexually, provide a rather direct reference to *Paris Is Burning*. As *One Moment in Time* progresses and we see fewer and fewer of these spectacularized images, it becomes increasingly evident that *Paris Is Burning* represents the dominant version of Latino gay and drag culture that *One Moment in Time* attempts to contest.[7] By making this introductory "citation" of the drag balls as they were seen in *Paris Is Burning*, then showing us aspects of a ball child's life that *Paris Is Burning* bypasses, all the while doing so in a manner formally coded as more "authentic," *One Moment in Time*, in a classic vogueing gesture, presents itself as more "real" than *Paris Is Burning*.

"Realness" here is the attribute of a performance that involves creating the best imitation possible in a manner so convincing, yet tacitly so illegitimate, that any notion of the real may be called into question. It is worth noting, too, that in the drag ball scenario, realness is not just a means by which to achieve a seamless identification (though identification is undeniably central to its operation), it is also an end highly valued in and of itself. It therefore also involves, from the point of view of its performer and those privileged to understand the performance as realness, taking pleasure in achieving such a remarkably accurate yet misleading imitation. In this sense it entails more than just, as Judith Butler describes it, "the ability to compel belief, to produce [a] naturalized effect." An essential part of its structure is based on undermining belief as well—an undermining that may then lead to a refiguring of the very notion of belief. As much as realness works "to the extent that it *cannot* be read" (her emphasis), it also *must be read* in order to work.[8] Much of its pleasure comes precisely from this paradoxical "reading" of what presumably cannot be read. Thus, formally speaking, *One Moment in Time* attempts to outdo—and takes pleasure in outdoing—the realness of *Paris Is Burning* as an authoritative representation of Latino gay and drag culture by posing as a documentary but being a fiction. This is obviously not meant to imply that this video is "untrue" or even less true than a traditional documentary, or in this case *Paris Is Burning*. The effect of this documentary fiction is to cast a fictive shadow on both *Paris Is Burning* and documentary more generally while still partaking of the truth claims of an authenticated positionality. If *Paris Is Burning* attempts to reveal what lies beneath the "fake" postures of the balls through the "real-life" codes of documentary, the documentary pose in *One Moment in Time* calls into question the very notion that there is any "real" to reveal. The vying for "realness" (with the possibility of restructuring belief) is what remains after this questioning. As such, *One Moment in Time* is a docudrag—a fiction in documentary clothing; a documentary about drag.[9]

Docudrag

As a fiction in documentary clothing, *One Moment in Time* achieves certain effects within the politics of imitation. It is, to paraphrase Homi Bhabha's definition of colonial mimicry, "almost the same [as conventional documentary] but not quite." According to Bhabha, one of the effects of mimicry is that it "rearticulates presence in terms of its 'otherness,' that which it disavows."[10] Thus the fictional status of *One Moment in Time,* that which makes it "not quite" conventional documentary, in turn exposes the way most realist documentaries rely—yet disavow their reliance—on the narrative conventions of fiction. It is partly through this disavowal that realist documentary achieves its "presence," that which so effectively compels audience belief in its truth.[11] It is partly through the exposure of this disavowal then—that is, revealing itself as fiction—that docudrag achieves its "realness," that which both generates and ultimately disappoints audience belief in its truth.[12]

Yet, in mimicking realist codes, *One Moment in Time* does not merely achieve a vanguardist, formalist self-reflexivity; nor do its critical effects remain entirely at the formal level, for this strategy also enables it to enact an impressive cultural displacement at the level of content. Let us reiterate that we are discussing a video made by Latinos about queer Latino culture. As such, *One Moment in Time* uses first-person voice-over narration, "indigenous" jargon, complex "archival" footage, and so on, all to help construct a plausible, but markedly and importantly nonwhite, universe for Hector/Tiffany in which s/he stands, along with h/er friends and family, and even h/er "intended" audience, firmly in the center of that drama. This centering strategy may again recall, and help to clarify, one of the ideals of vogueing competitions, which, as a ball child explains in *Paris Is Burning,* involves wanting to look and live "as well as" (in contrast to "like") those privileged by the dominant culture. For indeed, what is being imitated (and appropriated) here is nothing other than the *privilege* usually reserved for those who represent the dominant culture, the very same privilege that normally allows the dominant to so casually and repeatedly "overlook" gay and nonwhite cultural forms and expressions, and that functions best when it is itself overlooked.[13] In this sense, the deceptively simple cinematic strategy of allowing "the other" to enjoy the privilege of dominating the filmic frame can be-

come a complex and noteworthy, if provisional, form of political critique and self-assertion, especially in view of the historic absence and
marginalization that have shaped filmic and videographic representations of racial, ethnic, and sexual otherness.[14] Interestingly, the video's
formal strategy of revealing itself as fiction can be seen to ultimately
underscore the status of its contents as (still) just a fantasy, at once a
type of experiment in, and critique of, privilege. It is in this usurpa-
tion (albeit fantasmatic) of privilege and displacement of whiteness
that the video reflects the important variation Homi Bhabha adds to
his definition of mimicry: it is "almost the same [as conventional doc-
umentary] but not white."

Of course this does not mean that whiteness is not referenced in
One Moment in Time. Rather, it is radically relativized in the narrative representation of Hector/Tiffany's desire. This relativization (as
opposed to exclusion) of whiteness ironically allows "race" and ethnic difference to casually yet thoroughly permeate the video's construction, making its imitative strategies of form and content read-
able along these lines. The ethnic/racial distinctiveness of this text, in
other words, derives not from any ideal of pure difference but from
its simultaneous refusal to disavow or be subsumed by the influence
of its other(s). If, in terms of form, *One Moment in Time* can be said
to neither disavow nor be subsumed by the influence of conventional
documentary, for instance, a similar dynamic gets played out even in
the very details of its content, as evidenced, say, in the "respectable"
Chanel-like suit Tiffany wears when we first see her. Although the
suit is perhaps in part interpretable as a signifier of a desire to be
white, it is also recontextualized by her unmistakably queer Latino
gestures and language as she wears it. Tiffany's desire, here shown to
be informed — but not determined — by whiteness, is thereby also,
and importantly, marked as nonwhite. Indeed, the one (and only) sequence in the tape where images of white women do appear, generally alongside images of women of color, is anchored by Tiffany recalling how Raymond "never disrespected" her, how he preferred her
even over "the most beautiful" — and real — women. Even though this
scene also expresses Raymond's wish that Tiffany were a real woman,
thus spurring Tiffany's desire to change her sex, the narrative never
suggests that she sought to whiten herself to better fit her own or
Raymond's ideals. This is remarkable since much of the recent critical
writing on vogueing and drag, especially in regard to *Paris Is Burning*,

Tiffany tells her story in *One Moment in Time.*

has seen the practices as primarily a matter of idealizing white womanhood.[15]

In fact, womanhood in *One Moment in Time* is at times anything but idealized. This text, though it articulates an important critique of heterosexuality, whiteness, and the documentary form precisely through its representation and imitation of woman, occasionally lapses into an unexamined misogyny by means of an avowed distaste for the female body, whether surgically constructed or otherwise. Although Hector and friends clearly admire the accoutrements of womanhood as masquerade (evident, for instance, when they dress up in drag for fun), its grounding in the body (born male or female) incites a crisis of representation (and revulsion) for them and for the text. Like some of the recent writing about drag and transsexuality, *One Moment in Time* draws the line precisely at the naturalized site of the body for the gender denaturalizations it would endorse. Symptoms of this somewhat arbitrary demarcation and the representational crisis it engenders are not only Hector's campy but less than convincing drag, but also the text's troubling forays into sexism. Hector/Tiffany tells us, for instance, that as a boy "I liked to rap to fish all the time.... I liked to bother them, you know, play with their heads a little." "I wasn't incompetent,"s/he says, "I was just *not* interested" (h/er emphasis).[16]

If *One Moment in Time* idealizes anything at all as a docudrag text, then, it is a textualized notion of imitation itself. It is in terms of both senses of docudrag—a fiction in documentary clothing and a documentary about drag—that the tape achieves its striking adequation of form and content. Treating an already imitative practice, drag, the video imitates the codes of the filmic practice that purports to best imitate reality itself, documentary. *One Moment in Time* thus inscribes the problematics of imitation and realness as the central aspiration of documentary filmmaking as such.

In her chapter about *Paris Is Burning* entitled "The Golden Apple," Peggy Phelan suggests that just such an imitative strategy, where form mirrors content and where they both try to mirror already existing representations, might have been an improvement on Livingston's work because it would have enacted the "radical epistemology of her subjects," and provided "a filmic 'match' for the represented real her performers seek." Phelan suggests that like voguers, films about vogueing might themselves vogue by ransacking "the codes of the filmic real" to seize "an appropriative epistemology not *about* cross-dressing but indebted to its wisdom."[17] *One Moment in Time* does quite a bit of this ransacking, resembling at times public-service announcements, commercial advertisements, docudrama, police drama, suspense thrillers, music video, and of course, realist documentary. Rather than trying to straightforwardly represent the real, in the style of *Paris Is Burning, One Moment in Time* instead vogues to achieve realness: here the text "reads" the realism of *Paris Is Burning* as a competitive (yet ultimately unsuccessful) attempt at realness.[18]

Leaving aside the larger philosophical question of whether a "filmic match" is always a desirable ideal or if it may in fact turn out to be the ultimate ruse of realism, we can safely surmise that *One Moment in Time,* in its vying for realness, strives to embody a "filmic match" for its subject. And its subject, here, the drama of a body trying to "match" a gender, is the very drama of embodiment. By positing these relations between text and body, *One Moment in Time* encourages us to think about documentary textual practice in terms of the bodily practices of drag and transsexuality. In other words, (its crisis over the female body notwithstanding) it prompts us to see documentary realism, like drag and transsexuality, as an attempt to imitate and embody the codes and ontology of the real; to construct the real through its adaptive embodiment; to see it, that is, as a form of real-ness.[19] It is this transmutation and implication of a gender challenge into a documentary challenge that makes this particular confluence of factors intriguing. According to Judith Butler, drag exposes the fact that gender is an imitation for which there is no original. The naturalness or reality of gender, she argues, is the (belated) effect of its repeated performance. The ceaseless repetition of the performance is made necessary, even compulsory, because no one ever gets gender completely right.[20] Extending Butler's insights to *One Moment in Time,* we might argue that docudrag exposes the ways in which doc-umentary might be a performance for which there is no real, that the effect of the historical real, which documentary is said to capture, is produced in and through the repetition of documentary codes and is not prior to them.

Yet to argue that documentary helps to construct the reality it pur-ports to merely record, and to acknowledge that such reality is itself only available in ways mediated by representation, is not to do away entirely with the possibility of a specific relation between documentary as a category of filmmaking and a reality or history, now conceived as constructed and even in regress. This relation between a mediated real and a documentary practice, which in part helps to create rather than reflect it, has yet to be fully anatomized. In other words, to see documentary as drag does not necessarily require that it become in-distinguishable from fiction. Just as it is the *difference* between drag and realist gender that allows us to see the naturalizing pretensions of realist gender as just another form of drag, it is the *difference* be-tween docudrag and documentary realism that allows us to see the latter's naturalizing pretensions. It is not enough to point out, as Carol-Anne Tyler lucidly has, that such differences are erased by the bottom line of drag (and docudrag) theory, namely, that gender, and also doc-umentary, are merely imitative performances, just drag.[21] Some dis-tinction needs to be recognized, however ethereal or difficult to pin down, not only between drag and realist gender but also between docudrag and documentary, if only because in both cases the latter remain powerfully sanctioned performances, whereas the former are, to varyingly punitive extents, strongly discouraged. That the distinc-tion remains (as of yet) not definitively named need not be taken to mean that it does not exist, nor that is devoid of identifiable sociocultural implications. There are historical precedents (think of the historical construction of homosexuality, especially lesbianism, and/or racial/ethnic passing) that testify to the possibility of producing powerful and palpable knowledge effects even without the benefit of being "named." The distinctive difference between drag and realist gender, between docudrag and documentary, can be said to be, in this sense, a queer difference, one that awaits its "proper" signifier, with all the ambivalence that entails.[22]

Our focus so far has been primarily on documentary form in relation to drag theory. Let us now turn our attention to transsexuality, which the video in some ways constructs as the excessive and inappropriate logical conclusion of drag practices. If, as we have been suggesting, docudrag is alignable with an "imitative" theory of gender, which shows all gender reality, and by extension documentary realism, to be drag, how does the concept of transsexuality in relation to documentary fit with or complicate this picture?

Transdoc

The concept and practice of transsexuality sits uneasily in most recent theory about drag. As Ann Cvetkovich succinctly puts it, "the desire to be a 'real' woman [or man] implicitly rests on an essentialist conception of gender.... It re-establishes the fixed gender roles that cross-dressing and drag might challenge."[23] For much contemporary drag theory, then, transsexuality takes gender too seriously. It is not parodic or campy enough. For our purposes here, this "deadpan" quality of transsexuality is the first hint at its correspondence with documentary, also traditionally understood to be more "deadpan" than parodic or campy.

Other "explanations" of transsexuality have not been particularly generous either. Transsexuality has been considered, for instance, as a rather literal and thus quintessential form of fetishism;[24] as a homophobic response to same-sex attraction; and (at least in male to female transsexualism) as a threat to lesbian feminism—an assertion of unwelcome male privilege in biologically defined "women's space."[25]

One Moment in Time, for its part, offers its own implicit theory of transsexuality. It understands transsexuality not exclusively as an issue of gender, but also as a problem of sexuality, particularly as an effect of compulsory heterosexuality. Hector wants to become Tiffany not so much for h/erself (not, say, because s/he feels "trapped in the wrong body") but, importantly, to please Raymond, to be able to marry Raymond. Two simultaneous (and perhaps mutually exclusive) readings of transsexuality are offered. On the one hand, *One Moment in Time,* by understanding transsexuality in terms of sexual attraction, at least conceptually transfers the phenomenon from the realm of the purely individualistic and psychological to the space of the relational and the social. This has the advantage of explicitly eroticizing and politicizing transsexuality, something much drag theory as well as theory about transsexuality itself, tends to downplay.[26] On the other hand, there exists a subtext within the film, underscored by the opening song and reiterated by the final outcome of the narrative, that suggests that transsexuality is also necessarily a regressive move within the politics of homosexuality. Toward the end of the video, *One Moment in Time* slips unexpectedly into a moralizing tale wherein transsexuality becomes an irreversible and excessive transgression with tragic consequences. In actually having his sex (or gender) reassigned, Hector, an otherwise admirable, proud gay character, has gone too far. Gay, even drag, culture becomes the more natural, more appropriate form of gender and sexual expression. The celebratory opening song is telling: over images of the drag balls, Bishop Carl Bean sings, "I'm happy, I'm carefree, and I'm gay. I was born this way." Although this sentiment contributes to the centering effect discussed earlier by partially displacing heterosexuality along with whiteness, it can also be read as an attack on transsexuality (understood as a defection into heterosexuality). To be gay and male here is natural, biologically determined, and decidedly preferable to being transsexual and female.

This reviling of transsexuality and the female sex signals some of the dangers of centering when it is seen not as a strategy but as the goal of empowerment. It is by now a commonplace of poststructuralist theory to say that centering practices unavoidably produce their own exclusions; and *One Moment in Time* is no exception to this rule. By attempting narratively to posit Black and Latino gay male and drag culture as the center of its ideal world, it would, were it successful, unfortunately perpetuate the marginalization and exclusion of transsexuals and women from the privilege of that position.

Before offering our own comments on transsexuality, we'd like to briefly attempt to situate ourselves in relation to it. We each, for various reasons, have a complex and at times "inappropriate" relation to our assigned genders. It is important, however, to assert that this understanding of our, and indeed most people's, implication in gender discomfort does not amount to a "transgendered," much less a transsexual, experience.[27] We want to acknowledge publicly the bravery of, and the risks taken by, transgendered people and to clarify that what we have to say may be inspired by these lived experiences, but does not represent a definitive comment on them. Somehow transgenderism and specifically transsexuality continue to be discussed in academic fora as if no one participating in them inhabits that identity. Our discussion, which at times may continue to abstract from the historicity of these practices, does not presume to speak for transgendered people, though it does take into account the possibility of speaking to them.

Instead of surveying or responding to how transsexuality has been understood as homophobic, fetishistic, essentialist, or antiessentialist, we would prefer to consider more specifically some of its implications for documentary practice and, in terms of *One Moment in Time,* for docudrag. Like documentary, transsexuality is made possible by certain modern technological developments and is predicated on an enabling contradiction that involves the relations between these technological developments and their actions on "nature." Like documentary, transsexuality tends to believe in a sacrosanct, constant, and essential reality while at the same time insisting that this reality is changeable, that it can be acted on in a secular and technologically transformative way—a reality posited in order to be deposed. Both of these transformative practices implicitly recognize the *power* mobilized by what counts as the real, even if that "real" only appears in its discursive trappings. Here, documentary and transsexuality, as imitative practices, align with the concept of realness, which also posits, genuinely engages, and tries to embody the real it simultaneously deconstructs. Since both their aims are indeed to be considered "real,"[28] transsexuality and documentary, as forms of realness, may begin to offer ways not only to deconstruct but also to intervene in and reconstruct what passes as reality. They can then highlight not only the performative quality of the real, as do drag and docudrag, but also the potentially transformative quality of the practice of realness. As transsexual theorist Sandy Stone suggests in her article "The *Empire* Strikes Back: A Posttranssexual Manifesto," the transsexual body can be seized upon as "a reconstructive force."[29]

As we implied earlier, an important part of the transformative potential of realness is its implicit understanding of reality as structured and sustained by belief. Realness at once compels belief and calls attention to the arbitrariness of that compelling. As forms of realness, documentary and transsexuality engage this insight as they actively attempt to produce a "fit" between belief and the real, one that more often than not requires alterations. In the process of producing such a "fit," reality itself is revealed as a regulated, "well-stitched" phenomenon, but one that is nonetheless changeable because inherently produced and thus differently (re)producible. By means of their "illegitimate" yet believable productions of the real, the practices of realness show that what passes as reality both *requires* a specific history and ontology conceived of as legitimate and hence performing as legitimating and *necessitates* a thoroughgoing erasure of other historical and ontological possibilities, other versions of the real—even as they simultaneously rely on and underscore the abiding and constituting force of the reality they mimic. If documentary has traditionally concentrated on manipulating belief in a mostly unquestioned reality by means of often downplayed cuts and augmentations, transsexuality's mimicry suggests that not only belief, but reality "itself," may at times be in need of some cuts and augmentations. In both cases, realness can be understood as the demonstration of reality as *structured* by belief, a kind of mimetic decoupage of the real.

A possible blind spot in our analogy between transsexuality and documentary would certainly be the idea that transsexuality does not so much re-create history as it necessitates an active erasure of it. Transsexuality, even more than drag, is considered to rely on invisibility for success. Passing is often thought to be the ultimate aspiration of all transsexuals, entailing the eradication of any reference to their preoperative life, thus requiring that they erase their history.[30] Although it can be argued that documentary as a form of filmmaking also necessitates an active erasure of its own history, aspiring as it so often does to appear as a "window on the world," it must also be remembered that in film-historical terms documentary has also been seen as *the* force for inscribing history on film. In its best tradition, documentary tries to *make* history, no matter how contested or mediated that term.

Thus, if it has been useful to begin to think about documentary in a manner "indebted to the wisdom" of drag and transsexuality, we may also want to think about transsexuality in a form indebted to documentary's wisdom, in particular the wisdom produced by documentary's special, if not entirely transparent, relation to history. Indeed, Sandy Stone's posttranssexual manifesto, though it of course makes no direct reference to documentary practice, constitutes a call for transsexuals to write their erased histories, which would "map the refigured body onto conventional gender discourse and thereby disrupt it." Stone describes "the *intertextual* possibilities of the transsexual body" (her emphasis) in ways that resemble our discussion of the disruptive capabilities of the docudrag text.[31] She sees it as able to generate intriguing dissonances by means of its similarities to and differences from the rigidly polarized and thus limited discourse of gender. We too have attempted to offer docudrag as a way of problematizing and expanding the limitations of discussing documentary in terms of the rigid polarity often imposed on it, that of reality/fiction. And yet, although Stone speaks of the *post*transsexual, her use of Judith Butler's accounts of drag and butch/femme relationships to explicate this future body harbors the disadvantage of threatening to collapse transsexuality back into just another form of drag. Surely, transsexuality and drag, though related—even crucially overlapping at points—are not identical in all aspects. Nor are the insights available by considering documentary in terms of transsexuality simply reducible to the theoretical illuminations enabled by (docu)drag.

Interestingly, as we have mentioned, *One Moment in Time,* as a docudrag text, does not narratively treat transsexuality as having the disruptive potential Stone attributes to it. As a documentary—no matter how contested the term—about transsexuality, *One Moment in Time* answers Stone's call to write the history of the transsexual body; yet the way it does so indicates that such an act of inscription may not always or necessarily be disruptive. Consequently, it also raises questions about whether docudrag as we have been discussing it is always necessarily disruptive.

If all docudrag is a way of inscribing the history of a body, this inscription in *One Moment in Time* seems indelibly marked by a pronounced fear of irreversibility—of permanent and indelible changes on the body—brought about by the decision to alter one's sex. As Tiffany herself puts it, "Once its gone, its gone, chil'." Tiffany's inability to fully reconcile herself to this decision is symptomatized in the narrative by her loss of control and identity as she kills Raymond, in a fit of rage, for abandoning her after her "gender reassignment," then tries to rationalize the murder to his mutilated body. "It was like I was not me," she says to a lifeless Raymond, "I was just hurt." This momentary lapse into insanity (perhaps, the text suggests, the same insanity that led Hector to go through with the operation in the first place; "I don't know what got into me," s/he says about the operation) indicates both a radical dislocation between the speaking subject and h/er actions and a relocation of that subject in an identity alienated from its "true" (male) gender. Who is the "I" and who is the "me" in these quotations? The text implies here not only that the transsexual is never fully reconciled with the sex change itself, let alone any actions taken "post op," but also that s/he is, in fact, never fully "authentically" changed by it. The ensuing denial, "I was just hurt," obliquely refers to castration, yet to be hurt might also imply that one can heal, that the damage is *not* irreversible.

Moreover, the pronouncedly melodramatic staging of this loss of control, executed in horror-movie style with eerie music and a proliferation of abrupt close-ups, can thus itself be read as symptomatic of the text's own inability to reconcile itself to the irreversible fact of the transsexual. According to this logic, it is only apparently ironic that for all its insinuation of a connection between transsexuality and murder, *One Moment in Time* consistently refuses to accept the permanence of death. There is the reference to Hector's twin sister who died at birth, named Tiffany, a character clearly reincarnated in Hector's surgically altered body. Hector himself never fully disappears once Tiffany is (re)born, as seen in comments like "I was not me," where the "me" refers to "the real me," that is, Hector. And, of course, there is the death denial extraordinaire, the figure of Raymond himself, the lifeless addressee of the entire spoken narrative. Viewed in this light, the revelation that this documentary has been a fiction all along—which culminates a series of "shockingly melodramatic" revelations in the piece, most notably that Hector is (also) Tiffany, and that s/he killed Raymond and has been talking to his mutilated dead body all along—appears as a textual attempt to guard against and (re)gain control over the disturbing finality of these narrative events. The fictional status of *One Moment in Time* may serve to reassure us, as it seems to want to reassure itself, that the sex change and the murder never actually occurred.

The question "Is transsexuality *really* an irreversible decision?" is, in fact, a valid and necessary one. Why isn't it possible to have more than one gender reassignment in a lifetime? This seems to be at least partly an arbitrary determination, one that deserves further (re)consideration.[32] However, whether or not the operation is finally (ir)reversible may be less to the point here than the *perception* that transsexuality is an irreversible phenomenon. That perception, true or not, wields its own power, has its own realness. To think politically about transsexuality these days may involve considering how we might make strategic decisions and affirm identities that for the time being at least appear permanent and for that reason daunting or untenable. All the recent focus on the need for provisionality (for adaptability to a changing political climate) within the politics of identity, and on the need to secure the future resignifiability of politically useful terms (to make sure that their meanings and their status as sites of identification are open to change), though undeniably extremely important, should not obscure the fact that the need also exists at times to make choices and assume identities that appear permanent (such as, for example, the decision to assume an HIV+ identity). This is not to imply that these decisions, once made, foreclose the possibility of their changing significance, or even entirely disappearing in the future, nor that efforts to resist permanence must inevitably be doomed or flawed.

Indeed, in its almost desperate effort to reverse the one thing that may ultimately resist reversibility, death, *One Moment in Time* poses yet another challenge to documentary theory, which has itself on more than one occasion "used" death as the final arbiter for distinguishing fiction from documentary. Bill Nichols insists that in documentary, as opposed to fiction, "death is not a simulation but an irreversible act."[33] Of course, in documentary, as in fiction, we are talking about the *representation* of death, which is literally reversible (the film or video can be run backward), and figuratively reversible (the film or video enacts repeated "resurrections" of the dead with each viewing). "Death" itself, while certainly less reversible than its filmic representation in documentary or fiction, is (as our quotation marks imply) one of the very things *least* knowable apart from its representations and in that sense never self-evidently "real," even in documentary. By straining to reverse death, *One Moment in Time* as docudrag reveals that which has been taken most stubbornly to signify "reality" in documentary as the bedrock token of documentary's own attempted "realness."

Just as the "perception of irreversibility" persists with regard to transsexuality, the perception of irreversibility with regard to documentary representations—and not only of death—persists as well, wielding tremendous cultural, ideological, historical, and historiographic power. These perceptions are not without their contradictions, both in terms of documentary and in terms of transsexuality. In the case of transsexuality, though scientific and social authority will insist on the necessary permanence and completeness of the sex change once made (no doctor, having performed a gender reassignment, will reverse it), the post-op transsexual's claims to a rightful place in our regulated reality will remain, to many, in dispute. In a roughly symmetrical manner, much recent criticism has focused on delegitimating what traditional documentary perceives as its rightful claims to reality. Indeed, the deconstruction of documentary realism in its most extreme forms has reached the point where any distinction between fiction and documentary seems untenable. Yet need this lead to the delegitimation of documentary as a practice? While the claims that any representational practice makes to approximating a reality perceived as unproblematically "there" need to remain in question, might taking a cue from transsexuality not help to reorient the terms of discussing documentary away from a kind of critical annihilation of the practice, toward an exploration of its potential in altering the very perception of reality as necessarily permanent or irreversible, in contributing to the delimitation of the real? How might documentary's historically unique relation to the real be exploited to highlight these transformative aspects of realness, adjusting and refiguring the dynamic relation between belief and the real? What would a documentary practice be like that did not depend for its political effects on the perception that its statements be "definitive," in some sense irreversible? What if documentaries could be viewed without resentment as contestable, reversible from the start? And could this practice make effective, "constative" statements nonetheless? Could it still achieve the spectacular knowledge effects documentary is capable of producing in its audience by means of its specially engaged mimesis of what it takes to be actuality—that is, neither evacuate its unique relation, say, to an actual death, nor claim definitively, objectively to have captured it? What are the possibilities for the transdoc—and for continuing to affirm the validity of a filmic practice, which, because of its historical and political effectivity, is worth affirming despite its apparent insistence on fixed, permanent identity?

Subversion?

Returning to the issue of the relations between drag and transsexuality, we have meant to suggest that though transsexuality can certainly be made to fit, if uncomfortably, within the discourse of drag generally, it can also be the source of some complications within that discourse, as well as within the concept of docudrag. In addition, we have suggested that transsexuality, like drag, contains within itself some potential insights for a revitalized documentary practice. We have said that transsexuality and documentary are linked through their particular relations to technology and history. We have also commented, following Sandy Stone's arguments, on how the revelation of a transsexual's history can work to subvert gender (and sexual) norms much in the way that the revelation of a documentary as fiction can work to subvert unquestioned realism. That this worthwhile approach to the politics of transsexuality (and documentary) threatens to collapse it simply into (docu)drag is not its only drawback. *One Moment in Time* reveals further limits to the subversive potential of both these types of revelations. The piece does write the erased history of a transsexual, but in a manner arguably less than liberatory for transsexuals and for our understanding of gender and its relation to (homo)sexuality. The piece does deconstruct the distinction between documentary and fiction and thus problematizes the assumptions of realism, but in a manner that can also work to contain the potential disruption of our realist ways of knowing gender. *One Moment in Time* thus renders the subversive qualities of revelation more compromised than might at first appear. As can be argued about the revelation of the drag queen as such in the popular film *The Crying Game*, revelations, in and of themselves, can as easily consolidate as subvert our regime of truth. No doubt, as we have been discussing them, drag and docudrag fundamentally depend on revelation for their political and subversive effects. Although neither drag nor transsexuality need be entirely reduced to this problematic, revelation has nonetheless played a significant role in the way both have been taken up in contemporary theories of representation. Transsexuality, in particular, precisely because (rightly or wrongly) it has been so closely associated with passing (i.e., with eluding representation) as opposed to revelation, may offer an opportunity to shift the focus of this problematic in ways that are, if no more politically reliable than revelation, at least as provocative for thinking about documentary. As for subversion, it remains, when it is identifiable, temporally delayed and representationally treacherous. Although we may trace some of its effects, it will always be an elusive event — a moment in time — not easily or entirely locatable in any formal or contentual textual strategy. To put it plainly, subversion depends on its context, though that term too is not entirely transparent.

Incidentally, because its subversive qualities, wherever or whenever they appear, do not reside entirely at the level of form (or, for that matter, content), *One Moment in Time* resists the tendency of much contemporary film theory to locate "authentic" subversion in formal ingenuity. By positing productive parallels between gender/subaltern theories and documentary theory, *One Moment in Time* as docudrag can be seen as part of the tradition of filmic deconstructions of transparency, authenticity, and authority, alongside the works of filmmakers like Trinh T. Minh Ha, Rea Tajiri, Marlon Riggs, and Isaac Julien. These filmmakers often explore questions of cultural, racial, and sexual otherness through formally innovative techniques of imitation-with-a-difference. Considered as part of this tradition, *One Moment in Time* enables us to contemplate the aura of inherent radicality that often accompanies these works largely because of their formal innovations. Which is not to say that these texts are not subversive, but to suggest that if deconstructive texts like these are not inherently radical, neither are texts that employ "realist" strategies inherently reactionary.[34] That this depends on context is recalled in the way that *One Moment in Time* jockeys for realness. Realness allows us to understand the scenario that enables — and circumscribes — subversion as an interested, partial, necessarily incomplete yet nonetheless invaluable (re)assessment of what counts as real, of history and our place in it. It thus encourages us to see documentary practice as characterized not by a privileged aesthetic link between the documentary and the real, but as an engaged and embattled attempt to *pass* as real in a history laden with issues of representation, power, and desire. In other words, realness helps us to pose the political link between representation and the real that much documentary, no matter how politicized, has tended to efface.

Fiction and Imitation: A Rereading

The significance of fiction for *One Moment in Time* bears further scrutiny. As we have been discussing it, fiction has admittedly become a messy repository for the text's ambivalences and our own ambivalences about it. We have, for instance, made much of the fact that the video is fully revealed as fiction in the end; yet, as we have also mentioned, there are hints that the piece is a fiction throughout. What might be the significance of these hints? We have, in addition, suggested that the video's fictional status can as easily be read as reassuring as it can be experienced as discomfiting. Is the text, or our reading of it, thus irretrievably self-contradictory? Or, can the status of fiction in *One Moment in Time* be made to accommodate the seemingly chaotic elements of the text through a more nuanced reconsideration? Might these elements resolve, upon further examination, into an identifiable, if not entirely rational, logic? And what is the relation of fiction to the text's practices of imitation anyway? How might our own text benefit from a rereading?[35]

Before attempting to answer these questions, let us acknowledge that they are prompted in regard to a set of assumptions about drag theory. Eve Sedgwick has keenly criticized the work of those scholars intent on "straining [their] eyes to ascertain whether particular performances (e.g., of drag) are really *parodic and subversive* (e.g., of gender essentialism) or just *uphold the status quo*. The bottom line," she wittily concludes, "is generally the same: kinda subversive, kinda hegemonic."[36] This is, we concur, an apt characterization of much of the queer critical work that has lately appeared on drag, and one that, to some extent, admittedly applies to our own work here as well. However, to continue teetering along with this academic balancing act has not been our ultimate goal. Rather, we see the ambivalence that centrally informs drag and transsexuality — namely, that as imitative practices they must engage and rely on the very terms they would contest and that as deconstructive practices they must themselves be objects of the very critique they enable — less as an indication of a political impasse than as a potential source of political productivity with important resonances for documentary. Drag and transsexuality perform their agendas and derive their political usefulness, not despite, but precisely by means of, their constitutive ambivalences. Reading the docudrag text in and through these moments of logical crisis, we introduce another dimension of docudrag: it is a text that works with, and not despite, its constitutive ambivalences, for it is these precisely that make it most politically, culturally, and aesthetically challenging.

Let us try to work this out by rereading the function of fiction in *One Moment in Time*. As we stated earlier, fiction, the quintessential site of ambivalence for this text, crucially structures yet is disavowed by the documentary form. *One Moment in Time,* as a docudrag text, enables this observation by drawing attention to this disavowal. Examined more closely, however, the tape may help to even further specify the significance of this observation in the context of queer Latino culture. In fact, it is not so much the concept of fiction in general as it is specific genres of fiction—that is, horror and melodrama—that *One Moment in Time* most explicitly incorporates within its documentary pose. Not coincidentally, these genres are the very narrative forms most typically associated with representations of racial, ethnic, and sexual otherness, from *King Kong* to the clichéd image of the tragic drag queen (often of color) most recently and dramatically exemplified by pre-op transsexual Venus Xtravaganza in *Paris Is Burning*. By mimicking these particular fictional forms as part of its imitation of documentary, *One Moment in Time* directly comments on the heretofore unacknowledged codes by which queer and transgendered Latinos have been traditionally represented in documentary as well as fiction (when represented at all). Perhaps this strategy of including traditional signifiers of queerness and *latinidad* at the formal level might also constitute an attempt to redress *Paris Is Burning*'s formal disregard of those very cultural perspectives.

One Moment in Time most resembles the genres of horror and melodrama in its final sequence. And so, as an instance of a kind of condensation of the text's queerness and *latinidad,* let's revisit this scene. We have already described some of its aesthetic features, precisely in terms of fiction, as "melodramatic" and "executed in horror-movie style with eerie music and a proliferation of abrupt close-ups." Although we read the irruption of these features in the text as signs of the video's difficulties in dealing with irreversibility, what most effectively stands out in this climactic scene of ultimate revelations is arguably less the shock of these revelations than the blatantly

The delayed reaction shot of a dead Raymond from *One Moment in Time.*

citational terms used to frame them. Here the video is unabashedly imitating not only, as we said, the formal conventions of horror and melodrama, but also in its dialogue and content, shamelessly quoting — and reversing the fate of — Venus Xtravaganza herself, who, as documented in *Paris Is Burning,* is killed by a trick and found dead in a cheap hotel. In *One Moment in Time* it is the transsexual who kills the "trick" (as Tiffany refers to Raymond earlier). And it is no coincidence here that after the murder Tiffany reiterates the conventional discourse transsexuals learn to reproduce in order to be approved for sex change, or, "sorry," as she sarcastically clarifies, "gender reassignment" — the very same dreams recited by Venus in *Paris Is Burning*: I just want to be normal, have kids, is that so terrible, and so on.[37] Tiffany's plea of innocence thus eloquently, if ironically, testifies to Venus's own inculpability for the circumstances that in real life link transsexuality and murder and that are responsible for her own death.[38] It is impossible to fully grasp the significance of this scene without registering these intertextual references.

Considered in relation to the text's practices of imitation, then, the status of fiction in *One Moment in Time* produces yet another

layer of meanings, acquires yet another set of resonances. If, for instance, the video has hinted at its fictional status throughout, most
notably and campily through Hector/Tiffany's "obvious" imitation of
woman, this can now be reread not only as an indication of the text's
crisis over the female body, but also in terms of how queerness, historically aligned with imitation and camp, thoroughly permeates the
text alongside race and ethnicity. That the final scene must appear both
discomfiting and reassuring, that it must also be the point at which
the text becomes most like a morality tale, can now appear as both
constrained by and straining to transcend the historical limitations that
attend representations of queer and transgendered Latino empowerment. An important cue that the tape is not merely re-creating these
familiar and oppressive representations, but also taking a critical distance from them, is provided by the Whitney Houston song that lends
the video its title, and that closes the final sequence. Lip-synched twice
in the piece by Tiffany, the song each time interrupts the flow of narrative events that threaten to become overwhelmingly tragic, and all
too familiarly oppressive, by celebrating a point of transcendence and
abandon "beyond" the narrative, the first time for the drag queen,
the second for the transsexual. Featuring lyrics like "Give me one
moment in time, when I'm more than I thought I could be ... I will
be free," the song, considered in terms of its narrative placement, can
appear ironic, making that celebrated "moment in time" seem re-
grettably short-lived, if not downright dystopic. As an extradiegetic
interruption of, and comment on, the narrative, however, its "no re-
grets" disco diva sentiments also allow the text to register an admiration for the bravery of transgendered people and to offer Tiffany
as a heroine, even as, in the final sequence, it continues to moralize
about the excessive transgressions of the transsexual. Likewise, the
video's persistent denial of death can now appear not only "desperate," but also as a rather inspiring form of wishful thinking, especially in view of the pervasive violence against transgendered bodies
that caused Venus's particular fate.[39]

By rereading the relationship between fiction and imitation, we
can embrace many of the text's ambivalences, and, without disregard-
ing their often troubling persistence, acknowledge that it is precisely
through these most salient sites of logical crisis that the tape is able
to articulate some of its most trenchant social criticisms. Surely it is
significant that only by harnessing extranarrative mimetic devices (lip-

Credit sequence from Felix Rodriguez's *One Moment in Time.*

synched lyrics, extratextual references and reversals, etc.) can the text "plausibly" register the transsexual as a heroine who transcends tragedy; just as it is of profound political importance that the scene of her empowerment (Tiffany killing Raymond and continuing to demand of him an answer for her suffering even after his death) seems only imaginable in the context of fiction.

What the empowerment of the transsexual implicitly demands in this final scene, then, is also the aspiration of all documentary: not to be considered fiction, even as it heroically persists in its practices of imitation. By situating the transsexual explicitly within a self-consciously fictional and mimetic scenario, however, *One Moment in Time* also illustrates an important difference between transsexuality and documentary. Although the tape uses its docudrag structure to expose documentary's disavowal of fiction, it constructs the transsexual as less concerned with and dependent upon such a disavowal than with a questioning of the ontological requirements that legitimate what passes as real. Why, for instance, can't Tiffany be considered a real woman, if she has, as she puts it, "a pussy to prove it"? A documentary practice less invested in realism than realness might attempt not only to convincingly, yet "illegitimately," reinscribe the real but also to question the boundaries that police it. Such a practice could very possibly negotiate the ideological and practical minefield that politically committed, innovative, yet nonetheless realist-based documentary has become. As a filmmaking strategy, realness is indebted to the wisdom of both drag and transsexuality: if, as docudrag, *One Moment in Time* keeps its own claims to reality in question, it nonetheless continues to posture as "real," more "real" in fact than *Paris Is Burning*, thus demanding a reassessment and an augmented definition of the real. In other words, it absorbs the representational challenges of transsexuality, as well as drag, into the representational interventions entailed in the concept and practice of realness.

Notes

1. This paper is based on a rarely seen video that we were fortunate enough to see in one of its only public screenings, at the 1992 Look/Out gay and lesbian video festival in New York. The decision to write about and theorize such a low-budget, low-visibility tape was not made lightly. We believe that it is important to view this type of work as having as much relevance to the field of documentary and film/video studies generally as a better-known piece. Such seldom seen tapes often contain important commentary on such high-profile issues as the construction of specific audiences and the appropriation of mainstream representational practices, to name just two of the concerns we will be discussing here. The politics of distribution and exhibition are such that films and videos like this one often get overlooked (by virtue of their production standards as much as the cultural values and perspectives they represent or challenge). This oversight itself is worthy of further investigation and critical attention.

2. bell hooks, "Is Paris Burning," in *Black Looks: Race and Representation* (Boston: South End Press, 1992), 145–56.

3. This is not to suggest that all ethnographic strategies produce such a distancing effect but that there are those that do. For specific discussion about ethnographic strategies in *Paris Is Burning*, see Peggy Phelan, "The Golden Apple," in *Unmarked* (New York: Routledge, 1993), 93–111; and Marcos Becquer and Jose Gatti, "Elements of Vogue," *Third Text* 16/17 (autumn–winter 1991).

4. Some of the films of Michael Rubbo (*Daisy: The Story of a Facelift, Solzhenitsyen's Children, Waiting for Fidel*) provide clear examples of this documentary strategy. Also, many "reflexive" ethnographic films do this, as do many PBS-style expedition and nature docs. In terms of contemporary realist documentaries, *Roger and Me* is perhaps the most notable example. When fiction films apply this strategy, they are borrowing documentary techniques so as to approximate documentary verisimilitude.

5. Hector is a long-standing member of the House of Xtravaganza in "real life" and his drag name is Tiffany.

6. It is important to note that the video rarely ever entirely convinces us of its documentary status; it merely plays with the possibility of verisimilitude, campily taunting and tempting audience belief in its truth claims. Hector/Tiffany's halfhearted attempt at drag throughout (Hector is not and never has been "flawless" as a woman) is one such giveaway.

7. We realize that this is indeed an expanded version of "dominant."

8. Judith Butler, "Gender Is Burning: Questions of 'Appropriation and Subversion,'" in *Bodies That Matter: On the Discursive Limits of Sex* (New York: Routledge, 1993), 129.

9. In that *One Moment in Time* is a fiction in documentary clothing (dragging as a documentary), it is related to many films — *Zelig, Spinal Tap, No Lies, Culloden, War Games, Far From Poland, Daughter Rite*. The difference between these films and a docudrag film is that they do not also treat drag and/or issues of transgender as their subject, nor are their forms so closely related to that of their subjects.

10. Homi K. Bhabha, "Of Mimicry and Men: The Ambivalence of Colonial Discourse," *October* 28 (spring 1984): 132.

11. This heavy but unspoken reliance on fictional narrative conventions is present in all documentaries to one degree or another, never more present than in the documentary style that has the loftiest aspirations toward truth: American Direct Cinema, with its penchant for major media events and other built-in narrative eventness, that is, national elections (*Primary* and *The War Room*), rock concerts (*Don't Look Back* and *Truth or Dare*), and so on.

12. Some documentary theorists have discussed the "displeasure principle" many spectators seem to experience upon finding out that what they believed to be a documentary was really a fiction. See Vivian Sobchack, "*No Lies* Direct Cinema as Rape," in *New Challenges for Documentary*, ed. Alan Rosenthal (Berkeley: University of California Press, 1988), and Bill Nichols, *Representing Reality* (Bloomington: Indiana University Press, 1991), 161. This displeasure is not entirely dissimilar to the apparent displeasure experienced by a straight man upon discovering he is in bed with a transgendered man (witness *The Crying Game*).

13. For a further discussion of the problems inherent in in/visibility politics see Phelan's *Unmarked*.

14. It is noteworthy that although this video succeeds in reversing racial and cultural hierarchies, the displacement of heterosexuality remains a consciously articulated but not fully achieved fantasy. Midway through the video, Hector/Tiffany fantasizes in voice-over about a world where heterosexuals experience the same discrimination and violence that gay people confront every day. Imagine, s/he says, if "the world was the other way around." Although there are many apparent problems with a simple reversal strategy as a challenge to the source of power inadequacies, and although, as we shall show later, centering strategies inevitably enact their own set of exclusions,

the empowering affective charge of such a strategy and its freshness in film history cannot be denied or easily dismissed.

15. See, for instance, hooks, "Is Paris Burning." Some exceptions to this position can be found in the writings of Ann Cvetkovich, "The Powers of Seeing and Being Seen: *Truth or Dare* and *Paris Is Burning*," in *Film Theory Goes to the Movies*, ed. Jim Collins et al. (New York: Routledge, 1993), and Peggy Phelan, *Unmarked*.

16. In this scene, Hector is shown talking to a "random female" (as she is referred to in the credits) on the street, who seems flattered if skeptical. His convincing masculine posture here, complete with beard, is as much of a drag performance, in the context of this video, as when s/he dons a dress.

17. Phelan, "The Golden Apple," 103.

18. "Reading," in drag ball idiom, is the art of finding the flaw in apparently flawless representations.

19. Butler also sees the central connection between realness and embodiment. She states: "[The] effect [of realness] is itself the result of an embodiment of norms, an impersonation of a racial and class norm, a norm which is at once a figure, a figure of a body, which is no particular body, but a morphological ideal that remains the standard which regulates the performance, but which no performance fully approximates" (Butler, "Gender Is Burning," 129).

20. Judith Butler, *Gender Trouble: Feminism and the Subversion of Identity* (New York: Routledge, 1990).

21. Carol-Anne Tyler, "Boys Will Be Girls: The Politics of Gay Drag," in *Inside/Out*, ed. Diana Fuss (New York: Routledge, 1991), 32–70.

22. See Eve Kosofsky Sedgwick, *Epistemology of the Closet* (Berkeley: University of California Press, 1990), Lee Edelman, *Homographesis* (New York: Routledge, 1994), D. A. Miller, "Secret Subjects/Open Secrets," in *The Novel and the Police* (Berkeley: University of California Press, 1988), and Judith Butler, *Gender Trouble*.

23. Cvetkovich, "The Powers of Seeing and Being Seen," 159.

24. Marjorie Garber discusses this point in her book *Vested Interests: Cross-Dressing and Cultural Anxiety* (New York: Routledge, 1992). She cites Robert Stoller among others as holding this view.

25. Transsexualism is thus accused of being both essentialist and antiessentialist, depending on the context. For a further discussion of these issues, see Judith Shapiro's article "Transsexualism: Reflections on the Persistence of Gender and the Mutability of Sex" and Sandy Stone's "The *Empire* Strikes Back: A Posttranssexual Manifesto," both in *Body Guards*, ed. Julia Epstein and Kristina Straub (New York: Routledge, 1991). To this day the Michigan Women's Music Festival restricts entrance to all but those who were born female, and physically removed a transsexual woman from the premises in 1992.

26. See Sue Ellen Case, "Towards a Butch-Femme Aesthetic," in *The Lesbian and Gay Studies Reader*, ed. Henry Abelove et al. (New York: Routledge, 1993), and Cvetkovich, "The Powers of Seeing and Being Seen." See

also Michael Moon and Eve Kosofsky Sedgwick, "Divinity: A Dossier, a Performance Piece, a Little-Understood Emotion," in *Tendencies* (Durham, N.C.: Duke University Press, 1993), 215–51.

27. Here we are using the term "transgender" as a kind of umbrella term for a range of practices of gender crossing or blending, including, but not exclusive to, transvestism and transsexuality.

28. And of course, this would be a necessarily expanded version of "the real."

29. Stone, "The *Empire* Strikes Back," 295.

30. Stone writes that "the highest purpose of the transsexual is to erase him/herself, to fade into the 'normal' population as soon as possible. Part of this process is known as *constructing a plausible history*—learning to lie effectively about one's past" (ibid., 295; her emphasis). Judith Shapiro also discusses "passing," though less directly in terms of history ("Transsexualism," 255–56). Of course, some transsexual activists such as Stone and Kate Bornstein argue for the need to *not* pass, to assert the right of transsexuals to their past, present, and future self-manifestations.

31. Stone, "The *Empire* Strikes Back," 296–97.

32. Science constructs and legitimizes its own infallibility and remystifies gender by making sex reassignments a one-shot deal, as if, having made the determination once that the patient was a viable candidate for the operation, the medical establishment couldn't possibly be proven wrong later and have to reverse its position.

33. Nichols, *Representing Reality,* 237.

34. Alexandra Juhasz's article in *Screen* (summer 1994), "They said we want to show reality, all I want to show is my video: The Politics of Feminist Realist Documentaries," takes up this question of realism as politically efficacious, in opposition to the accepted wisdom within certain sectors of the field of feminist film theory at least, which have relegated realism to the realm of the politically regressive.

35. Antonio Benítez-Rojo develops the concept of "rereading" in an entirely different context in his provocative book *The Repeating Island: The Caribbean and the Postmodern Perspective* (Durham, N.C.: Duke University Press, 1992).

36. Eve Kosofsky Sedgwick, "Queer Performativity: Henry James' *The Art of the Novel*," in *GLQ: A Journal of Lesbian and Gay Studies* 1.1 (1993): 15; her emphasis.

37. In order to be considered for "gender reassignment," transsexuals are subjected to a panoply of disciplinary medical practices that evaluate the viability of their candidacy. Many transsexuals have negotiated this demeaning system of surveillance by mastering these discourses and reproducing them at will, in order to achieve their desired ends. Tiffany's comment here implies this type of knowing stance, yet by treating the issue so dismissively the video also suggests that these disciplinary practices are *not* the central problematic by which ball children understand the importance of transsexuality in their lives.

38. As transgender activist Leslie Feinberg states in the video *Outlaw* (Alisa Lebow, 1994; distributed by Women Make Movies), "Life expectancy is *the* issue [for transgendered people]."

39. As forms of wishful thinking, the text once again aligns its imitative practices, as well as its fictional components, with the concept of realness, whose status as a fantasy of identification we wish neither to downplay or ignore. There is no ultimate achievement of realness; like realism, it remains an impossible ideal, paradoxically only realizable in projection, both psychologically and filmically speaking. That realness is never self-coincidental, however, does not mean that it may not have significant effects in the real. As a theory of the real, its inherent "failure" may also be a source for its creative and metamorphic potential, that which keeps the reality it mimics necessarily at once believable and dynamically doubtful.

From Exile to Ethnicity: Nestor Almendros and Orlando Jiménez-Leal's *Improper Conduct* (1984)

Marvin D'Lugo

All profound changes in consciousness, by their very nature, bring with them characteristic amnesias. Out of such oblivions, in specific historical circumstances, spring narratives.

Benedict Anderson[1]

The Liminal Text of Exile

The Nestor Almendros/Orlando Jiménez-Leal documentary about the repression of homosexuals in Cuba, *Improper Conduct* (1984), affords a rare view into the processes that have transformed the identity of Cuban exiles into a distinct Cuban American cultural ethnicity. Originally produced as a denunciation of the Castro regime's treatment of homosexuals and thereby intended to shift liberal sentiment against socialist Cuba, the film nonetheless articulates its strident political position with conspicuous marks of textual vacillation.

One reason for such textual instability may derive from the seldom acknowledged fact that *Improper Conduct* is not merely a simplistic right-wing propaganda vehicle, but a complex and multilayered text that conjugates the condition of exile with issues of sexual identity in surprising ways. It is addressed simultaneously to the liberal international audience that favors socialist Cuba (thus, the denunciation of the persecution of gays) and to the Cuban exile audience that needs reaffirmation of its identity (thus the metaphorization of homosexuality as an "otherness" marking the shift from exile to ethnicity). How the latter audience—itself marked by intense homophobia—is addressed and refigured as an ethnic community is the most surprising characteristic of *Improper Conduct*.

The film is centered on a series of often moving interviews by political exiles that form an oral history of human rights abuses and

171

institutionalized homophobia during the first two decades of Castro's rule. This oral history is enunciated by individuals who in many instances are distanced by at least a decade from the events they describe. While forming the centerpiece of the film, these interviews are appropriated into a political discourse that appears, at times, to run counter to the personal narratives being recounted and to the film's own alleged progay and lesbian stance.

As a result of this conceptual hybridity, *Improper Conduct* seems marked by textual instabilities that are more reflective of an exilic sensibility than of the political diatribe of which the film has so often been criticized.[2] Hamid Naficy sees the kind of ambivalence that characterizes the film as common to numerous works of political exile. Speaking of the paradigmatic condition of such texts, he notes: "The exilic ambivalence stems from holding two essentially incompatible positions or attitudes simultaneously, one involving the disavowal and the other the recognition of difference — racial, ethnic, historical, and knowledge and power differences that exist between host and home cultures."[3]

This ambivalence becomes apparent in telling ways at about the midpoint of the narrative when the film abruptly shifts focus from its recounting of human rights abuses during the first decades of revolutionary Cuba to a depiction of aspects of contemporary life in the Cuban American community of Miami. The sequence begins with contemporary newsreel footage of the Miami skyline as seen from a vehicle moving along an expressway as it approaches downtown, followed by a series of clips of Spanish-language television commercials from south Florida. Instead of maintaining this new focus on the evolution of Cuban exilic culture in the United States, however, the action cuts immediately to scenes from Cuban theater group productions in Miami's Little Havana that lampoon both Castro and social conditions in Cuba. Thus the sequence recuperates its original political focus but only after having elided questions of homosexuality and opened up a space of interrogation about the historical processes that have temporalized the condition of exile and given rise to a distinctive Cuban American ethnicity.

By giving prominence to the artifices of representation — recycled television images and the staginess of theatrical impersonations — the sequence reinscribes an acute moment in what Benedict Anderson would call "the biography of nations, which, like the photograph, simultaneously records a certain apparent continuity and emphasizes its loss from memory."[4] Here we see a formulation of the hybridity of exilic experience when two nearly simultaneous and overlapping histories—one of diaspora and exile, the other of an emerging cultural identity of Cuban Americanness—are tellingly expressed through their own visual icons. Understood in the context of a gradual realignment of cultural affiliations, the sequence does not simply contradict the overt ideological position that the film as a whole appears to promote; rather, it suggests, almost as an inadvertent gesture, the presence of a counternarrative in which exilic culture, fixated on the past, is refigured as the emergent ethnicity of Cuban Americanness.

Recognizing this textual and conceptual ambivalence, Ana López has recently described *Improper Conduct* as a text of the first generation of Cuban American filmmaking, marked by its impassioned political focus, but pointedly signaling the entrance of a new ethnic discourse within the ostensibly "exilic" one. López situates the film within a contemporary Latin American tradition of exile cinema and argues that, by virtue of its production outside of Cuba and the exile status of its authors, the film should be considered as an example of the first generation of Cuban cinema of exile in which one can discern the diasporic formation of "a specific 'Cuban-American' identity." López goes on to characterize films of the Cuban diaspora by their "attempt to contain the traumas of exile by repeating and denouncing the actual experience (the history of departures) and by symbolically reconstructing the 'lost' home (within) in a new imagined community."[5] Indeed, the discursive ambivalence of the Little Havana sequence confirms the sense that the film's underlying cultural frame of reference is not merely the result of its site of production outside of Cuba, but a consequence of the elaboration of a new cultural position defined in historical, cultural, and ultimately cinematic terms.

Speaking of the subjective positionality produced by exile, Naficy, for example, notes how the condition of "deterritorialization" produces "a threshold state in which the liminars or the exiles live on the threshold between two cultures" (85): "Located in the slipzone, where home and host cultures overlap and slide over and under and past each other, the liminar exiles are in between the structural force field of both social systems, and as a result they are able to question, subvert, modify, or even adopt attributes of either or both cultural systems" (86–87).

As Zuzana Pick argues, a positionality that is at an ambivalent distance from the authority of both cultures "has social and political ramifications that affect subjective consciousness and inform cultural production."[6] Pick identifies a series of features that appear to have informed the discursive regularity of a number of Latin American films of exile. The most substantive of these she describes as "foreground[ing] a consciousness inflected simultaneously by structures of feeling and affiliation. The ambivalent merging of memory and otherness is a site of struggle where identification is dialectically anchored in nostalgia and resistance" (159).

Indeed, *Improper Conduct* appears to be a work in which, as Pick describes, the dialectical structuring of historical experience, not only of exile but of emerging ethnic and cultural realignments, is the central organizing concept. Historically situated on the interstices of cultures and temporalities, where the experience of Cubanness transformed into Cuban Americanness is still profoundly unstable, the film bears the indelible textual marks of that instability. To consider it in its appropriate cultural context, therefore, requires that one abandon the simple Manichaeism that has characterized so much of the polemic surrounding the film up to the present and address it in terms of its textual complexity as that textuality mirrors an equally complex historical situation.

The Containment of Time

The cornerstone of the film's problematic and the pivot of its enunciative apparatus is a notion of narration that equates the chronology of events with historicity. After an initial sequence that establishes the historical and thematic foci as the political repression and exile of homosexuals, the film fixes on a series of facts, dates, and individual testimonies in order to promote the sense of a coherent and unified chronology and a stable discursive position through which the viewer may follow this history of human rights abuses in Cuba. A total of twenty-six interviews detailing the chronology of institutional policies of homophobia in Cuba between 1965 and the early 1980s comprise the basic design of *Improper Conduct*. Each interview is punctuated by supporting newsreel images and voice-over commentary to help identify each interviewee. Twenty-five exchanges form what we have already identified as an oral history of human rights abuses under the Castro regime. The twenty-sixth, the only one not filmed by Almendros and Jiménez-Leal, is an interview with Fidel Castro shot by French television in 1979 and used in the final part of the film to characterize the regime's denial of human rights violations as political hypocrisy. Throughout the film, the interviews and their supporting archival footage are strung together through the use of an offscreen male voice that provides continuity by linking the various historical events and periods described. More than merely offering a sustained historical narrative, however, this disembodied voice—never identified, never connected to an "authorial" image—provides a narrational omniscience that works in tandem with the images to produce the effect of historical "truth"; that is, it supports the testimonial force of the interviewees by providing the viewer with a series of "other" documents, usually newsreel footage, that appear to confirm and expand upon the interviewee's words.

Thus the narrator's voice serves a suturing function, mobilizing in the name of historical veracity the chains of images that it explains in support of the words of the interviewees. The mix of voice-over narration, interviews, and newsreel images consequently produces a textual redundancy in which the narrator's commentaries are often echoed by testimonies that, in turn, are reinforced by other commentaries from seemingly "different" perspectives. The initial effect of this redundancy is to blur the simple lines of chronology by reiterating certain "facts" from a variety of interpretive positions. Yet the voice-over narration ultimately operates to maintain a sense of linear chronology by continually introducing pieces of new information in the accumulated narrative of state abuse of human rights.

Such a construction seems designed to mask what critics have often pointed out is a very narrow chronology. Although appearing to cover the first twenty-five years of the Castro regime, *Improper Conduct* actually focuses on only two periods of pronounced homophobic policies: 1965–67 (the period of the notorious UMAP work camps) and the 1980 Mariel exodus.[7] Implicitly, both are made to function as metaphors for a larger history as confirmed by Almendros in the prologue of the published script of *Improper Conduct*: "the persecution of homosexuals in our film may serve ... as a metaphor for the general suppression of civil liberty in Cuba."[8]

In fact, the larger textual operation of the film may also be described as a chain of metaphoric substitutions in which historical events covering nearly twenty years seem not so much to move in a temporal progression as in a reiterative pattern, continually emphasizing through the accumulation of eyewitness narratives the same scenario of repression that has transformed Cubans into exiles. Such a stylistic feature clearly reinforces the identification of *Improper Conduct* as an example of exilic textuality in which the appearance of chronological historicity camouflages the exilic fetishization of the past.

Nowhere is this metaphoric undermining of chronology more explicit than in the precredit and opening sequences of the film that function as a frame for the ensuing text. Formulated as a juxtaposition between the protest march staged outside the Peruvian embassy in 1980, which occasioned the Mariel exodus, and the newsreels reporting the defections of members of Alicia Alonso's Cuban National Ballet in Paris in 1966, the linkage of images from Havana 1980 and Paris 1966 effectively displaces the chronology of human rights abuse by foregrounding from the very start the exilic scenario. Such an inverted ordering of events, posed as the "backdrop" to the film's opening credits, underscores the synchronic condition of the exilic historical reconstruction that will be presented in the ensuing text by its formulation of two key narrative tropes: the traumatic deterritorialization in which Cubans see themselves as being forced to give up their homeland, and the demonization of Fidel Castro as the "author" of that involuntary exile. In this way the chronological axis of the film cedes to the more potent synchrony of reiterated stagings of exile.

Restaging Identity

As a presumed historical documentary, the narrative attempts to frame the audience's attention around its own construction of the past. Yet, as the film's opening sequences illustrate, that notion of history is problematized by its underlying exilic project. As we examine the interplay between the interview situations and the narrational apparatus in a number of key sequences, we may begin to see how, in fact, that tension between historical representation and the exilic fetishization of the past destabilizes the text.

Two interviews in particular — ironically the only sequences of the film in which Cuban homosexuals are explicitly identified — point up this tension. The first example begins as the camera tracks along New

Interview of Luis Lazo in *Improper Conduct*, directed by Nestor Almendros and Orlando Jiménez-Leal.

York's Forty-Second Street locating Luis Lazo, who is then shown being questioned by the offscreen voice of Jiménez-Leal about Lazo's treatment as an openly gay man in Havana. While recalling the oppression of gays in Cuba, Lazo gives evidence of his assimilation into the host culture by making reference to his clothing, attire that would have landed him in jail in Havana. In the second interview, Caracol, a transvestite performer in a Manhattan cabaret who is interviewed in drag before and after a performance, follows a similar course in which the images of a contemporary "emancipated" cross-dressing identity are juxtaposed against the verbalized history of homophobic treatment in Cuba.

Both sequences are marked by a double staging: the first is inherent in each retelling of persecution in Cuba that has been necessarily "staged" for the camera; the second, less inevitable but ultimately more revealing, is the foregrounding of each interviewee's present situation in the United States. The first artifice is clearly apparent in any number of the twenty-five interviews with exiles, but in these two interviews, it appears especially pronounced. This is particularly strik-

Interview of Caracol before performance, from *Improper Conduct*, directed by
Nestor Almendros and Orlando Jiménez-Leal.

ing in the way the camera tracks after Lazo as he walks along Forty-
Second Street, attempting to simulate a casualness to the encounter
between filmmakers and interview subject.

As Lazo and Caracol are seen recounting their experiences of persecution in their homeland, both are engaged in what amounts to the
restaging of their own personal identity since leaving Cuba. This level
of artifice is literalized in Caracol's case in that the interview is con-
ducted before and after his cabaret performance while he is in costume. This double staging and the distension it underscores between
the two levels of each interview—the retelling of persecution, and
the foregrounding of the interviewee's present situation in the United
States—reveal one of the essential unverbalized themes of the film: the
ways in which people's circumstances have evolved from the fetishized
exilic past to the present time of the film's telling, thereby opening
the text to a series of dialogical readings that thwart the static focus
of the exilic theme. As the sound track reiterates the single paradigm
of oppression in Cuba, the film's visual track betrays the stasis of
that theme by documenting the truism that time does not stand still

and that people do change.[9] It is the reality of change, of the temporality of emergence, that the elaborate narrational apparatus of *Improper Conduct* attempts futilely to disavow.

There is a particularly telling moment at the end of Caracol's description of his arrival in the Mariel exodus to south Florida when he reflects upon his Cuban identity: "There is a saying, if you don't love your land you don't love your mother. I must not love her. I don't miss Cuba."[10] This is the first point in the film in which the viewer can see clearly beyond the political narrative to the glimmers of an emerging new cultural agency, the voice of the subject who has given up his identity as a Cuban and who, in a very literal sense, is shown restaging his identity as well as his nationality and his sexuality.

Caracol's statement effectively unhinges the text from its Cuban roots and enunciates a position that subverts the exilic obsession with the homeland, revealing the underlying tension of exilic culture as a crisis of the temporality of national identity and affiliation through the filter of sexuality. Through their active restagings of their own identity, Caracol and to a lesser degree Luis Lazo bring the audience to understand that what is really at stake in the fetishized chronology of *Improper Conduct* is a reconstruction of the ideal of the homeland as the center of existence of those who have formulated this exilic discourse.

In a revealing description of the process of making the film, Almendros describes the elaboration of the mise-en-scène of the interviews:

> During the filming we placed our interviewees in settings that, at the same time they documented their new geographic or social situation after their exile, maintained a certain neutrality so as not to introduce any element of distraction that might take away from the key element in each frame, which was the interviewee's face. We tried to make these settings or scenes pleasant (we usually asked the interviewees to choose a place of their own preference). In this way we created an ambience that lent itself to trust. At times the setting was in total contradiction to the drama of some narrations. We thought that this dialectic would enrich each sequence.[11]

What Almendros sees as the "total contradiction to the drama of some narrations" is, in fact, the tension between the symptomatic marks of an exilic culture, focused through its political thematics on the ideal of the abandoned *patria,* and a counterforce that intuitively seeks accommodation in a culture other than Cuba and that gravitates toward what we have already identified as the in-betweenness of cultural hybridity.

The insistence on the leitmotif of "restaged identity" begins to suggest a much more complex dynamic inadvertently in operation in the film: precisely the dispersion/fragmentation/reiteration of individual and collective identity that in the postmodern context Antonio Benítez-Rojo calls "the repeating island" and that clearly undermines the genealogy of Cubanness that is at the heart of the film's political chronology.[12] Such reconfigurations of exilic experience are not merely a few fleeting moments in the film. Rather, in their numerous expressions, these slippages of identity and affiliation from Cuban to Cuban Americanness form part of a complex textuality that is transposed into a variety of contexts beyond the filmmakers' ability to contain, beyond, perhaps, even their awareness that such representations gradually undermine the political project of their film.

One needs to consider the full range of the twenty-five interviews included in *Improper Conduct,* especially the ways in which the variety of personalized mise-en-scènes undercut the interviewees' verbal narrative, to recognize the richness and breadth of this phenomenon. Taken separately, certain sequences may suggest the peculiarities of an individual's self-placement. Viewed within the matrix of a total film structure, however, they appear to underscore insistently the gradual shift away from the exilic reconstruction of a Cuban national imaginary toward an emergent hybrid cultural formation.

Ends and Beginnings

The film's failure to contain its historical subject matter suggests that there is a profound dynamic at work here rooted in the problematic juncture of simultaneous and overlapping histories. It is the liminal temporality of an imperfect subjectivity that, as Homi Bhabha says of migrant subjects, "seeks its proper name within the scene of genealogical indebtedness."[13] Neither denying its origins in a Cuban cultural identity nor suppressing the hybridity that defines its host culture, this is an emerging subjectivity that looks back, but seeks not to restage the past, nor to disavow it. Rather, the subject who emerges from the images of *Improper Conduct* implies a refiguration of an idea of affiliation for individuals positioned by geography and history on the margin between cultures.

The full implication of this struggle for expression between dual discursive modalities is underscored in the film's final sequence. René Ariza, a Cuban writer and actor who arrived in south Florida during the Mariel exodus, is seen in an amusement park performing in a puppet theater for children. What at first distinguishes this scene from nearly all of the preceding interviews is the presentation of Ariza in the carnivalesque clown makeup of his job. In striking ways this theatrical mask links him to Caracol's earlier presentation. But unlike Caracol, Ariza delivers his interview in a pointedly unself-conscious way, as if the theatrical persona were truly his identity. Ariza's choice of being interviewed in costume, as well as the strategic placement of this interview as the final sequence of the film, serves to foreground for the audience the very condition of staging and performance of identity that, in fact, has gradually gained ground in the film.

Ariza's final soliloquy begins in the vein of most of the other verbal histories, as denunciation: "To be different, to be strange, to have improper conduct, is something that is not only prohibited, but may also cost you imprisonment" (105). Then, abruptly, he switches focus to voice a deeper and more troubling scenario:

> I think this has been in the Cuban character for a long time, and it's not peculiar to Castro; there are many Castros and we have to look out for the Castro that each one of us has inside. It's an attitude that we take hold of.... It's a vicious circle and one becomes completely paranoid, a paranoia that feeds everyone, that nurtures those who pursue as well as the ones they pursue, since the pursued at times look like the pursuers. (105–6)

Read against the film's opening sequences that present the demonized Castro as the cause of exile, Ariza's notion of a multiplicity of Castros appears implicitly to question the political source of the exilic discourse of which it is a part. As such, the scene crystallizes the underlying tension between two different sensibilities, two different temporal perspectives on exile, that have characterized the film's textual instability throughout. The final image of *Improper Conduct*, the freeze-frame of Ariza staring into the camera, sums up the underlying meaning of the film's textual instability as it appears to move its audience toward a self-conscious reflection on the process of slippage from exilic temporality to that of an emerging cultural consciousness beyond the confines of the past.

182   Marvin D'Lugo

Notes

1. Benedict Anderson, *Imagined Communities*, rev. ed. (London: Verso, 1991), 204.

2. For discussion of how the film was critiqued by writers on the left, see especially Dan Georgakas, "*Improper Conduct*," *Cineaste* 14.1 (1985): 45–48; Ruby Rich, "Bay of Pix," *American Film* 7X.9 (July–August 1984): 57–59; Michael Chanan, *The Cuban Image* (London: British Film Institute, 1985), 5–7; Marvin Leiner, *Sexual Politics in Cuba: Machismo, Homosexuality, and AIDS* (Boulder, Colo.: Westview Press, 1993), 51–52.

3. Hamid Naficy, "Exile Discourse and Televisual Fetishization," *Quarterly Review of Film and Video* 13.1–3 (1991): 87.

4. Anderson, *Imagined Communities*, 204.

5. Ana M. López, "Cuban Cinema in Exile: The 'Other' Island," *Jump Cut* 38 (June 1993): 53–54. An expanded version of this essay appears in the first section of this volume.

6. Zuzana M. Pick, *The New Latin American Cinema: A Continental Project* (Austin: University of Texas Press, 1993), 158.

7. Lourdes Arguelles and Ruby Rich have observed as well how the film conveniently omits any discussion of the status of gays and lesbians in pre-Castro Cuba, and avoids any information that would help the viewer contextualize Cuban homophobia in other areas of Latin America. See Lourdes Arguelles and B. Ruby Rich, "Homosexuality, Homophobia, and Revolution: Notes Toward an Understanding of the Cuban Lesbian and Gay Experience, Part I," *Signs: Journal of Women in Culture and Society* 9.4 (1984): 683–99, and "Part II," *Signs* 11.1 (1985): 120–36.

8. Nestor Almendros, *Conducta impropia* (Madrid: Editorial Playor, 1984), 21. This translation and all others from the published script are my own.

9. Marvin Leiner notes that implicit theme as he observes the narrowness of the film's historical treatment of the status of gays in Cuba. He writes: "these interviews are important as oral history protesting the institutionalization of homophobia. But there is something very static about the film as a whole. It focuses on an aspect of human rights in which significant improvement has taken place, yet the film tells us nothing of these changes and implies that conditions of twenty to twenty-five years ago are the conditions of today" (Leiner, *Sexual Politics in Cuba*, 51–52).

10. Almendros, *Conducta impropia*, 58.

11. Ibid., 20.

12. For Benítez-Rojo, the salient historical features of Caribbean culture transcend the localism of specific nationalities in the region and point to a broader cultural fabric that is antithetical to the parochial conception of homeland implicit in the Almendros/Jiménez-Leal notion of Cuba. See Antonio Benítez-Rojo, *The Repeating Island: The Caribbean and the Postmodern Perspective* (Durham, N.C., and London: Duke University Press, 1992), 3.

13. Homi K. Bhabha, *The Location of Culture* (London: Routledge, 1994), 242.

Media Destructionism:
The Digital/Laser/Videos of
Raphael Montañez Ortiz

Scott MacDonald

Raphael Montañez Ortiz has been making valuable contributions to contemporary culture, including contemporary film culture,
since the late 1950s. That he is not well known, especially among "film
people," is a function of his tendency to work outside conventional
understandings of art, and, especially in recent years, at the intersections of various media technologies: the works that will be the focus
of this discussion are neither films, nor videos, nor computer art, nor
laser art—though each of these four technologies is a crucial dimension of the process that produces the works. On one level, Ortiz's refusal to function within one particular arena of aesthetic history and
influence parallels his ethnic heritage. As a "slum kid" who grew up
on New York's Lower East Side in the thirties and forties, a member
of the first Hispanic family in his neighborhood, Ortiz developed outside the centers of social power, "with no resources for anything beyond working at the Educational Alliance and the Henry Street Settlement."[1] And even his own particular "Hispanic" heritage can hardly
be described simply: Ortiz's roots reach back through Puerto Rico
not only to Portugal and Spain, but to Ireland and to the indigenous
Yaqui people of northern Mexico.

The scope of this essay does not allow anything like a thorough
review of the many incarnations of Ortiz's career as an artist, but
a brief review of at least those works that have involved film will
provide a context for the more detailed discussion of recent work
that follows. Ortiz made his first films when he was a student at
Pratt Institute during the late fifties, and from the very beginning he
declared himself an innovator. Although much of the earliest work is
lost, several films from 1958 remain, including *Cowboy and "Indian" Film, Newsreel,* and *Henny Penny: The Sky Is Falling.*[2] The

first two are minilandmarks in what has come to be called "recycled cinema."[3]

Finished the same year as Bruce Conner's influential *A Movie, Cowboy and "Indian" Film* and *Newsreel* are at once related to Conner's work and distinct from it.[4] Like Conner, Ortiz did not have the economic means to shoot his own footage. In order to satisfy his desire to make movies, he bought inexpensive 16mm prints of films that were widely available in local drugstores and camera stores, and reedited them. Conner's method in *A Movie* was to accept the literal actions occurring within individual shots, but to change their impact by arranging the shots into an entirely new and imaginative continuity. Ortiz's method combined his developing fascination with his Yaqui heritage and an interest in the Dadaist tactic of appropriating found objects:

> I would chop the films up with the tomahawk and put them into a medicine bag. I would shake it and shake it, and for me the bag would become a rattle, and I would chant with it.... I was imitating indigenous ritual to find my place in it. When I imitated it long enough, and felt comfortable in it, *then* I would reach into the medicine bag, pull out pieces of chopped up film, and splice them together.[5]

As a result of this unconventional process, the continuity of the films Ortiz worked with—Anthony Mann's *Winchester '73* (1950), with James Stewart, in *Cowboy and "Indian" Film*; a Castle Films newsreel in *Newsreel*—is utterly shattered. Images are sometimes right side up and forward, sometimes upside down and backward. And not only do the successive images follow each other with virtually no suggestion of their original continuity, but the sound we hear with any given image bears no particular relation to it. Further, Ortiz includes not only the imagery that was part of what the original film audiences saw in theaters, but bits of Academy leader and even the informal notations written on the strip of 16mm leader that precedes the Academy leader on many prints: "For me, every bit of celluloid contained the life of what that film was about."[6]

Whereas Conner's *A Movie* creates a grim, though generally entertaining, vision of modern life, Ortiz's *Cowboy and "Indian" Film* and *Newsreel* are not entertainments. Rather, they are indices of the process that was used to create them, and, by implication, of an ideology that sees conventional cinema and the visions of the world it promotes as more than simply misguided and in need of Conneresque send-up. For Ortiz, the ethnic ramifications of the western were (and remain) deeply problematic, because the genre not only tended to re-confirm a vision of North American history that was disastrous for the indigenous peoples but undercut Ortiz's sense of his own self-worth: how could *he* identify with the Euro-American "good guys"? His cinematic response, therefore, was not irony, but an attack on the cultural artifact that most clearly represented for him the suppression of the indigenous (and the Hispanic) in history and within himself. By editing the shards of *Winchester '73* and the Castle Films newsreel into montages that emphasize the distance between the original films and what we're seeing, Ortiz announces his distance from the enterprise of conventional cinema and all that it represents.

And yet, Ortiz's destruction of the western and the newsreel does have a constructive dimension—beyond his refusal to accept a set of oppressive conventions. Indeed, this constructive dimension of Ortiz's "destructionist" art was to fuel his outrageous performance work during the sixties and more recent decades, as well as the digital/laser/video deconstructions that have occupied him since 1985. It is evident even in the grotesque *Henny Penny: The Sky Is Falling* (Ortiz has also called it *Chicken Little*). Only the imagery of *Henny Penny*—a series of hand-held 8mm images of a chicken slaughterhouse in Brooklyn leads to a series of extended close-ups during which chickens are partially decapitated, thrown into metal funnels to be bled, and twitch in the throes of death—dates back to 1958; the current sound is from a later performance during which Ortiz "cleaned" a piano with a chicken, killed the chicken, and destroyed the piano with an ax, then walked around the performance space scattering feathers on the audience.[7] For most viewers of almost any ideological bent, the close-up killing of the chickens would seem little more than a visual assault. But more was involved: the dying spasms of the chickens, Ortiz explains, were "a clinging to life, a positive thing, a life reflex like the heartbeat."

In the nursery rhyme, Chicken Little's fear of the sky falling is needless hysteria, but for real chickens in the real world, "the sky is falling" all the time. Conventional, capitalist cinema's function has been to provide adult nursery rhymes that help audiences believe that essentially all is well with the world, regardless of what is actually going on, as a means of maintaining the film industry's economic viability. Ortiz's unpleasant little film is the diametric opposite: it's a

Ortiz performs a piano destruction concert in 1967. (Photo courtesy of Raphael Montañez Ortiz.)

"life reflex," a clinging to reality in the interest of psychic health. Those twitching, not-quite-dead chickens were, and remain, a metaphor for the usually passive film consumer, and their very real spasms are a metaphor for the "spasm" caused by this filmmaker's interruption of the smooth predictability of our pleasures. What Ortiz did with random, montage editing in *Cowboy and "Indian" Film* and

Pope blessing the bomb in *Newsreel* (1958). (Photo courtesy of Raphael Montañez Ortiz.)

Newsreel, he does with a continuous, unflinching gaze in *Henny Penny: The Sky Is Falling*. The sky is falling for the chickens and for the viewers.

During the sixties, Ortiz was centrally involved with performance work, little of it incorporating film, though in general his approach remained close to the early film work.[8] Often, Ortiz would devise a ritualized process that would lead to the destruction of objects that encoded problematic elements of the larger culture. For a time, he chopped up pianos with his ax: "Sound is an important part of indigenous ritual, and the drumming sounds of the pianos that resonated when I chopped them apart were an expansion of their voice, so to speak: for at least a moment they had an indigenous voice." Some of this sixties (and later) performance work has been documented and discussed by art historians, and in at least one instance it was inspirational in the realm of pop psychology. In the introduction to *The Primal Scream*, Arthur Janov describes how one of his patients, a college student, changed Janov's approach to therapy by describing how he had seen a performance during which Ortiz enacted the trauma of a child who has lost his parents, by spasmatically tearing off his clothes, gorging himself with milk and vomiting it up, and releasing what Janov would later call "the primal scream."[9]

Although the violence in Ortiz's performances was always symbolic, always "violence" with the fundamentally constructive purpose of eliminating real violence (as Ortiz has said, "Destruction has no place in society—it belongs in our dreams; it belongs to art"),[10] by the 1970s, even the symbolic violence he worked with was becoming more gentle, as is clear in his video documentation *Past Life Regression* (1979), where Ortiz directs several people into past-life regressions during which their contact with previous lives sometimes expresses itself in "spasms" of laughter. And by the 1980s, his discovery of the possibility of using the new digital, laser, and video technologies as a means of ritually reworking moments from conventional cinema (and video) allowed him to devise an almost sedentary process for responding "violently" to the overt and implicit psychic violence promoted and marketed by the media.

In the late seventies and early eighties, Ortiz experimented with a variety of ways of generating imagery on the computer, or, to be more precise, of using the computer as a device to transform one form of imagery into others. As he became more adept with digital technology and with laser and video technology, he discovered he could electronically "chop up" cultural artifacts and give elements of these artifacts a new shape/motion/sound, more fully in touch with those fundamental (and frequently spasmodic) psychic/physical realities the smooth continuity of conventional cinema represses. Specifically, he began to explore the classic cinema by recording or buying laser disc versions of films, and then using his Apple+ and IIe (and the computerized directory for the laser disc) to access those sets of frames that seemed to hint at deeper implications worth exposing and recontextualizing. Ortiz began exploring these passages by playing them over and over, forward and backward, at different speeds—and with different modifications to the sound (a Deltalab Effectron II sound-effects generator is hooked into his system). Each finished piece is performed (and recorded on a three-quarter-inch VCR) during a prolonged engagement with this source material.

Although Ortiz's electronic process is more time-consuming than chopping things up with an ax, his earlier commitment to indigenous ritual remains central: "I have to go through thousands, millions of possibilities. I give myself up to it. I'm there working with it, just chanting and chanting the passage, until finally it's a prayer, a ritual." For Ortiz, these performances are rituals, electronic incantations, during which he makes sustained contact, not only with fundamental levels of the original cinematic artifacts, but with his own unconscious and with the "unconscious of the culture," which is expressed within the original films. The jagged, phased repetition of the visuals and sound in the finished pieces has the potential to affect viewers, in Ortiz's view, in a manner akin to indigenous drumming and chanting. His interruption of our expectations offers us an opportunity to experience something of the rhythms of heritages not empathetically represented in much mainstream popular culture. Ortiz's electronic ritual has produced dozens of works available on video (see the film/videography at the end of this essay). They reveal a wide range of particular concerns, and a process of evolution within Ortiz's general approach. Some discussion of a few of the more memorable of these works can serve as an introduction.

The Kiss (1985)

The Kiss is a six-minute video that recycles a few seconds of Robert Rossen's *Body and Soul* (1947), starring John Garfield and Lilli Palmer, a film about a boxer whose obsession with financial success threatens but ultimately fails to destroy his relationships with a painter (Palmer), whom he falls in love with and then marries, and with his mother (Hazel Brooks). In *The Kiss* Ortiz reworks a seven-second passage made up of parts of two shots at the end of a scene at the painter's apartment when the painter and the boxer are beginning to fall in love, plus a less-than-a-second passage of a street scene. In

Ink-jet print of digitalized video image from Ortiz's *The Kiss* (1985), by Carol Kinne. Kinne's image encodes the motion in Ortiz's video graphically as a series of horizontal strips.

Ortiz's film, the street scene functions as a frame around the central action of the kiss; in *Body and Soul,* it occurs during an entirely different part of the film.[11] In the original film, the boxer and the painter kiss at her front door, just as the boxer is leaving her apartment. After a moment, the painter pulls away and pushes the boxer out the door, and closes it. Rossen cuts from the close-up of the kiss to a long shot of the boxer standing in the hallway outside the door. The boxer then turns and walks away from the door, looks at the drawing the painter has made of him, smiles in his excitement at this new relationship (and at the fact of the kiss), and walks down the stairs. In *The Kiss,* we see only the kiss at the door and the opening moment of this second shot: the boxer outside the door.

Ortiz's exploration of this seven-second excerpt is interesting on several different levels. In the first place, the reconstituted motion produced by Ortiz's electronic process is visually arresting and often magical. What is, in *Body and Soul,* basically a conventional gesture, nearly invisible within the trajectory of the developing relationship, becomes in *The Kiss* a fascinating display of repetitive motion, reminiscent of

Eadweard Muybridge's animation of human and animal movements with the Zoopraxiscope and of Etienne-Jules Marey's "chrono-photographs."[12] On the most basic level, Ortiz's process transforms the expected into something quite unusual. Most contemporary viewers are probably unfamiliar with Rossen's *Body and Soul* (though it holds up reasonably well after thirty years, as a result of Palmer's sensual performance as an experienced, self-aware European—and the elegant cinematography by James Wong Howe). For those who recognize the film, Ortiz's visual pyrotechnics seem even more arresting because of the relative visual simplicity of the original passage.

Although Ortiz accepts the "found object" of the brief sequence from a Hollywood film as his raw material, he organizes his repetitive recycling of the passage into a structure of his own, in this instance a structure nearly symmetrical in time. In *The Kiss,* we first see a man (without prior awareness of the Rossen film, we have no way of identifying more than his gender) in an apartment house hall-way—the superimposed street scene is fading out as we first see the hallway; then we are inside the apartment as a woman (we see her from behind and can identify only her gender) opens the door; for several seconds we see both man and woman from behind in a retinal collage as the two meet in the doorway; they kiss for several minutes; then she pushes him out the door, closing it behind him; and we see the man again, as at the beginning, outside the door; the street scene dissolves in and lasts just slightly longer than at the beginning.[13] At the beginning of Ortiz's video, we are seeing the man and woman in reverse—though there's no way of knowing this from *The Kiss*—and at the end, we see it forward.

The kiss itself is extended by more minimal movements forward and reverse, and the rhythm of these movements, when combined with the implications of the imagery itself, causes the lovers' approach to the kiss, the kiss itself, and the exit from it to seem overtly sexual. Although they are standing up, their reconstructed motions suggest sexual intercourse and the flailing movements of erotic abandon and orgasm. Ortiz has invested the conventional gesture of the abbreviated Hollywood kiss with the sexual energy—the "spasm"—that it implies (and represses) within the original scene. In *Body and Soul,* after all, the painter's abbreviation of the kiss is a function not of desire, but of societal "rules" about sexuality. Within the context of the late 1940s, the experienced European painter is meant to seem a little "loose" (the fighter, and Rossen, seem to admire her courageous independence and integrity, but know she tests the limits of the strict American social mores of the period). Indeed, her independence is particularly evident when she invites the boxer into her apartment after their first meeting, and when she exposes her desire for him by participating in the kiss. Her abbreviation of the kiss proves she remains essentially a "good girl" by conventional standards. Of course, the societal rules that determine the action within this scene had effected Hollywood's self-interested capitulation to Motion Picture Producers and Distributors Association standards: we know that implicitly Hollywood agreed to repress the painter's desires, and to force her to "close the door" on the aroused boxer, as a part of a much more general concern for the industry's financial stability within a sexually energized, but repressive, society.

Ortiz's expansion of the kiss into a virtual act of intercourse is a gesture of defiance with regard to this repressive and sexist (the *woman* must say no; the man is allowed to continue his pursuit until he's stopped) convention—and a sustained act of defiance at that. Six minutes may be—at least according to contemporary public comment— a brief duration for passionate intercourse, but since Ortiz's method expands a minimal amount of information into a sustained visual experience, most viewers (and particularly those unacquainted with experimental forms of film and video) experience *The Kiss,* and the kiss, as lengthy, rather than brief. Rossen may defy the conservative moral standards of his time by creating a film in which we particularly admire the painter for her healthy awareness of her own passion, but Ortiz goes much further by liberating the character's passion and allowing its expression.

Still other implications of *The Kiss* declare themselves if we think in terms of a parallel, and perhaps a reference, to the Edison Studio's 1896 Mary Irwin-John C. Rice kiss, a film that, in its close-up focus on sustained kissing, prefigures what became and remains one of the most inevitable filmic gestures. If Edison's kiss can be seen, at least in retrospect, as a sign of the evolution of viewership from popular theater as the dominant public art form to cinema (the Irwin-Rice kiss was well known to Edison's audience as part of the popular play *The Widow Jones*), Ortiz's decision to make *The Kiss* suggests, at least in retrospect, two levels of his own evolution as an artist. First, Ortiz's electronic process for "destroying" imagery is part of the electronic revolution that is quickly transforming public audiences for "film" into spectators of videotapes and laser discs. Indeed, for Ortiz digital and laser technology represents an advance over the essential narrowness and linearity of the mechanical technology of cinema, by representing the open nature of consciousness: Ortiz's digital/laser apparatus provides instant access to any moment in the films he explores, just as our consciousness allows us "access" to anything we remember (and as our unconscious provides access to much that we've "forgotten").

Ortiz's decision to transform the societally inspired self-repression of the painter into full participation in her passion also gains meaning from a personal transformation Ortiz has described:

> Unlike men, women don't have to go up to the mountain and starve to death, or freeze to death; they don't need to go to extremes of deprivation or of pain in order to achieve revelation. No. They take a nap and dream. Inner vision work became important to me [in the 1970s] when I realized there are more subtle aspects of deconstruction: the destruction of the ego, of normal consciousness, in dreaming.... That then created an important link for me in my relationship with women, and I wanted to make that more subtle, matriarchal form of revelation central.

In fact, the body of work that begins in the year *The Kiss* is made — the digital/laser/videos — is, in general, a form of revisionist dream exploration: Ortiz reenergizes the fabrications of the Hollywood "Dream Factory" with what he has discovered by making the "matriarchal form of revelation central." Of course, Ortiz has not eliminated his "male side," but by 1985, he was more interested in embracing the "female" within him. In *The Kiss*, the "male" has come in from his doings in the outer public world (a world outside the intimacy of this new relationship with a woman) to explore the inner, passionate world of art, of sexuality, and of the psyche, regions gendered female by the society in which Rossen made *Body and Soul* while Ortiz was just reaching puberty.

By liberating the passionate sexuality of the painter in *The Kiss*, Ortiz may be chanting his own personal development from "slum kid" (from a New York City neighborhood like the boxer in *Body and Soul*) to artist, and expressing his pleasure in learning to unite "male" and "female" approaches to life—and destructionist art—via his new digital/laser/video process.[14]

Dance No. 1 (1985)

Made the same year as *The Kiss, Dance No. 1* can represent a somewhat different kind of exploration made possible by Ortiz's electronic system—an approach to deconstruction/reconstruction that was to inform a long series of "dance" pieces. *Dance No. 1* is a three-minute forty-seven-second reworking of a ten-second passage from *Citizen Kane* (1941). Unlike *Body and Soul,* Orson Welles's film is well known to almost anyone with a serious interest in media; and for many viewers this nearly instant recognition can be expected to create a somewhat different experience.[15] On a very basic level, *Dance No. 1* suggests that even the most widely admired classic film can become raw material for Ortiz's destructive creation. The specific ten-second passage Ortiz remakes occurs at the beginning of Bernstein's reminiscences of Kane: Kane and Jedediah Leland (Joseph Cotton) have entered the *Enquirer* office, followed by Bernstein (Everett Sloane), who has just fallen through the door. Ortiz focuses on a portion of a single shot that begins when Mr. Carter is shaking hands with Bernstein, the new business manager, and ends just as Carter is realizing that Kane means to take over his office. *Dance No. 1* is about the public, rather than the private, about the social "dance" of contemporary life.

Whereas *The Kiss* is structured symmetrically (perhaps as an implicit sexual metaphor for the man's "entry," then "exit" from the woman), *Dance No. 1* begins at the conclusion of the excerpt and moves—in Ortiz's usual repetitive, cycling manner—back to the beginning. At first, we see Kane and Carter circling around each other; and, near the end, Carter, Leland, and Bernstein move forward in synchronization, over and over, like a mechanized chorus line. The original moment excerpted from *Body and Soul* for *The Kiss* is virtually silent (Ortiz does add a rhythmic electronic sound), but in *Dance No. 1* the characters' voices are reworked into a sound piece reminiscent of Hollis Frampton's *Critical Mass* (1971) within which we can hear some particular words clearly: Kane's "Mr. Carter," and Bernstein's "How do you do?"

For most viewers of *Citizen Kane*, I would guess, the particular shot Ortiz recycles is one of the film's more high-spirited moments (it reflects Bernstein's respect and admiration for Kane): Kane's takeover of the stodgy *Enquirer*. Carter assumes Leland is Kane (Leland looks more like a "gentleman") and Carter's realization that Leland is only the drama critic is quickly followed by Kane's introduction of Bernstein, a Jew, as managing editor — a change sure to conflict with Carter's assumptions about class and ethnicity. But although viewers may admire Kane's progressive tendencies, Ortiz chose this scene because he was aware of an aspect of it that undercuts this progressiveness. Indeed, his representation of the ten-second passage so that its primary directionality is the opposite of the original scene is a way of suggesting that in some senses what is happening needs to be reversed. There is, after all, a cruelty in this moment in *Citizen Kane*. By dint of (unearned) money and the power that comes from it, Kane is able to walk in and turn the lives of the *Enquirer*'s management and staff upside down; and it is clear during *Citizen Kane* that Kane quite enjoys the process. For Ortiz, who has spent a good deal of time contemplating the workings of colonialism and the general implications of the power of class, this moment in Kane hides (at least from many viewers) a pattern that undercuts Kane's pretensions of installing a more progressive regime at the *Enquirer*.

The reality is that no change in class control is occurring at this moment in *Citizen Kane*. Kane, Leland, and Carter are members of the same privileged level of society. We may see Kane's hiring Bernstein as managing editor as progressive, compared to what we assume Carter's hiring policies might be; but just before the shot recycled in *Dance No. 1*, Bernstein has arrived at the front of the *Enquirer* building on a separate wagon from Kane and Leland, poised atop a pile of furniture. And his literally falling into the *Enquirer* office is a vestige of the pattern of Jews (and all other identifiable non-European-American groups)-as-clowns so pervasive during Hollywood cinema's "golden days." Whether one is fully enough aware of *Citizen Kane* to recognize the implicit anti-Semitism, Ortiz himself can hardly have failed to note the hypocrisy of the scene's pretensions to class-progressiveness. Indeed, Ortiz's introduction of an electronic "spasm" into the passage can be read as a destructionist's revenge on the privileged class's tendency to ignore those outside their offices.

The problematic implications of the overtly upbeat scene are invisible to so many viewers—in Ortiz's view, at least—because of a formal dimension of *Citizen Kane* that can easily go unnoticed: "It's the dance of the characters that allows us to forget what's really going on. For me, this 'funny' scene hid something cruel that needed to be exposed. We experience the humiliation [of Carter] *and* how Carter is pulled into the dance, and we forget his humiliation as he's dancing." Although the "dance" in *Citizen Kane* happens so quickly that we overlook its subtle impact, Ortiz's reversing of the scene and his extending it to twenty-two times its original length are meant to provide viewers with the opportunity to see (and hear) the formal dance that originally helped to disguise these problematic implications.

Dance No. 1 is Ortiz's means for venting his anger at his disenfranchisement from economic privilege in general, and from the artistic privilege represented by the Hollywood film industry. These implications are confirmed by his reworking the sound of the original passage so that it has a different, more obvious "beat"—and so that the characters "chant" the same sounds and phrases over and over. Ortiz incorporates the conventional narrative ritual of this canonized classic within his own indigenously inspired cine-ritual.

To put all this another way, Ortiz moves into *Citizen Kane* and "takes over," turning the lives of the film's characters and the film itself "upside down." He does to the institution of classic cinema what Kane is doing to the traditional "institution" of the *Enquirer*—and, in a sense, what Welles's flamboyant expressionism as director of *Citizen Kane* did to the conventions of Hollywood realism. And Ortiz makes this institutional attack on at least two levels: he revises a film that the institution of film history came to define as a masterpiece, and he interrupts the formal/thematic flow of the action; that is, he subverts and recontextualizes the "institution" of the linear rhetoric of classic cinema that *Citizen Kane* so brilliantly revised and reconfirmed.

My Father's Dead (1991)

During the ten years Ortiz has been working with his digital/laser/video setup, he has finished more than forty pieces. His explorations have in some cases remained close to the 1985 work—Ortiz's interest in the "dance," for example, remains strong, as is clear in *Dance No. 22* (1993), in which he enhances the already frenetic energy of a passage from *A Night at the Opera* (1935). In other cases, the finished pieces reveal significant modifications of approach. One notable development is Ortiz's increasing tendency to combine multiple excerpts from particular films, and passages from different films. I have already mentioned his use of the brief moment of the street scene from a separate sequence of *Body and Soul* as a framing device for his exploration of the kiss in *The Kiss,* but in many films the juxtapositions of originally separate sequences are more obvious. *Expulsion from the Garden* (1991) combines two distinct passages from *King Kong* (1933), as does *Gonna Get Me a Gal* (1991); and *Raw Oysters* (1991) weaves together three distinct passages from Welles's *The Magnificent Ambersons* (1942). *If You Don't Want It Anymore* (1987) intercuts between a passage from the black-and-white *Body and Soul* (from a scene in which the boxer comes back to the painter's apartment to return her portrait of him) and color imagery of fighter planes attacking; *Man Has Man Has Always* (1986) combines a passage from a Road Runner cartoon and a shot of a rocket launch; and *Here's Looking at You, Kid* (1991) is made up of a reworked sequence of Bogart and Bergman at the end of *Casablanca* (1942) and imagery of the Crossroads nuclear test (the first underwater A-bomb test, July 25, 1946, at Bikini Atoll in the Pacific).[16]

One of the most interesting of Ortiz's pastiche works is *My Father's Dead,* which combines brief excerpts from three films in such a way that, for most viewers, the excerpts are probably not readily identifiable.[17] One of the three passages is a gorgeous color image of a building exploding, from Clint Eastwood's *High Plains Drifter* (1973)—though nothing in the explosion makes this identification likely, except perhaps for the most obsessive Eastwood fan. The second excerpt includes two visually obscure color shots—one in close-up, the other in long shot—of a "caveman" (Everett McGill) and a "cave woman" (Rae Dawn Chong) fucking, from Jean-Jacques Annaud's *Quest for Fire* (1981). The third is a color shot of a child saying "My father's dead!" from John Boorman's *Excalibur* (1981). The unusual mixture of imagery in *My Father's Dead* is emphasized by the abrasive, disconcerting montage Ortiz constructs from the three excerpts. There are forty-one cuts from one excerpt to another (in the following order: explosion/sex/explosion/sex/explosion/sex/explosion/child/explosion/child/sex/child/explosion/child/explosion/sex (close-up)/explosion/child/explosion/child/sex/explosion/child/explosion/child/explosion/

sex/child/explosion/sex/child/explosion/child/explosion/child/sex/ explosion/sex/explosion/sex/explosion/child) and nearly continual interruptions within each moment of each excerpt. Each of the three excerpts has a very different sound: Ortiz's quick cutting rhythm, enhanced by his sound-effects generator, causes the repetitions of the exploding building to suggest a machine gun; the sex scene is accompanied by explicit sexual grunts; and the phrase, "My father's dead!" is repeated in various, generally decipherable segments.[18]

Together, the three disparate passages can be read in a variety of ways, either by exploring what the excerpts seem to reveal intrinsically, with no reference to their original sources, or by reading the brief passages as references to their original sources and exploring the complex network of associations implied by Ortiz's juxtapositions. That *My Father's Dead* (and other Ortiz pastiches) can be approached in these two different ways is part of the challenge and excitement of his work—and it can also be seen as a defiance of the general tendency of commercial media to enforce a single, "correct" reading of narrative action: for Ortiz, interpretive openness is part of the larger process of cultural liberation.

If we ignore the different sources of the excerpts and approach the film as if Ortiz's rapid-fire intercutting enforces a symbolic continuity (it would be difficult to find a literal continuity, since the couple having sex seem almost a different species from the child), we might construct one or another Oedipal drama. We could argue that the child's implicit witnessing of the "primal scene" has created a psychic "explosion" that on some level destroys the child's understanding of "father" and the apparent coherence of the home. Or, we might say that for the child, the death of the father, as a result of whatever violence is playing itself out in the destruction of the building, has been a psychic detonation that is expressed in the abruptness of Ortiz's intra- and inter-shot editing. What seems most obvious and general in the sequence, however, is the precariousness of family life, as a result of the combination of the violent forces of society (represented by the explosion and confirmed by Ortiz's jagged editing) and the powerful, primitive urges that move us from within (represented by the "animalistic" sex). The child is poised between these two forces and, like all children, must find a way to construct a life in the margin between them.

My attempts to make at least a quasi-literal coherence from *My Father's Dead* can themselves be read as metaphor. The fact that the excerpts in *My Father's Dead* have been so completely removed from their original context that, for most viewers, they have no connection with their origins is Ortiz's way of responding to the traditional power of the patriarchal film industry. Traditional entertainment film has relied on narratives in which problems are developed and solved within a predictable structure, the illusion of seamless verisimilitude, and the coherence of a single, "correct" reading of events. For Ortiz, the simplicity and directness of conventional narrative is an illusion, the maintenance of which serves the interest of the "Fathers" of commercial cinema and the larger social forces they represent—an illusion to be exploded in the interest of a healthier society. In a sense, the distraught child is the conventional viewer. As we confront Ortiz's disconcerting vision, we are displaced from our traditional cinematic pleasure—our media world is blown to smithereens—and we are left on our own to fabricate a new continuity from the shards Ortiz presents, to create new meaning from Ortiz's de- and reconstructed images. We are "cave people" again, and our dislocation is the stimulus of our new freedom and a new sensuality.

On at least one level, of course, Ortiz reveals himself as a part of the very system he defies. His access to videodiscs of films is a function of commercial concerns: he chooses to work with films that the film industry deems are likely to make a profit in the home video market, that is, with films that have enjoyed some commercial success. As a result, no matter how fully Ortiz tries to obscure his sources, the excerpts he uses will be, to some degree, identifiable—at least on the part of those of us with the interest, time, energy, and resources for tracking down these sources. In the case of *My Father's Dead*, an identification of not only the general sources of the three excerpts, but the particulars of these excerpts as they function within the narratives from which Ortiz "liberates" them, leads to further readings of *My Father's Dead*, readings that suggest the (conscious and/or subconscious) connections that resulted in Ortiz's choice of these particular excerpts and these particular films, as well as dimensions of the culture that produced the original artifacts (and, by extension, Ortiz's responses to them).

The excerpt from *Quest for Fire* is part of a sequence, pivotal in that film's narrative and ideology, during which the Ray Dawn Chong character uses the "missionary position" with her partner for the first time, enforcing their psychic, as well as physical, coupling. That this new incorporation of the woman's preference occurs in conjunction with the discovery by the explorers from the fireless tribe, that fire can be created, not just stolen from Nature or from other tribes, suggests that the process of civilization, with which we as viewers are asked to identify, is a function of *both* technological development and women's sexual liberation. The technology of the fire is identified with the fire between the couple, and this "fire" leads to the Rae Dawn Chong character's decision to leave her own people (where women are less brutally treated than in some tribes, but where her individuality remains oppressed) and join her partner in a new tribe, where her first action is to rescue him when he cannot create fire with the device they have brought with them from her tribe.

The explosion from *High Plains Drifter* occurs just after the Eastwood character has had sex with a young woman who is part of a plan to betray him by distracting him so that several cowardly men of the town can ambush him as he relaxes after the sexual encounter. The explosion is created by the drifter as he instinctively understands their plan and responds to their aborted ambush. Later, we recognize that the Eastwood character is the Devil, who has come to Lago to punish the town's corrupt refusal to live by law, the savage murder of their previous sheriff by the town bullies, and the other townspeople's cowardly refusal to intervene.

The young child who says "My father's dead!" is Uryen's daughter Morgana, who grows up to become Merlin's rival in necromancy as mythic revenge for her father's betrayal and death at the hands of Uther, who — just after Morgana has instinctively felt and said "My father's dead!" — returns to Uryens's castle to father her brother Arthur (King Arthur) with her mother Igrayne.

A thorough discussion of the many implications of Ortiz's interweaving of these three references would require a chapter in itself, but it is worth noting that all three source films are about mythic pasts — the American West, Arthurian England, "the dawn of civilization" — and about the importance of sexuality (its liberation, its corruption) in the formation of community: one might even say that the more "modern" the mythic past referred to, the more thoroughly corrupt it seems, especially in its relationship to sexuality. Further, each excerpt is taken from a particular sequence during which characters reveal their instinctive awareness of levels of reality beneath socially accepted appearances. One relatively straightforward reading of this set of parallels is to see them as metaphors for the process Ortiz hopes to engage us in: the process of looking beneath the socially accepted surface levels of some of our social artifacts as a means of revealing their oppressive tendencies, and reconnecting us with the spiritual/ sensual "fire" deep within us as a means of fueling a progressive re- construction of society.

Ultimately, Ortiz's refusal to stay within the "world" of a particular mythic narrative in *My Father's Dead,* and more fundamentally, within the "world" of a particular technology (in all his digital/laser/videos), is his means of "killing the Father" and "marrying the Mother." Tra- ditionally, if one has wished to thrive in the world of film history, one has accepted the tools and processes that have been institution- alized during the historical development of film. And one has been rewarded, economically and otherwise, within a system that has priv- ileged film, that has dealt with it as if it were a separate and distinct medium with a history all its own. Even in academic institutions where media is studied seriously, a clear distinction between film and video, and between these and other image-making activities, has often been promoted. For Ortiz, the application of technologies that mirror the holistic (Ortiz often calls it "holographic") reality of consciousness to the history of film, which has traditionally attempted to reduce the complexity of life to linear (dare I say phallic?) narrative devel- opment, is essentially an attempt to reestablish a psychic wholeness that can confirm the complex nature of the realities we face and are. For Ortiz, our cinematic "father" (the motion-picture medium) is dead, and his children (the various electronic media) are beginning to use their patrimony to right the psychic wrongs that have come down to them, including the traditional marginalization of the mother and of those whose ethnic heritages have lain shattered beneath the industry fathers' seamless illusions of image, continuity, and history.

Film/Videography

The listing below includes all the film and video works I am able to locate, as of summer 1994. The title is followed by my best guess—in collaboration with Ortiz—of the year of completion (some pieces are dated differently on different listings). The original gauge or format of the piece is followed by the length, to the nearest quar- ter minute. (On video copies of the pieces, Ortiz has not been consis-

tent in his indications of length; as a result, I have timed nearly all
the videos and films with a stopwatch—exceptions are marked with
an *, and even though on some copies sound begins with the credits,
my time designation never includes the credits.) Following the length
are indications of whether a piece is black and white, color, or both;
and whether a piece is silent or has sound. The listing is chronological according to year, but I have not attempted a chronological ordering of digital/laser/videos completed within individual years: pieces
completed during a single year are listed alphabetically.

In North America, Ortiz distributes much of his work: he can be
reached at 315 Harper Place, Highland Park, NJ 08904 (908-846-
2690). In Europe, Ortiz's distributor is 235 Media, Spichernstrasse
61, D-50672 Cologne, Germany (02-21-52-21-35; Fax: 02-21-52-27-
41). 235 Media has some work Ortiz does not, and vice versa. The
early films are currently available on video only.

Cowboy and "Indian" Film. 1958. 16mm; 2 minutes; black and white;
    sound.
Golf. 1958. 16mm (with holes punched into frames); *20 minutes;
    black and white; sound.
Henny Penny: The Sky Is Falling (a.k.a. *Chicken Little*). 1958. 8mm;
    7 minutes; black and white; sound.
Newsreel. 1958. 16mm; 1¾ minutes; black and white; silent.
Sports Gems. 1959. 16mm (with holes punched into frames); *9 min-
    utes; black and white; sound.
Piano Destruction Concert, London, England. 1966. 16mm; 4½ min-
    utes; black and white; sound.
Destruction Room, Judson Church. 1967. 16mm; 4½ minutes; black
    and white; sound.
Past Life Regression. 1979. ¾-inch video; 26 minutes; color; sound.
Beach Umbrella. 1985. ¾-inch video; 7½ minutes; color; sound.
Bridge Game. 1985. ¾-inch video; 12 minutes; black and white; sound.
Dance No. 1. 1985. ¾-inch video; 3¾ minutes; black and white; sound.
Dance No. 2. 1985. ¾-inch video; 2½ minutes; black and white; sound.
Dance No. 3. 1985. ¾-inch video; 4¾ minutes; black and white; sound.
Dance No. 4. 1985. ¾-inch video; 3¼ minutes; black and white; sound.
Dance No. 5. 1985. ¾-inch video; 9 minutes; black and white; sound.
Dance No. 6. 1985. ¾-inch video; 2¾ minutes; black and white; sound.
The Kiss. 1985. ¾-inch video; 6 minutes; black and white; sound.

The Kiss, Version II. 1985. ¾-inch video; *4½ minutes; black and white; sound.

What Is This? 1985. ¾-inch video; 9¼ minutes; black and white; sound.

Back Back Back Back. 1986. ¾-inch video; 7 minutes; black and white; sound.

Couplett. 1986. ¾-inch video; 4¾ minutes; black and white; sound.

Good and Evil. 1986. ¾-inch video; 20¼ minutes; black and white; sound.

Man Has Man Has Always. 1986. ¾-inch video; 2½ minutes; color; sound.

pushAnn pushAnn. 1986. ¾-inch video; 3¼ minutes; black and white; sound.

You Bust Your Buns. 1986. ¾-inch video; 5½ minutes; color; sound.

Chamber Music Group, No. 1. 1987. video installation; 3 tapes of *30 minutes for 3 separate monitors; color; sound.

Christ. 1987. ¾-inch video; 3½ minutes; color; sound.

If You Don't Want It Anymore. 1987. ¾-inch video; 3½ minutes; black and white/color; sound.

They Bombed the Speak. 1987. ¾-inch video; 5¾ minutes; black and white; sound.

Welcome. 1987. ¾-inch video; 5½ minutes; color; sound.

Election Promises. 1988. ¾-inch video; 7¾ minutes; black and white; sound.

Mischievous Shadows. 1988. ¾-inch video; 3½ minutes; black and white; sound.

Shadow Boxing. 1988. ¾-inch video; 3 minutes; black and white; sound.

Expulsion from the Garden. 1991. ¾-inch video; 4 minutes; black and white; sound.

Gonna Get Me a Gal. 1991. ¾-inch video; 3 minutes; black and white; sound.

Here's Looking at You Kid. 1991. ¾-inch video; 3¾ minutes; black and white; sound.

My Father's Dead. 1991. ¾-inch video; 3¾ minutes; color; sound.

Now You've Done It. 1991. ¾-inch video; 3¼ minutes; black and white; sound.

Raw Oysters. 1991. ¾-inch video; 6 minutes; black and white; sound.

The Briefcase. 1992. ¾-inch video; 13 minutes; black and white; sound.

The Drowning. 1992. ¾-inch video; 3¾ minutes; color; sound.

*If We Believe That Man's/Womyn's Soul Has Not Reached Its Fulfill-
ment ... Is It Right ... Is It Wise ... to Tamper with the Problem?*
1992. ¾-inch video; 6½ minutes; black and white/color; sound.

Mr. Marechal Have You Seen This Photograph? 1992. ¾-inch video;
5¾ minutes; black and white; sound.

Our Thoughts Are Made of Clay: Horse Women of the Apocalypse.
1992. ¾-inch video; 7¾ minutes; black and white; sound.

That's the Way I Feel about Him. 1992. ¾-inch video; 3¼ minutes;
black and white; sound.

Dance No. 22. 1993. ¾-inch video; 7¼ minutes; black and white; sound.

Elvis: The Premonition. 1993. ¾-inch video; 4½ minutes; color; sound.

Fred and Ginger. 1993. ¾-inch video; 6¾ minutes; black and white; sound.

Gonna Get Gonna Get Gonna Get a. 1993. ¾-inch video; 8 minutes;
black and white; sound.

Send Him to the Capital. 1994. ¾-inch video; 7¼ minutes; black and
white; sound.

Slam Dance. 1994. ¾-inch video; 8¾ minutes; black and white; sound.

Kiss Number Also. 1994. ¾-inch video; 6¼ minutes; color; sound.

Behind It All. 1995. ¾-inch video; 20¾ minutes; black and white/
color; sound.

Ragtime Piano. 1995. ¾-inch video; 6½ minutes; black and white;
sound.

Notes

1. From an unpublished interview with Ortiz, recorded in January and
February 1994. Unless noted, all other statements attributed to Ortiz are from
this interview. The Henry Street Settlement was/is a community center on the
Lower East Side, where Ortiz began going as a seven-year-old. There he de-
veloped his interest in music, worked with puppets, and learned to play pool.
At the Educational Alliance, a larger institution serving a similar function,
Ortiz learned crafts and participated in other activities.

2. Dates in the text and in the film/videography indicate the year when
a piece was finished. Ortiz says he worked on *Cowboy and "Indian" Film* in
1957, but finished it the following year. In two other films made during the
same period — *Golf* (1958) and *Sports Gems* (1959) — Ortiz used a hole punch
to make holes in sequences of frames from films he had bought.

3. William C. Wees has established himself as the chronicler of "recycled cinema" (also called "Found Footage Film"). See his *Recycled Images*
(New York: Anthology Film Archives, 1993) for an overview. See also Ce-
cilia Hausheer and Christoph Settele, eds., *Found Footage Film* (Lucern: Viper/

Zyklop Verlag, 1992), a catalogue for a retrospective of found footage cinema sponsored by the Swiss group Viper in 1992.

4. Although his work has come to define the field, Conner didn't invent recycled cinema. That distinction probably belongs to Joseph Cornell, who first used George Melford's *East of Borneo* (1931, starring Rose Hobart) as raw material for his *Rose Hobart* (1939) and continued to explore the approach for nearly fifteen years. Like *Cowboy and "Indian" Film* and *Newsreel, Rose Hobart* recycles a single film, but Cornell's later work prefigures Conner's—and Ortiz's—combining multiple recycled sources within individual films.

5. For Ortiz, Dada's critique of traditional Western assumptions about art was closely related to the critique implicit in indigenous ritual. Like many young artists of the time, Ortiz's awareness of cultural history developed on several fronts simultaneously, resulting in useful parallels.

6. This inclusion of evidence of the material elements of film, in addition to the photographed imagery, in recycled cinema was already an element of the Joseph Cornell recycled films of the 1940s.

7. Over the sounds of the performance, we hear a narrator—Ortiz himself—describing what's going on in the performance, as if he's reporting a news event. In earlier presentations of *Henny Penny: The Sky Is Falling*, Ortiz played tape-recorded sounds of chickens. The current sound track makes clear that the imagery is less a document of the slaughterhouse than a symbolic ritual. The sacrifice of chickens is an important element in the Caribbean ritual of Santeria—a reference Ortiz makes in various works. And, of course, our society has "ritualized" the mass killing of the animals our diet demands.

8. The most complete discussion to date of Ortiz's performance work is Kristine Stiles's overview in *Raphael Montañez Ortiz: Years of the Warrior 1960/Years of the Psyche 1988*, published by El Museo del Barrio in New York City on the occasion of a 1988 retrospective of Ortiz's work. The catalogue includes two brief essays by Ortiz, detailed listings of publications by and about Ortiz, and visual documentations of Ortiz's performances. Ortiz was the founder of El Museo del Barrio and served as its first director.

9. See Arthur Janov's introduction to *The Primal Scream* (New York: Dell, 1970), 9. Ortiz also performed a piano destruction on the *Tonight Show* after talking about his work and Destructionist Art with Johnny Carson.

10. Ortiz quoted in *Raphael Montañez Ortiz*, 4.

11. This street scene is a close-up of a portion of a single shot near the beginning of *Body and Soul* during the fighter's drive from training camp to his old neighborhood on the eve of his final heavyweight title defense. *The Kiss*, like other early digital/laser/video pieces, was constructed of images Ortiz transferred from a 16mm print of *Body and Soul* onto laser disc via video, and I assume that for the street scene that frames the kiss, Ortiz moved the video camera closer to the print. Ortiz remembers the shot differently: during our interview he indicated that the framing image was part of the speakeasy bombing sequence. Examination of *Body and Soul* makes clear that this sequence was not the source of the image.

12. A number of other filmmakers have explored similar effects. Ken Jacobs's Nervous System performances use a two-projector device Jacobs invented as a means of exploring moments of his own and others' films. The most widely seen Nervous System works, at least recently, are *XCXHXEXRXRXIXEXSX* (*Cherries*), *Two Wrenching Departures*, and *The Sub-Cinema*, each of which has existed for years in various versions. The Austrian independent filmmaker Martin Arnold has used a homemade optical printer to create works that are remarkably like Ortiz's digital/laser/videos. Indeed, because Arnold saw some of Ortiz's work before making his own, his *Pièce Touchée* (1989) and *Passage à l'acte* (1993) may owe Ortiz a debt—though a close examination of both Ortiz's and Arnold's work reveals considerable differences in both form and attitude.

13. There is a second, shorter version of *The Kiss*, made during the same period as the version I'm discussing. According to Ortiz, it eliminates the material at the beginning and the end of the longer version, focusing on the kiss itself.

14. That Ortiz may have identified with the boxer seems particularly likely since Charlie Davis's mother in the film is identified as Jewish and, to a degree, an outsider in the neighborhood—as Ortiz was at first in his Manhattan neighborhood.

15. At the beginning, Ortiz's fascination with finding and exploring moments of "dance" within narrative development led him to particular films over and over: *Dance No. 2* (1986), *Dance No. 3* (1986), *Dance No. 4* (1985), and *Dance No. 6* (1985) are recyclings of passages from *King Kong* (1933), as are the later pieces *Gonna Get Me a Gal* (1991), *Expulsion from the Garden* (1991), and *Gonna Get Gonna Get Gonna Get a* (1993). *Citizen Kane* provided material for *Shadow Boxing* (1988), *Mischievous Shadows* (1988), *Election Promises* (1988), and *If We Believe That Man's/Womyn's Soul Has Not Reached Its Fulfillment ... Is It Right ... Is It Wise ... to Tamper with the Problem?* (1992). *The Grand Illusion* (1935) and *The Magnificent Ambersons* (1942) have also supplied material for several pieces.

16. The most elaborate of Ortiz's pastiche works is *If We Believe That Man's/Womyn's Soul Has Not Reached Its Fulfillment ... Is It Right ... Is It Wise ... to Tamper with the Problem?*, which includes excerpts from *Dr. Jekyll and Mr. Hyde* (the 1941 Victor Fleming version, with Spencer Tracy and Ingrid Bergman), *Quest for Fire* (1981), *High Plains Drifter* (1973), *Moby Dick* (1956), *Citizen Kane*, and *King of Kings* (1961).

17. All three excerpts are quite brief. The four-shot sequence of the explosion in *High Plains Drifter*, only part of which is used in *My Father's Dead*, is eight seconds long. The sex in long shot lasts nine seconds, as does the close-up (though, here too, only a portion of each shot is reworked). And the child says "My father's dead!" in a four-second shot.

18. Ortiz's exploration of sound is as varied as his exploration of visual image. In some cases, he generates a regular rhythm from a minimal bit of the original film sound track. In other cases, he subtly modifies and rephrases

passages of original dialogue, creating a variety of effects. And for still other digital/laser/videos, Ortiz uses modifications of one passage of the the sound track over both its original imagery and over imagery from a very different part of the original film. In *Expulsion from the Garden,* for example, we hear King Kong's (modified) grunts as we see Jack Driscoll kissing Ann Darrow earlier on the boat.

Collaborative Public Art and Multimedia Installation: David Avalos, Louis Hock, and Elizabeth Sisco's *Welcome to America's Finest Tourist Plantation* (1988)

C. Ondine Chavoya

> 1,950 mile-long wound
>   dividing a *pueblo*, a culture,
>   running down the length of my body,
>   staking fence rods in my flesh,
>   splits me splits me
>   *me raja me raja*
>
> This is my home
> This thin edge of
>   barbwire.[1]

Introduction: Video and Border Art

Video as a part of multimedia installation has become a prominent fixture in museum programming and exhibition, blurring the boundaries between film/video practices and the visual arts. This essay examines *Welcome to America's Finest Tourist Plantation,* San Diego Bus Poster Project (January 1988), a collaborative project by artists-activists David Avalos, Louis Hock, and Elizabeth Sisco. *Welcome to America's Finest Tourist Plantation* was originally staged as a public art project: an exterior bus poster and a media event. Mounted and viewed on the back of city buses, the traveling poster catalyzed a visceral public response, generating dialogue in the print and broadcast media. Situated at the intersections of public and informational space, the project ultimately developed into a discursive performance. The interplay of reactions and opinions transformed the collaborative project into a participatory, collective one.

Documenting the mass-media response was an integral component of the project. The artists collected the multiple, competing views that were expressed in the press, art criticism, and editorials; media artist-collaborator Louis Hock recorded and edited the electronic media coverage. This documentation, in the form of a book and video, was exhibited in the subsequent museum installation. I will examine the mass media's function in the creation of the discursive performance and consider how the mass-media dialogue takes on another function when it is introduced into the museum as "video" within an installation format.

Welcome to America's Finest Tourist Plantation developed through what is known as border arts, which examine the relations of power at the U.S.-Mexico border in artistic and cultural terms. El Centro Cultural de La Raza in San Diego, California, has been instrumental in the promotion, exhibition, and scholarship of border arts. Larry T. Baza, executive director of El Centro Cultural de La Raza, affirms:

> The founding of the Centro, 23 years ago [1970], was in itself a cultural and political statement that still speaks to the art and issues relevant to the lives of the Chicano and Mexican people of the border region. The establishment of the Centro came as a part of the growth of the Chicano movement, which, put simply, is driven by self-determination and works toward the attainment and maintenance of full civil rights for people of Mexican descent in the United States.[2]

Since 1984, el Centro has sponsored and housed the Border Art Workshop/Taller de Arte Fronterizo (BAW/TAF) as its "active visual arm."[3] David Avalos, a cofounder of the Workshop, coordinated BAW/TAF's activities from el Centro while a member from November 1984 to November 1987. At the time of *Welcome to America's Finest Tourist Plantation,* he was an artist in residence at el Centro.

Border art has been produced by Chicana/os, Latina/os, Mexicans, and multiethnic allies invested in cross-cultural exchange and coalition. As such, these aesthetic and political activities have often been collaborative. As Philip Brookman explains, "Collaborations between artists of diverse ethnic backgrounds and experiences have continued in San Diego, creating a methodology that has crossed boundaries often imposed by cultural institutions and artists themselves."[4] By late 1993, Elizabeth Sisco, David Avalos, and Louis Hock had collaborated on four projects, while participating in a number of other collaborative projects in San Diego. One way of understanding the contribution of these collaborations to multiculturalism is through their impact within the public sphere. In this respect, Avalos contrasts his collaborative work with identity- and community-oriented art: "We don't have a group name because we're not a group. It's that simple. We have to be understood as individuals looking for a forum, not a community."[5]

The historical context for collaborative border arts, evident in *Welcome to America's Finest Tourist Plantation,* is the United States' master-narrative: its self-definition as a nation of immigrants. However, the contradictions of this narrative are a lived reality at the U.S.-Mexico border. Except when it was economically advantageous to the United States, the narrative has been aggressively mobilized in support of physical and ideological policing of "undesirable" immigrants from the south. This has been accomplished through capricious immigration policies, discrimination, and violence. A 1986 exposé in the *San Diego Union,* "The Border at Tijuana: 'One Square Mile of Hell,'" represents the border region as an abject zone of impending pollution, one that threatens national security and the national identity.[6] By evoking proximity and penetration anxieties, the article gives credibility to this alleged threat with epitaphs such as the "hell at our doorstep," "invasion from Mexico," and "flood of illegal aliens." The article contends that "the nation's most porous border at San Diego, the most out-of-control, is an open invitation to terrorists, drug smugglers, and international criminals — the dregs of the earth and certainly the enemies of freedom." Although some would counter that this alleged invasion irrigates the state's powerful agricultural industries and prosperous service-based tourism economy, the public discourse was framed within a rhetoric of war.

In fiscal year 1986, a record 1.76 million undocumented Mexicans were arrested crossing the border. Despite formidable legislation to "control" immigration, 1992's arrest projections surpassed the 1986 record, with 40 percent of these occurring along the San Diego-Tijuana border. A press story on the border in the year of the Quincentennial "reads like a preparation for war,"[7] or rather the maintenance of U.S. military actions abroad to legitimize an internal, domestic war on immigration: "The Bush Administration plans to announce a series of stepped up enforcement measures to handle what may be more than a million apprehensions this year. The measures include hiring hundreds of new border patrol agents, issuing counterfeit resistant work permits and using military vehicles left over from the Persian

Gulf to patrol border areas."[8] Also in 1992, the U.S. military and the Border Patrol cooperatively engineered a thirteen-mile steel fence constructed from materials recycled from Desert Storm to defend and secure the Pacific coastline from "invaders."

A reign of vigilantism has been introduced at the border to defend the nation from the "Brown Terror," commanded by "patriot" groups and organizations such as the Alliance for Border Control, Light Up the Border (led by San Diego's former mayor, Roger Hedgecock), and Border Watch (affiliated with David Duke and the Ku Klux Klan). The violence and injustices committed by such crusades are in addition to the much larger abuse and human rights violations committed by the Immigration and Naturalization Service and the San Diego police department against Mexican migrant workers and Chicanos (83 percent of reported abuse).[9] Such vigilantism and violations depend on the mass media to both circulate and frame the discourse on national identity within xenophobtic terms. As one San Diego resident declared on a talk-radio program:

> If you don't seal the border, *you're going to destroy the United States as an identity.* ... Things have gotten out of hand, so far out of hand, not only here but in Germany, England, Sweden, and everywhere else, that there is invasion by the third world. Things have gotten completely out of control.... If they don't come here legally, they should be immediately deported or shot at the border.[10]

Welcome to America's Finest Tourist Plantation strategically intervenes in the public sphere in order to reframe and expand the existing media discourse on national identity. The project specifically focuses on historical and contemporary discrimination arising out of immigration policies and media discourse. Moreover, the project connects immigration control to the more general policing of public space. In this way, Avalos, Hock, and Sisco challenge the prescribed notions of public space and call for an examination and reconsideration of the codified functions of the "public."

Welcome to America's Finest Tourist Plantation

The image here is not of art becoming life, but of life passing through art as a function of place. In another place, one would need another art.[11]

In January 1988, Avalos, Hock, and Sisco launched a "public art ambush" known as the San Diego Bus Project.[12] With monies from one of the city's arts organizations, Combined Arts and Educational Council of San Diego County (COMBO), the artists purchased advertising space on the back of one hundred buses in San Diego's transit bus fleet. In addition to making the project public, this strategy sidestepped the rampant censorship that followed the conservative backlash against public/federal funding for the arts. Existing outside a specific art context, the bus poster reached an audience that included "more than 80% of San Diego's population."[13]

The 21 × 72-inch poster montage bore an incisive welcome to San Diego residents and visitors — "Welcome to America's Finest Tourist Plantation." This parody of San Diego's self-defined civic slogan, "America's Finest City," canvased the county for over a month. The poster depicts a series of brown working hands to reveal how San Diego's civic slogan is founded on and maintained by the labor, services, and exploitation of undocumented workers within the city's service industries. In the press release, the artists discussed their parody as a means to point out that the city defines itself "on the fantasies of non-residents rather than the needs of most of us who live and work here, including the undocumented Mexican worker."[14]

On the right side of the poster, a woman's hand reaches toward a hotel door where a placard reads "Maid Service please." On the left, a pair of hands scrapes food off a plate. In the center, a pair of hands is shackled in handcuffs by an INS/Border Patrol agent, with a prominently displayed holstered weapon. This last image, a detail of a larger print, was photographed by Sisco when she witnessed an INS raid on a city bus. The detained individual was removed from the bus, handcuffed, and more than likely deported. As symbolic redress, Sisco states, the poster places individuals removed in INS raids from city buses back onto them. By channeling attention to the issues of tourism, immigration, and racism, the project called attention to the social structure that sustains San Diego's contradictory policy and attitude toward undocumented workers.

The poster was by design not the "product" in and of itself, but rather a catalyst for public dialogue. As Avalos points out, "We don't create these controversies. They already exist.... It wasn't yet a debate because it was one-sided."[15] By visually and publicly representing San Diego's dependency on and exploitation of undocumented labor, the project created both a public spectacle and a civic scandal, and was heavily debated in the printed press, television news, and in day-to-day conversations. Once the dialogue was in full swing, the

David Avalos, Louis Hock, Elizabeth Sisco, *Welcome to America's Finest Tourist Plantation*, 1988. (Photo by Elizabeth Sisco. Courtesy of Elizabeth Sisco, Louis Hock, and David Avalos.)

performance was set in motion and the (public) discourse took prominence over the (art) object.

Throughout, the use of tax monies dominated the news coverage. One *Los Angeles Times* headline read: "Bus Poster Art Taxes Officials' Patience."[16] The mass media's coverage primarily focused its commentary on the "inappropriate" use of civic funds, contending that the city was indicted with its own money. The irony that the press subsequently jumped on was that a significant amount of the funds used to purchase the advertising space was raised from the industry under critique, San Diego tourism, through the hotel room tax.[17] Typical print headlines included "Bus Art Takes Controversial Route," and trite although telling comments such as "One group's artistic statement has turned into another's public relations nightmare."[18]

The "Great Art Debate"[19] exerted considerable force and took on spectacular proportions, because it was intentionally scheduled to kick off as San Diego prepared to host its first Super Bowl. The tourist industry's preparations for Super Bowl XXII was the talk of the town because of the opportunity to showcase "America's Finest City" to the expected eighty thousand-plus visitors and the international television audience. To put this in perspective, one must take into account the fact that tourism ranks as the third-largest industry in San Diego—the military being first and manufacturing second. By 1988, it was estimated that San Diego's tourist industry would generate approximately 2.5 billion dollars per year; and the city banked on an additional 104 million dollars in Super Bowl-related revenues. As a slur on this self-portrait, *Welcome to America's Finest Tourist Plantation* was perceived as cracking the foundation of a lucrative and successful image campaign, and, hence, the city's economic future.

Despite the heated debate and protests mounted against the poster, it remained in transit and on view. Some posters were vandalized; others were stolen and soon after replaced.[20] One local citizen declared, "What the city needs is an art dictator!" and subsequently volunteered to take the position once it became available to ensure that this type of art would not offend the city again.[21] But the project, as Avalos noted, "resisted everyone's efforts to dominate it. We ... were no more in control of the events we initiated than those government officials

KCST Channel 39, San Diego Evening News, "Finest Art," January 7, 1988.

frustrated in their attempts to remove the image from city buses."[22] Although the project was not explicitly censored, and an art dictator was not appointed, the city's funding procedures for public art were modified, and the transit board's policy on advertising was accordingly changed. In fact, before the month was up, San Diego mayor Maureen O'Connor began modifying the city's art funding guidelines "to make sure nothing like this happens again."[23] The city proposed to instate its own city-run and -funded Commission on Arts and Culture, which would supervise and administer all public art funding. In essence, this commission was created to replace, or force out, COMBO, the arts organization that administered the grant monies to Avalos, Hock, and Sisco.

A few months later, in June, the Metropolitan Transit Development Board instituted new guidelines that required the board's general manager to remove "any advertisement, public service or other display deemed to be objectionable." The guidelines to determine what is defined as "objectionable" were changed to include ads that "might be considered as derogatory towards any aspect of the law enforcement profession." The previous rules protected only the police and the legal profession, a loophole that apparently did not protect the Border Patrol.[24]

Public Art

Aiming to illuminate the absence of public space, the artists have created a public forum within a conceptual space.[25]

Public space is a site for the examination and discussion of the relations of power; it is also a site of access to the relations of power. The project, in presenting these issues, manifested the consequences of its topic, demonstrating what happens to individual rights when public space is too bureaucratized or monitored. The press release for the project, written by the three artists, stressed the issue of public space: "The immigration laws attempt to deny a space for the undocumented worker, while at the same time, their space is clearly recognized by the local economic forces."[26] The artists then outlined their strategy:

> Why: Assume that there is no such thing as public space in San Diego. The few plazas that lie dormant before their corporate towers await an "art" at the service of public relation campaigns. The City fills its space with work that buffs its image as a fitting housekeeper for tourist attractions. Private enterprise has papered over the space that remains with commercial advertising.
> If we further assume that the logical forum for public issues is public space, then it follows that the first task of the public artist would be the creation of such a public space.
> And if the art that potentially occupies such space is to continue to be a target of the city's hostility, then public artists will increase their chances of survival by making that target a moving one.

Through the process, the collaborators imaginatively created a new space for public art—a space usually reserved for corporate ads to create and incite consumers—from which to enlist a public dialogue. The form of address appropriated the strategies of mass-media advertising, although the terms of advertising were reversed and unsettled. During this time advertising space was reclaimed and utilized to create (and incite) an involved, engaged public in a dialogue with complex and multiple components. I will examine how this debate unfolded in the press and on television as a mass-mediated "performance," before considering the artists' video appropriation of this coverage within a multimedia installation.

The Press Coverage

We intend to create something that is provocative and engenders a public discussion. It is public art, not art in the public. The work is defined by its performance in the community.[27]

Competing views on the poster continued throughout the project. But, with the exception of brief allusions to previous San Diego public art controversies, neither the media nor the public carried the debate over to the broader questions of public space that the artists outlined.[28] Instead, most press features can be encapsulated in the sentiments expressed by David B. Dreiman for *La Jolla Light,* who reported Avalos, Hock, and Sisco's "rear-end showcase" as yet another example of the "excesses of the free speech movement." Dreiman used the forum to "point out that no one forces our undocumented visitors to crawl through the fence to get here," and that immigration laws as currently enforced provide "some visitors with a free ride back across the border."[29]

At the time, the local papers were deluged with caustic commentary and letters to the editor, including a series of letters written in response to earlier published letters. An array of diverse subjects and opinions surfaced in these letters, including the status of undocumented workers in city industries, militarization of the border, immigrant bashing in political rhetoric, and discrimination and racism directed against Chicanos. Some also took this occasion to review and scrutinize the history and policies of many of the local conservative newspapers.[30] A few local papers printed discriminatory and offensive terms such as "wetback" or "illegal" in both their articles and in the letters submitted to them. This then spawned a new series of editorials on the terms of identity, mass-media representation, and community self-definition. One letter to the *San Diego Union* stated:

I am sick of the carping, the lectures, the griping and complaining, the endless demands. If they do not want to be dish washers here, let them stay home and wash dishes in Mexico.... All they contribute to us is illness, medical costs, dope, gang violence, increased crime, and an additional burden on our educational system with their huge, out-of-control birthrate. I have had it up to my ears with the illegal immigrants and their 'rights.' ... Let us face it, Mexico will never change. They will always be takers; we will always be givers.[31]

The author, Mary Gustafson, soon received history lessons on the Mexican-American War and the appropriation of California from a variety of enraged respondents, including one whose temper was sparked by Gustafson's "ignorance and pea-sized brain."[32] Another response, by Jesus R. Cabezuela, commented:

The only thing I felt were feelings of sorrow for Mary Gustafson because it's obvious she's suffering from a severe mental disease called racism. For your information, Mary, the soil under the one foot you're standing on is part of Mexico, or was until your ancestors decided to instigate a war to forcibly take it. The people you call "uninvited" are, in reality, returning to the homeland of their ancestors which was stolen from them.[33]

A letter to the editor that fueled a heated discussion (also printed in the *San Diego Union*) proclaimed, "I haven't talked to a single San Diego resident who gives diddly-squat about the city bus posters that suggest that wetbacks are somehow martyrs."[34] The *San Diego Union* was called on this piece, in particular for printing an "inaccurate and unacceptable terminology."[35] The paper responded by acknowledging that the word "wetback" was derogatory and apologized to the offended readers. However, the paper refused to apologize for printing the term, not because of freedom of speech or the press, but because the editor did not consider the word to be "in the same class with the clearly racist terms offered for comparison," such as "nigger" or "kike." If it were in the same "class," the editor would have substituted another term, such as "illegal."

In effect, this dialogue created a substantial examination (or, rather, exhumation) of the social-economic relations that make the tourist industry possible. Whether or not these heated exchanges constituted a "dialogue," they did nonetheless present a number of viewpoints as well as establish the need for open debate.

Television Coverage

Electronic media coverage included four television editorials, eight news spots, a cable talk show featuring the artists and an industry spokesperson, a National Public Radio report, and excerpts from a local public television special, *Super Week Report,* that had as one of its topics the poster controversy.[36]

Television coverage and editorials achieved a semblance of diverse viewpoints, through brief interviews gathered from the artists, COMBO representatives, mayoral officials, Tourism and Visitors' Bureau representatives, and the public. However, this semblance of multiple viewpoints was accomplished by deflecting the topics away from the social, economic, and political issues of undocumented labor in San Diego, focusing instead on the hotel-motel business, but never fully understanding or representing the tourist industry as a complex of interrelated businesses and services. In general, television coverage defended the city by downplaying the role of undocumented labor in the city's economy. The coverage typically took a "while it once may have been the case, it is no longer true" stance with regard to San Diego's dependency on undocumented workers. A similar disclaimer was taken by the tourist industry: "While they [undocumented workers] are found almost anywhere, no industry is dependent on them."[37] Such disclaimers were enhanced by temporally distancing the footage of INS raids in the hotel industry to the prereform era: 1986. In so doing, these broadcasts reinforced rather than explained or examined what was so threatening about the issues the poster raised.

The question of the poster's legality and the constitutional rights of the artists was a heated topic as well. Inquiry into legality, free speech, and freedom of expression was initiated by industry and city officials, not the artists. Television broadcasts often engaged in rhetorical shifts that allowed them to distinguish between freedom of speech and freedom of (artistic) expression. Paul Downey of the mayor's office commented in a television interview, "The First Amendment gives us the right to express opinions. The question is if taxpayers' dollars should be spent to promote a message many people find offensive and on public transportation."[38] Threats of censorship were invoked when two television editorials were delivered by station presidents who condemned the project and called for its immediate removal.[39]

Perhaps the most effective rhetorical strategy used by the news media (and industry advocates) involved positing a public that could not, or would not be able to, understand the poster. Repeatedly claiming that the poster was indecipherable, the media then granted themselves the authority to interpret and translate for the public. In this

way, they could set the terms of the debate around their own interpretation and ideological framework, rather than that of the artists.

The most engaging coverage consisted of forums modeled on debate and dialogue. One, a cable talk show, "Face to Face," assembled
the three artists and tourist industry spokesperson Al Reese. Reese's
position mirrored that of the mayor's office, defending the city and
insisting that *Welcome to America's Finest Tourist Plantation*'s accusations were incorrect and inappropriate; he removed himself and
the tourist industry from the issue. His primary fear was not "artistic
expression" but that the project was targeted toward the international media; he feared that the media's attention would tarnish the
city's reputation with a deceptive and misleading assertion. Dismiss-
ing the poster as unintelligible to the public, censorship was neither
an option nor an issue for Reese, as it was a harmless expression in
its indecipherability. Accordingly, it was the media that created the
controversy, not the art.

Despite Reese's indifference to the artists, "Face to Face" was the
television forum most responsive to the artists. The artists' stance
was firm: "People good enough to work here are good enough to
have full citizenship rights."[40] The artists' emphasis was to move away
from the media ploy of statistical inquiry to determine what exact
percentage of tourist labor is undocumented, asserting instead that
such number games inhibit the examination of the social structure
that makes the exploitation of undocumented workers possible. Avalos responded to Reese's scolding for spending the "city's money" by
shifting the focus to point out that the city-administered funding for
the project was generated primarily from nonresidents, visitors or
tourists, through hotel-motel occupancy taxes. This subtle yet telling
critique of the media exposed its coverage of the funding controversy
as misleading. As a further counterpoint, Avalos requested that Reese
divulge how much of the Tourism and Visitors' Bureau budget is supported by tax dollars—an amount totaling 74 percent.

Four newspaper columnists were assembled by the local PBS station in *Super Week Report* to review the stories of the week.[41] Here,
San Diego Tribune art critic Susan Freudenheim argued that the media and city officials' response to the project delivered a message that
"*art* is more frightening than the issues." Freudenheim then included
herself and media colleagues as active and crucial participants in the
project, concluding that the "message comes across as a collabora-

tive piece." This notion of the media's active collaboration was also implied by Channel 10 news commentator Michael Tuck. In his "Perspective," using some out-of-whack baseball analogy, he contended that in its coverage, the media gave fuel to the artists' cause and propelled their "little fluff pitch." Had the media ignored the project, the artists' "little slow-pitch of a sociopolitical message...would not have broken a Japanese window pane." Like others, Tuck concluded that the public would not understand the project and/or its inherent critiques without the media's assistance. In essence, although both Tuck and Freudenheim have differing opinions on the media's impact on the project, both clearly recognize the project for what it is, a discursive performance dependent upon public dialogue and the mass media to expand it into a collective performance.

Multimedia Installation

By design the poster was mobile; through media reproduction the image was further transported to doorsteps via newspaper accounts and into living rooms through local and national broadcasts. According to Hock, "the media coverage was not a means of evaluating the project but rather a component of the project."[42] As such, the artists subverted the very process by which mass-media or informational space constitutes public space. Compiling the mass-media coverage served to document the discursive elements of the performance for multifarious contexts. But, in compiling the television coverage, Hock did more than create an "objective" document. Instead, his careful editing of the material gives the video a cutting and humorous edge, juxtaposing clips in order to draw out an implied analysis of the media. The video then becomes a pedagogical tool, a sort of "How to Read the News."

By including excerpts from the opening scenes of the news broadcast itself and from commercials that followed the news segments on the art project, Hock is able to deconstruct the news stories by highlighting the similarity between media reportage techniques and promotion and advertisement. In one news story, for example, promotional snippets that market San Diego's tourist enterprise are included as part of the coverage: catchy jingles, grinning faces of happy tourist families, the bronzed bodies of a glowing San Diego, and stunning panoramas. In the video, the local newscasts are shown using the same technique and format in their opening sequence or trailer. In other instances, strategically unedited clips of commercials woven in between the newscasts draw attention to the commodification of Mexican and Latino/Chicano culture that coincided with the debate over "illegals" and public art funding. One of the commercial fragments — for "Tostada Howard" — features a nerdy Anglo male who sambas as he prepares his individualized Mexican entrée and expands his cultural horizons through consumption.

The video not only highlights the similar promotional techniques of the city, the local news, and the restaurant industry, but juxtaposes this image of consumption with the art project's much different call for dialogue and debate. As the project entered the institutionalized space of the museum, it developed yet another format — that of multimedia installation. The incorporation of video into an installation format enhances the concept of the fusion of informational and public spaces, revealing how the media have acquired and secured the function of public space in contemporary, urban U.S. society.

Two months after its premiere on San Diego's buses, the project had its first site-specific exhibition at LACE (Los Angeles Contemporary Exhibitions).[43] Since its debut at LACE, the project has traveled extensively across the nation and in Europe.[44] Occasionally the project traveled solely as a wall-mounted poster, and once as the book document.[45] The project's manifestations as installation have incorporated the poster and book, but more often than not as poster, book, *and* video. It is important to note, however, that the video has never been used to represent the project independent of the installation. Although the images originated as mass-media responses to a public event, their appropriation and exhibition necessarily took place within an art space. This model would be followed in all subsequent public art collaborations by Avalos, Hock, and Sisco.

Most recently, *Welcome to America's Finest Tourist Plantation* was exhibited with *America's Finest?*, San Diego Bus Bench Project (1990), by Deborah Small, Elizabeth Sisco, Scott Kessler, and Louis Hock. This multimedia installation of two collaborative projects traveled in *La Frontera/The Border* as "Untitled" (1991). In "Untitled," the bus poster was transformed into a reading table upon which the documentary book and video monitor are placed. Viewed from the *America's Finest?* bus bench, the closed-circuit monitor loops the video components for each project. By placing the spectator on the bus bench, the installation mimics the project's original public placement. As one is positioned on the bus bench, a theatrical relationship is established between the viewer and the videotape. Through minimalist aesthetics and placement, this theatricality yields to a pedagogically reoriented space. In effect, the installation transforms the space in which it is situated into a reading or research room for rigorous study—rather than for art appreciation.

The installation's emphasis on research acts serves to prevent aestheticization of the politics, processes, and effects inherent in the project. In the collaborators' statement for the exhibition *West/Art and the Law,* where the poster was exhibited without the media-installation documents, the artists reinforced the idea of process over object.

> Viewing the poster on a gallery wall the audience needs to be reminded that the art is to be found in the community's response and connection to the work. The art work was the catalyst for community discourse. It is hoped that the inclusion of the poster in this traveling exhibition will stimulate further discussion about the relationship between art and the law.[46]

There is understandable concern that the project will be misrepresented in the standard modernist techniques of museum display, exhibition, and curating, which attribute meaning on the basis of a work's visual qualities or objectness.

One of the most imaginative ways in which the project was situated was in the exhibition *Café Mestizo.* The exhibition itself was a site-specific installation that transformed a gallery space into an "ethnic" restaurant with the artist as the chef-waiter and the curator as manager.

Avalos authored the gallery/café menu, and takes on the additional role of maître d':

> Let's face it. The service is lousy and the fare is life threatening. But, if you feel like helping yourself, you can find a seat at the *Welcome to America's Finest Tourist Plantation* table, or at the *California Mission Daze* desk. Please be sure to read Cora's and Unca's story, *The Last of the Mohicans.* I know that you hate to read, so I've edited the *Cliff Notes* version for you. Then make your way to the back room, where something new is brewing.

Café Mestizo was a participatory, interactive exhibition installation that dialogued with American frontier literature, specifically the narrative of *The Last of the Mohicans.* By its inclusion, *Welcome to America's Finest Tourist Plantation* became a site within a metasite.

The nonironic consequence of *Welcome to America's Finest Tourist Plantation* museum "tour" as installation is that, although the documentation of the contestation are on view, the active involvement that the project originally incited does not register. Hock specifically cites as an example the *La Frontera/The Border* exhibition, which included *Welcome to America's Finest Tourist Plantation, America's Finest?*, and *Art Rebate*:

> [They] sat quite comfortably in the museum without a peep from anybody who was contesting *Art Rebate. Once the work entered the domain of the museum it was essentially removed from the public sphere.* It didn't have the voices of contention working with it. The museum is generally a sanctioned space, at least for work without explicitly sexual or religious content.[47]

Conclusion

Welcome to America's Finest Tourist Plantation is an aesthetic coalition of politics and production, performance and action, that bridges the diverse cultural communities addressed. In the public dialogues that the project catalyzed, the existing means of "imagining" community were engaged and often transformed, relying in the first instance (public art) on the mass media, and in the second (installation art) on video. As a public performance, *Welcome to America's Finest Tourist Plantation* reframed the media discourse on "illegal aliens" around questions of public space and how it set the terms for communal relations, cultural identities, class and cultural difference. As a multimedia installation, *Welcome to America's Finest Tourist Plantation* used video technology in order to appropriate mass-media representation, then resituated it as a pedagogical tool within art spaces. In this manner, video became part of a strategy to use the public art performance to subvert museum exhibition practices, though on much different terms than those of the original project. Whereas the bus poster incited (but could not control) mass-media discourse, the video installation used that discursive event for pedagogical or didactic purposes. As a consequence, as Hock noted, its success on this front was far less visible and "public" than the original poster. Nonetheless, in quite different ways, both projects provoked an examination of the historical and contemporary social relations that transpire and often collide at the U.S.-Mexico border.

Notes

I wish to thank the Museum of Modern Art for access to research materials. I would like to thank Lisa Cartwright, Robert Foster, Brian Goldfarb, and Karen Kosasa for commentary on earlier drafts. I am especially grateful to Gian Seminara for editorial assistance and critical insight.

1. Gloria Anzaldúa, *Borderlands/La Frontera: The New Mestiza* (San Francisco: Spinsters/Aunt Lute, 1987), 2–3.

2. Foreword, written in collaboration with Hugh Davies, director of the Museum of Contemporary Art, San Diego, in *La Frontera/The Border: Art about the Mexico/United States Border Experience* (San Diego: Centro Cultural de la Raza and Museum of Contemporary Art, 1993), ix.

3. Founding members: David Avalos, Victor Ochoa, Isaac Artenstein, Jude Eberhart, Sara-Jo Berman, Guillermo Gómez-Peña, and Michael Schnorr. For a detailed account and collection of projects, reviews, and membership, see *The Border Art Workshop, 1984–1991: A Continuing Documentation of Seven Years of Interdisciplinary Art Projects Surrounding Issues of the U.S.-Mexico Border* (San Diego: BAW/TAF, 1992).

4. Philip Brookman, "Conversations at *Café Mestizo*: The Public Art of David Avalos," in *Café Mestizo* (New York: Intar Gallery, 1989), 6–19.

5. David Avalos in Cylena Simonds, "Public Audit: An Interview with Elizabeth Sisco, Louis Hock, and David Avalos," *Afterimage* 22.1 (summer 1994): 8–11.

6. Edward L. Fike, reproduced in *The Border Art Workshop (BAW/TAF), 1984–1989: A Documentation of Five Years of Interdisciplinary Art Projects Dealing with U.S.-Mexico Border Issues,* ed. Jeff Kelley (San Diego: BAW/TAF, 1988), 41.

7. Susana Torruella Leval, "Border Watch: Local and Global," in *Green Acres: Neo-Colonialism in the U.S.,* ed. Christopher Scoates (St. Louis, Mo.: Washington University Gallery of Art, 1992), 60.

8. David Johnston, "Border Crossings Near Old Record; U.S. to Crack Down," *New York Times,* February 9, 1992, sec. 1, 1; excerpted in the *Green Acres* catalogue, 60.

9. A study released by the American Friends Service Committee on June 7, 1991, reported: "Of the 405 abuses reported, 73.4% (297) were committed by the U.S. Border Patrol, 9.6% (39) by the Immigration and Naturalization Service, 9.1% (37) by U.S. Customs, 5.9% (24) by local Law Enforcement Agencies (e.g., SD PD, National City PD, etc.), 1.5% (6) by Military (National Guard) and 0.5% (2) by 'others.' If we combine the Border Patrol with the INS, these two agencies alone committed 83% (336) of the total reported abuses." Of the victims, 31.3 percent were U.S. citizens and legal residents; 82.8 percent were Mexican American, which led the committee to conclude that "U.S. Citizens and legal residents suffered a disproportionately high number of abuses as compared to the other groups." Quoted in *The Border Art Workshop, 1984–1991,* 92.

10. Quoted in Kristen Aaboe, "Art in the Service of Equity" (October 1990); reprinted in *The Border Art Workshop, 1984–1991,* 48; my emphasis.

11. "Jeff Kelley on Border Art" in BAW/TAF, *Colón Colonizado,* Venice Biennale 1990, unnumbered pamphlet, available at the Museum of Modern Art Library. Originally published in *Art Forum* (March 1990): 23–25, under the title "A Border State of Art."

12. David Avalos, "A Wag Dogging a Tale/Un Meneo Perreando una Cola," *La Frontera/The Border,* 59–75, 74.

13. Reported in Susan Freudenheim, "Bus Art Scorns City's Smugness," *San Diego Tribune,* January 7, 1988, 1.

14. Project press release, "COMBO Public Art Project Takes to the Road," January 4, 1988: 2. Reproduced in Elizabeth Sisco, Louis Hock, and David Avalos, eds., *Welcome to America's Finest Tourist Plantation,* unnumbered book (archived in Museum of Modern Art Library) and distributed by Printed Matter.

15. David Avalos in Simonds, "Public Audit," 9.

16. Hillard Harper, *Los Angeles Times,* San Diego County Edition, January 7, 1988, 1.

17. The project also received funding from the National Endowment for the Arts and Art Matters. Additional support was provided by the La Jolla Museum of Contemporary Art.

18. Steve Schmidt, *San Diego Union,* January 7, 1988, A-1.

19. Channel 39, January 7, 1988.

20. In response to the thefts, the artists had the image commercially reproduced and made available to the public through a photo-duplicating service.

21. J. Thomas Baylor, "What City Needs Is an Art Dictator," *San Diego Tribune,* January 12, 1988, letter to the editor, B-6.

22. Avalos, "A Wag Dogging a Tale," 74.

23. Darcy DeMarco, *In These Times,* January 27–February 2, 1988.

24. Paul Krueger, "The Inside Story," *San Diego Reader,* June 23, 1988.

25. Project press release, January 4, 1988: 2.

26. Ibid.

27. Lewis Hock in Simonds, "Public Audit," 9.

28. These included the works of Vito Aconci and Christo, as well as Avalos's *San Diego Donkey Cart* installation outside the federal courthouse. For a national review of this installation, see "Sculpture Is Focus of Censorship Suit," *New York Times,* January 6, 1986, B1. See also David Avalos, "The Donkey Cart Caper: Some Thoughts on Socially Conscious Art in Anti-Social Public Space," *Community Murals* 11.3 (fall 1986): 14–15.

29. David B. Dreiman, "Bus Poster Artists Lack Sense, but Raise Important Questions," *La Jolla Light,* January 14, 1988. In contrast, a local Latina/o newspaper declared David Avalos as San Diego's miniversion of José Clement Orozco. See *La Prensa,* January 29, 1988, 4.

30. Open letter to Gerarld Warren, editor, and Helen Copley, owner of the *San Diego Union* from Ernesto Bustillos, La Unión del Barrio San Diego, published in *El Sol de San Diego,* February 11, 1988.

31. Mary M. Gustafson, *San Diego Union,* January 15, 1988, B-10.
32. Mrs. L. Fresquez, *San Diego Union,* January 21, 1988, B-6.
33. Jesus R. Cabezuela, *San Diego Union,* January 21, 1988, B-6.
34. Sheila Daniels, "No Class," *San Diego Union,* January 26, 1988, B-6.
35. *San Diego Union,* February 1, 1988, B-8.
36. Some of the headlines in news spots were "Poster Art Worth a 1,000 Angry Words" (Channel 10, afternoon, January 7, 1988), "Great Art Debate ... Comes at Worst Time" (Channel 39, January 7, 1988), and concluding remarks such as "may have bitten the hand that feeds them" (Channel 10, evening, January 7, 1988).
37. "Face To Face," Southwest Cable, Cox Cable, January 26, 1988.
38. Channel 39, January 7, 1988.
39. KFMB stations editorial TV8, AM and FM, delivered by Robert L. Myers, president and general manager, "Offensive Poster," January 12, 1988; and KCST-TV editorial broadcast by Bill Fox, president and general manager, "Super Goof," January 12, 1988.
40. Avalos, "A Wag Dogging a Tale," 74.
41. San Diego Channel 15, KPBS, January 20, 1988.
42. Hock in Simonds, "Public Audit," 9.
43. *RE: Placement/LACE* 10 Year Anniversary Exhibition.
44. *Le Démon des Anges — 16 Artistes Chicanos autour de Los Angeles,* curated by Pascal Letellier, traveled throughout Sweden, Spain, and France between May 1989 and December 1990. The exhibition was organized by Halle du Centre de Recherche pour le Développement Culturel, Nantes, France.
45. *By Any Means Necessary: Photocopier Artist's Books and the Politics of Accessible Printing Technologies,* Printed Matter Bookstore at Dia Center for the Arts, New York City, 1992.
46. Artists' statement for the exhibition *West/Art and the Law,* 1988–89.
47. Hock in Simonds, "Public Audit," 11.

Mass Media, Site Specificity, and the U.S.-Mexico Border: Guillermo Gómez-Peña's *Border Brujo* (1988, 1990)

Claire F. Fox

All major metropoli have been fully *borderized*. In fact, there are no longer visible cultural differences between Manhattan, Montreal, Washington, Los Angeles or Mexico City. They all look like downtown Tijuana on a Saturday night.

Guillermo Gómez-Peña[1]

From San Diego/Tijuana to "The New World (B)order"

Today, "the border" and "border crossing" are commonly used critical metaphors among multicultural and postmodernist artists and writers. According to Chon Noriega, however, these terms were first employed by Chicano and Mexican scholars in the 1960s and 1970s who referred to the experience of undocumented workers from Mexico crossing to the United States.[2] Since then, in Chicano arts and letters, the Borderlands has replaced Aztlán as the metaphor of choice in order to designate a communal space.[3] But even though the U.S.-Mexico border retains a shadowy presence in the usage of these terms, the border that is currently in vogue in the United States, both among Chicano scholars and those theorists working on other cultural differences, is rarely site-specific.[4] Rather, it is invoked as a marker of hybrid or liminal subjectivities, such as those that would be experienced by persons who negotiate among multiple cultural, linguistic, racial, or sexual systems throughout the course of their lives. When the border *is* spatialized in these theories, that space is almost always universal. "The Third World having been collapsed into the First," as the argument goes, the border is now to be found in any metropolis — wherever poor, displaced, ethnic, immigrant, or sexual minority populations collide with the "hegemonic" population, which is usually understood to consist of middle- and upper-class WASPs.[5]

228

Border Brujo (1990), a video directed and produced by Isaac Artenstein and featuring performance artist Guillermo Gómez-Peña, is one signpost of this theoretical shift from the site-specific to the global border, which in this case was also facilitated by the documentation and distribution of a live performance by means of video technology. The character and performance showcased in the video were created in 1988, while Gómez-Peña was a founding member of the San Diego/Tijuana-based Border Art Workshop/Taller de Arte Fronterizo (BAW/TAF). During that period of the mid- to late 1980s, U.S.-Mexico border issues were a central theme of Gómez-Peña's collaborative work. The release of the video version of *Border Brujo* roughly coincides with the artist's decision to de-emphasize the U.S.-Mexico border region, while nevertheless retaining the border as a metaphor to address general issues of cultural imperialism. Although Gómez-Peña has increasingly unmoored his border from the "transfrontier metropolis" of San Diego/Tijuana, viewers of *Border Brujo* will note that Gómez-Peña did not accomplish this by purging the border from his work, but rather by vastly expanding the border's potential meanings.[6] In this respect, Gómez-Peña's post-BAW/TAF work tends to resemble the "global border consciousness" characteristic of postmodern critical theory I just outlined.

This "expanded" U.S.-Mexico border, ironically, is not unlike the border that blanketed mainstream news media prior to the congressional vote on the North American Free Trade Agreement (NAFTA) in 1993. In *Border Brujo* and subsequent work, Gómez-Peña, like the news media, grapples with ways to broach the subject of "North American identity" in light of globalization's putative threat to national identities. In the United States and Mexico, national news and documentary sources constantly represent the border as a synecdoche of the nations it divides;[7] that is, developments on the border are perceived to be symptomatic of the overall status of U.S.-Mexican relations, and the importance of border events is presented from the point of view of national actors rather than local inhabitants. NAFTA's advocates and detractors appropriated this way of seeing the border in order to cast it as "the future" or "the cutting edge" of what is to occur throughout the North American continent, post-treaty. The last segment of *Border Brujo*, entitled "Hacia un Futuro Post-Colombino/Towards a Post-Columbian Future," foreshadows the recent trend in Gómez-Peña's work to represent the future of North America, in which a totalizing regime called the "New World (B)order" is opposed by progressive advocates of a "Free Art Agreement."[8]

At the close of *Border Brujo,* the Brujo addresses his spectators, whom he imagines to be scattered in distinct cities around the world, while he, in contrast, speaks from "the border" itself: "I am here in prison, right in the center of the wound, right in the crack of the two countries." Gómez-Peña's notion of the border as both a definite place and a "speaking position" evolved through his earlier work with BAW/TAF. BAW/TAF was, and still is, a group of Mexican, Anglo, and Chicano artists who engaged in collaborative multimedia and interactive arts projects about the U.S.-Mexico border region.[9] BAW/TAF artists were both present-minded and oppositional, insofar as their work responded critically to border issues such as immigration, human rights violations, and racism, and they were utopian in that they asked their audiences to "imagine a world in which this international boundary has been erased."[10] Site specificity—not just in terms of installation, but also of audience address and thematic issues—became a guiding principle of the group. Jeff Kelley aptly described BAW/TAF's project as an "art of place":

> An art of place is concerned less with the phenomenal and geological aspects of a place than with the cultural, historical, ethnic, linguistic, political, and mythological dimensions of a site. To some degree, of course, site and place are matters of interchangeable perception. Thus, we see site-specific art transformed into a place particular practice which represents the domestication and/or socialization of the '70s site, and defines approaches to art-making in which a place, a condition, or an occasion is seen and worked as the materials of human or social exchange. A place is not merely a medium of art, but also its contents.[11]

For Gómez-Peña, as for other BAW/TAF members, the border was always much more than a line demarcating national space. Emphasizing the social and cultural dimensions of the U.S.-Mexico border over topographical ones immediately gave "border consciousness" a certain mobility. As a phenomenological category, the border was something that people carried within themselves, in addition to being an external factor that structured people's perceptions.

Gómez-Peña's endeavors in performance art prior to the foundation of BAW/TAF (e.g., with Poyesis Genética,)[12] suggest that he was already working through ideas about liminal subjectivities before he attached them to the San Diego/Tijuana region. Emphasizing subjectivity as predominant over social geography, however, facilitated his later expansion of the border to encompass "the world." This shift is clearly evident in several essays he published in U.S. arts media during the period immediately prior to and following his break with BAW/ TAF. In his 1988 essay "Documented/Undocumented," for example, Gómez-Peña referred to the process of world "borderization,"[13] but he also privileged the deterritorialized perspective of the (U.S.-Mexico) border artist, which allowed him/her to act as facilitator of intercultural dialogue among ethnic groups. In his 1989 "The Multicultural Paradigm," Gómez-Peña extended the role of "border-crosser" to include all North Americans and all readers of his work:

> Today, if there is a dominant culture, it is border culture. And those who still haven't crossed a border will do it very soon. All Americans (from the vast continent of America) were, are or will be border crossers. "All Mexicans," says Tomás Ybarra-Frausto, "are potential Chicanos." As you read this text, you are crossing a border yourself.[14]

Gómez-Peña's next step was to make the border global. "From Artmageddon to Gringostroika," an essay published in 1991 in *High Performance,* found Gómez-Peña speaking of many geographical borders, from the Americas to the Iron Curtain. But geographical borders were all but upstaged in this essay by a new, temporal threshold. He wrote, "We stand equi-distant from utopia and Armageddon, with one foot on each side of the border, and our art and thought reflect this condition."[15] This apocalyptic look toward the next millennium, signified by a vertiginous time-space compression, has become a major theme of Gómez-Peña's post-BAW/TAF work.

Border Brujo, the Video

The release of the video version of *Border Brujo* in 1990 registers a shift in the artist's thinking about borders in relation to place, but one can see that this shift occurred as a result of a logical progression in his theorization of the border, rather than as a radical departure from it. In some ways the video is an anomalous conclusion to Gómez-Peña's involvement with BAW/TAF, for it was released just as the collective was in the throes of reorganization and shortly before Gómez-Peña was to denounce border art altogether in several highly publicized articles in 1991.[16] Artenstein, a Mexican-born filmmaker well known for his movie *Break of Dawn* (1988), about the rise of Spanish-language radio in Los Angeles, produced and directed *Border Brujo* after Gómez-Peña successfully toured the performance for two years (1988–90) in North America and Europe.[17]

The publicity for *Border Brujo* describes it as a performance "in which Guillermo Gómez-Peña transforms himself into fifteen different personas to exorcise the demons of dominant cultures. In English, Spanish, Spanglish, Ingleñol and Náhuatl-bicameral." People familiar with BAW/TAF's earlier work would note immediate continuities of theme, costume, iconography, and sets between *Border Brujo* and previous BAW/TAF projects. This was also not the first time that a BAW/TAF member had used video to record a performance.[18] For the most part, *Border Brujo* privileges documentation of Gómez-Peña's performance over experimentation with the video medium itself. Its camera movement and editing are relatively nonintrusive; other than alternation between medium shots and close-ups of Gómez-Peña, the camera only cuts for brief moments to extreme close-ups of the props that comprise the altar/set.[19] This simplicity of form, a characteristic of Gómez-Peña's performances during this period, has two antecedents, as he explains it. The first is from the performance art monologue movement of the late 1980s, associated with Eric Bogosian, Spalding Gray, Karen Finley, and Tim Miller, in which these artists sought to "rescue the spoken word"[20] from pyrotechnic spectacles. The second comes from a respect for the lack of access to technology under which many Chicano, Mexican, African American, and Native American artists must operate.[21]

In one portion of the video, the editing is uncharacteristically foregrounded, so as to highlight Gómez-Peña's "borderline" perspective. In the "Casa de Cambio" sequence, Gómez-Peña plays a Tijuana barker who advertises the various transformations of personal identity available to those who dare to cross the border.[22] The video rapidly cuts from camera positions to the left and right of Gómez-Peña, establishing an imaginary line that actually bisects his body. This technique represents a drastic departure from the way that Hollywood editing has used an imaginary borderline in narratives set in the U.S.-Mexico border region—namely, as a structuring device that segregates, rather than integrates, opposing elements of "cultural identities."

From its first intertitle, which asserts that "Language is the border," *Border Brujo* preoccupies itself with the perceptual and perspectival

Scene from *Border Brujo,* written and performed by Gillermo Gómez-Peña, produced and directed by Isaac Artenstein. (Photo courtesy of Max Aguilera Hellweg.)

definition of the border that I have associated with BAW/TAF. The Brujo incarnates a mosaic of parodic characters including a *mojado,* a *cholo,* a Texas redneck, and a transvestite, who are differentiated from one another by variations in costume, body movement, and speech. The idea of alternation among personae, spaces, and languages is in fact so integral to the performance that it raises the issue of whether Gómez-Peña would really like to see borders eliminated, or whether his work is indeed dependent upon borders to uphold the opposi-tions that he critiques. Gómez-Peña is not out to destroy differences so much as he attempts to effect abrupt collisions among various "subject positions," and to compel his audience to perform a similar kind of "border crossing." The gestures of religiosity and self-purification that punctuate *Border Brujo*'s segments, which include lighting candles, burning sage, the bell ringing of transubstantiation, and, most memorably, drinking from a bottle of Clairol Herbal Essence shampoo, also beg the question of just whose "dominant culture" demons Gómez-Peña is exorcising—his own or the audience's? Rather than adopting such a thematic in order to denounce the pervasiveness of U.S. mass media and commercialism, in the name of preserving some "authentic" national or local culture, Gómez-Peña instead turns this exorcism into an indictment of a monocultural point of view on the part of his implied audience. The Brujo's ritualistic gestures punctuate his entry into a liminal state in which the notion of an essential or stable identity is thrown into question.

The Brujo not only speaks in Spanish and English, but also in tongues, suggesting that the spectator has access only to a fragmentary view of the complex, hallucinatory reality to which the Brujo is privy. This disproportionate relation of knowledge and power between the Brujo and his audience is established from the very beginning of the video when the Brujo says, "Allow me the privilege of reorganizing your thoughts," and it is sustained throughout the video's often claustrophobic framing and Gómez-Peña's frequent eye contact with the camera. As he mutates from character to character, the Brujo speaks as many "I"'s, while frequently leveling accusations at a "you" who is seemingly stable, both in terms of location and identity. Very often this "you" would appear to be a white male cultural imperialist:

"I speak therefore you misinterpret me";
"I am in Tijuana, you are in San Diego";
"I exist, therefore you misunderstand me";
"How ironic, mister, I represent you, yet you don't represent me."

Self-reflexive comments scattered throughout the video also imply that this "you" constitutes part of the video's audience. At one point the Brujo chants, "If it wasn't for the fact that I wrote this text on a Macintosh and I shot my rehearsals with a Sony 8, I would really fulfill your expectations."

Grant Kester identifies Gómez-Peña's relationship to his audience, characterized by polemical statements and direct address, as typical

of what he terms the "rant" performance artists who came to prominence in U.S. "alternative arts" scene of the mid-1980s and early
1990s. Writing of Gómez-Peña, Karen Finley, and other artists, Kester
remarks that the "implied viewer ... is often a mythical father figure
conjured up out of the artists [sic] imagination to be shouted at, at-
tacked, radicalized, or otherwise transformed by the work of the performance."[23] According to Kester, "rant" performances turn upon a
tacit play between this fantasy audience composed of racist, sexist,
homophobic, white men to the "real" audience, drawn from the enlightened habitués of the "alternative arts" scene. The former camp,
of course, would be quite unlikely to attend such performances in
the first place, which leaves the "alternative arts" audience to engage
in a double identification:

> The audience of a performance by Finley or a Kruger installation knows
> that it isn't the "real" target of the outraged pronouncements on sex-
> ism or racial oppression. Rather they consume the work simultane-
> ously in the first person and the third person; imagining themselves as
> the intended viewer while at the same moment reassuring themselves
> of their own ideological superiority to this point of view.[24]

Thus, haranguing a phantom audience permits Gómez-Peña to enter
a bond of complicity with an audience of informed spectators. The
fact that this confrontational mode of address becomes a sort of in-
joke on those who are not actually present for the performance is
also suggested in Gómez-Peña's critical writings on multiculturalism
and cultural studies in the United States, where he subtly defines his
intended audience by who it is not.[25] Chicano nationalists are another
group besides conservative Anglos who are absented from Gómez-
Peña's implied audience. In *Border Brujo,* they are not directly addressed, but rather more delicately isolated from the imaginary audience: "They say I talk to Gringos; they say I wasn't born in East L.A.;
they say I left the committee by choice; they say I promote negative
stereotypes of my people." By eliminating these two "extremes" —
that is, Anglo and Latino separatists — Gómez-Peña rhetorically constructs a "middle" of sorts, which consists of those who, in his estimation, would be most receptive to hybrid cultural identities and "border
crossing."

Border Brujo's transformation from performance to video was
marked by additional features, however, which also suggest a shift in
the way Gómez-Peña conceived of his mass-media audience. For one

thing, in the earlier in situ versions of the piece, Gómez-Peña inter-
acted with the audience during the performance. He would shine a
flashlight on members of the audience and interrogate them in a parody of a Border Patrol agent, for example, and, at the end of the performance, he collected items from various members of the audience,
which he added to his altar/set for future performances or buried on
the U.S.-Mexico border. The video, on the other hand, does not portray an audience, nor does the camera ever cut to give a point-of-view
shot from Gómez-Peña's perspective. In the live versions, Gómez-Peña
often changed portions of his script to include the name of the place
where he was performing, and other site-specific information. Three
published versions of the script,[26] for example, include a great deal
of material about California, and more specifically about San Diego/
Tijuana. In the video version, on the other hand, there are fewer references to the location of the performance, and at one point Gómez-
Peña refers to "Sushi," the performance gallery that supported the
video's production. Finally, and perhaps most importantly, in the video
version Gómez-Peña deleted almost all of the large chunks of the script
that were in Spanish, as well as some of the more politically radical
critiques in English.[27]

It is worth remarking that many of these deleted portions of the
script became outtakes from the *Border Brujo* video, which were eventually recut into another much shorter piece, entitled *Son of Border
Crisis: Seven Video Poems* (1990). The latter video is sort of an alter
ego to the former. It contains more material in Spanish, and because
its roughly fifteen minutes of length are broken up into seven segments, the pace is aphoristic rather than sermonic. It even opens with
an exterior shot of Gómez-Peña in front of Sushi, pitching the show
to potential spectators through a megaphone. The second video was
released largely because of demand from Chicano and Latino film
festivals in the United States, and also from festivals in Latin America and Spain, to have a sample of Gómez-Peña and Artenstein's project that would fit in well with the time constraints of short subject
programming.[28]

"Art of Place" and the Exportation of Culture

As Gómez-Peña was moving toward a solo career based in
New York and gaining access to a broader "alternative arts" audience

through this video, he was simultaneously attacking the co-optation of the border art movement by major museums and galleries.[29] A key complaint on his part was that BAW/TAF, which had in some sense brought border art to the attention of the national arts community, was now being ignored by that same community. He criticized the La Jolla Museum of Contemporary Art (now the Museum of Contemporary Art, San Diego) for raising half a million dollars in order to "bring big names from out of town" for a four-year border art project.[30] Perhaps for Gómez-Peña, being "deterritorialized" from the U.S.-Mexico border region itself provided him with the rationale for abandoning an "art of place" in favor of the more general "New World (B)order." The border arts project to which Gómez-Peña referred was known as *Dos Ciudades/Two Cities,* and it culminated in 1993–94 with an exhibition called *La Frontera/The Border: Art about the Mexico/United States Border Experience,* jointly organized by San Diego's Centro Cultural de la Raza and the Museum of Contemporary Art. The Centro Cultural, founded in 1970 in the wake of the Chicano movement, had housed and sponsored BAW/TAF during Gómez-Peña's tenure with the group, and it had long been positioned as "alternative," in terms of both funding and constituency, to the "mainstream" Museum of Contemporary Art. Although the two institutions did achieve a rapprochement during the period of the *Dos Ciudades/Two Cities* project, Gómez-Peña was among several artists who declined to have their work included in the *La Frontera/The Border* show.[31]

In interviews, Gómez-Peña now refers to himself as a "cross-cultural diplomat,"[32] and one notes in his recent work an ever-increasing faith in the political effectivity of art and artists. BAW/TAF used to conceive of its artistic projects as working in concert with other activities such as journalism, education, and political activism; that is, art projects were but one aspect of the group's site-specific work. In a recent essay, in contrast, Gómez-Peña argues, following a prophecy of Joseph Beuys from the 1970s, that art became politics and politics became art by the second half of the 1980s.[33] He proceeds to create a continuum of "Performance Politics or Political Performance Art," under which he assembles many artists and activists in the United States and Latin America, based on their common use of performative strategies to achieve political goals.[34] To this new breed of grassroots artist-politician, Gómez-Peña contrasts certain conservative forces who have on several occasions appropriated performance art and progressive popular cultural icons in order to bolster state power.

The idea of the performance artist's power transcending that of the "nonaesthetic" political activist is identified by Gómez-Peña in several sources with a trip he took to the Soviet Far East as part of a binational human rights commission, where, he realized, "The artist as intercultural diplomat is able to cross many borders that political activists are unable to."[35] The idea is consistent with a trend in the work of many of the postmodern theorists, such as Henry Giroux, Iain Chambers, and D. Emily Hicks (the latter also a former BAW/TAF member and ex-wife of Gómez-Peña), who highlight certain professions as those that facilitate "border crossing." In texts by the latter theorists, "cultural workers," identified as artists, writers, educators, architects, and lawyers, among others, are portrayed as those having "primacy"[36] in processes of social transformation, because their jobs give them a unique position from which to "dialogue" with "Others."[37]

There are other reasons, however, that may account for the relative ease of such "border crossings" by professionals and intellectuals. The U.S.-Mexico border has rarely presented itself as a hindrance to artists, intellectuals, and tourists, for example, but then again these crossings are not demographically representative of other large-scale flows of border traffic that currently characterize the region, such as those of undocumented workers northward and U.S. capital southward. The de facto emergence of the metropolis as the site of "border crossings" in the work of the postmodern theorists, in the wake of allegedly collapsed national boundaries, has in a sense made it possible for intellectuals to cross borders while remaining in the same place, and simply by carrying out the duties of their profession.

Gómez-Peña's periodization of the art/politics merger in the late 1980s is concomitant with the emergence of an oppositional "artist/administrator" figure that Kester has identified as characteristic of the "alternative arts" sphere in the United States during the same period.[38] Artists whose work was deemed controversial or obscene by the National Endowment for the Arts and other government-supported arts funding agencies during the Reagan-Bush era were often publicized as victims of censorship, stemming from racism, sexism, and homophobia. On a thematic level, these artists linked their own victimization at the hands of the right wing to other forms of oppression such as poverty and homelessness. According to Kester, many "alternative" artists who gained notoriety during this period, among them several in the performance art monologue movement, based their work on a declared solidarity between artist and "the oppressed," and positioned themselves as spokespeople, if not as members, of their avowed constituencies. Gómez-Peña's self-presentation as a shaman in performances such as *Border Brujo* has clearly been read by academics, journalists, and others as that of a spokesperson for all "border-crossers." His descriptions of "border consciousness," for example, appear repeatedly in a recent article by an anthropologist about a transborder migration circuit of undocumented workers between Aguililla, Mexico, and Redwood City, California, but at no point in the article does the author quote his own informants regarding their daily life and consciousness.[39]

Gómez-Peña eloquently argues through *Border Brujo* that globalization, immigration, and mass media, among other factors, have effectively made it impossible to think of North American cities as culturally homogeneous. He does not elaborate, however, the fact that the deleterious effects of global economic restructuring are felt in some geographical areas more than others. Although art is produced on the U.S.-Mexico border under much more comfortable conditions than TV sets and other consumer products, it too is subject to exportation, as Gómez-Peña asserted when he repudiated the genre of border art. When an "art of place" finds itself decontextualized and distributed for mass consumption on a national or international level, then it becomes all the more important to differentiate between two "borderized" cities like Matamoros and New York; for often the distinction is not just spatial and national, but also one between production on the one hand, and consumption and distribution on the other. Gómez-Peña's globalized border overlooks the specificity of regions such as the U.S.-Mexico border, where nation-states continue to enforce differences within urban space. Making the border the global metaphor of an oppositional discourse also falls prey to facile appropriation by an equally globalizing U.S. nationalist expansionism. A recent headline in the *New York Times,* proclaiming northern Mexico to be "America's Newest Industrial Belt" and referring to Mexico as the "fifty-first state" in terms of the U.S. economy, illustrates how easily the border can be assimilated by U.S. industrial interests. There still *is* a border between "us" and "them," according to the logic of the *Times* article; it has simply been displaced southward.[40]

Locally based art movements linked to activist agendas, like that practiced by BAW/TAF, are still extremely rare on the U.S.-Mexico border, but meanwhile, "border art" flourishes in national arts media. One cannot see this phenomenon in terms of a simplistic opposition of site specificity to mass media, as though experimentation with mass media immediately signified inauthenticity and co-optation. Indeed, many of the grassroots organizations currently engaged in cross-border organizing employ communications strategies similar to those used on a smaller scale by Gómez-Peña, including video, fax, and E-mail.[41] In contrast to professional border artists, however, the grass-roots organizations do not necessarily isolate their videos, installations, and the like from the rest of their activities, as "aesthetic" artifacts. Perhaps, then, the key emphasis in promoting an "art of place" should be less on the formal or thematic qualities of a given work and rather on the supposition that performers and spectators alike are all actors in a common social struggle that takes place once the performance or video is over.

Notes

I would like to thank Dudley Andrew, Charles Hale, Tom Lewis, Kathleen Newman, Chon Noriega, and Andrew Ross for their valuable suggestions as I was writing this essay. Portions of this essay were delivered at the 16th Annual Whitney Symposium on American Art and Culture, May 1993.

    1. Guillermo Gómez-Peña, "The New World (B)order," *High Performance* 15.2–3 (summer–fall 1992): 60.
    2. Chon A. Noriega, "This Is Not a Border," *Spectator* 13.1 (fall 1992): 6.
    3. See, for example, Héctor Calderón and José David Saldívar, eds., *Criticism in the Borderlands: Studies in Chicano Literature, Culture, and Ideology* (Durham, N.C.: Duke University Press, 1991), and Gloria Anzaldúa, *Borderlands/La Frontera: The New Mestiza* (San Francisco: Spinsters/Aunt Lute, 1987).
    4. The following is a partial list of recent scholarly work that features the border metaphor: D. Emily Hicks, *Border Writing: The Multidimensional Text,* Theory and History of Literature 80 (Minneapolis: University of Minnesota Press, 1991); Iain Chambers, *Border Dialogues: Journeys in Postmodernity* (London: Routledge, 1990); Henry Giroux, *Border Crossings: Cultural Workers and the Politics of Education* (New York: Routledge, 1992); Trinh T. Minh-ha, *When the Moon Waxes Red: Representation, Gender and Cultural Politics* (New York: Routledge, 1991); Maggie Humm, *Border Traffic: Strategies of Contemporary Women Writers* (New York: St. Martin's Press, 1991); Renato Rosaldo, *Culture and Truth: The Remaking of Social Analysis*

(Boston: Beacon Press, 1989). The border metaphor also appears in semiotic and poststructuralist critical theory. See Jacques Derrida's "Living On: Border Lines," trans. James Hulbert, in Harold Bloom et al., *Deconstruction and Criticism* (New York: Seabury Press, 1979), 75–176; and, Jacques Derrida, "The Parergon," *October* 9 (summer 1979): 3–41. See also Thomas G. Pavel, *Fictional Worlds* (Cambridge: Harvard University Press, 1986).

5. Giroux writes, for example, "In the postmodern age, the boundaries that once held back diversity, otherness, and difference, whether in domestic ghettoes or through national borders policed by customs officials, have begun to break down. The Eurocentric center can no longer absorb or contain the culture of the Other as something that is threatening and dangerous. As Renato Rosaldo points out, 'the Third World has imploded into the metropolis. Even the conservative national politics of containment, designed to shield "us" from "them," betray the impossibility of maintaining hermetically sealed cultures.'" (*Border Crossings,* 57–58).

6. The term "transfrontier metropolis" is used by Lawrence A. Herzog in his book *Where North Meets South: Cities, Space, and Politics on the U.S.-Mexico Border* (Austin: Center for Mexican American Studies, University of Texas at Austin, 1990). See also Lawrence Herzog, ed., *Planning the International Border Metropolis,* Monograph 19 (La Jolla, Calif.: Center for United States-Mexico Studies, 1986).

7. This is an idea that I develop in my doctoral dissertation. I begin my study of this pattern of spectatorship with the U.S. Punitive Expedition in Mexico during the Mexican Revolution.

8. Guillermo Gómez-Peña, "The New World Border: Prophecies for the End of the Century," *The Drama Review: The Journal of Performance Studies* 38.1 (T 141) (spring 1994): 119–142; and Guillermo Gómez-Peña, "The Free Art Agreement *El Tratado de Libre Cultura,*" *High Performance* 16.3 (fall 1993): 58–63.

9. BAW/TAF's membership varied throughout the years 1984–89, although a core of founding members remained. In 1989 many new artists joined the collective, and only one original member stayed. Gómez-Peña discusses the dissolution of the group's core members in "A Binational Performance Pilgrimage," *The Drama Review* 35:3 (fall 1991): 39–40, and "Death on the Border: A Eulogy to Border Art," *High Performance* 14.1 (spring 1991): 8–9.

10. Guillermo Gómez-Peña and Jeff Kelley, eds., *The Border Art Workshop: Documentation of Five Years of Interdisciplinary Art Projects Dealing with U.S.-Mexico Border Issues, 1984–1989* (New York: Artists Space; La Jolla, Calif.: Museum of Contemporary Art, 1989), 20.

11. Ibid., 18–19.

12. Gómez-Peña, "A Binational Performance Pilgrimage," 27–32.

13. Guillermo Gómez-Peña, "Documented/Undocumented," *The Graywolf Annual Five: Multi-Cultural Literacy,* Rick Simonson and Scott Walker, eds. (Saint Paul, Minn.: Graywolf Press, 1988), 130.

14. Guillermo Gómez-Peña, "The Multicultural Paradigm: An Open Letter to the National Arts Community," *High Performance* 12.3 (fall 1989): 21.

15. Guillermo Gómez-Peña, "From Art-mageddon to Gringostroika," *High Performance* 14.3 (fall 1991): 21.

16. See note 9. BAW/TAF responded to Gómez-Peña in a manuscript entitled "Errata Historica" (unpublished, December 1991). Recently, David Avalos, founder of BAW/TAF, published his own recollection of the early BAW/TAF years, which responds to many of Gómez-Peña's claims about the demise of border art: "A Wag Dogging a Tale/Un Meneo Perreando una Cola," *La Frontera/ The Border: Art about the Mexico/United States Border Experience* (San Diego: Centro Cultural de la Raza and Museum of Contemporary Art, 1993): 52–93.

17. For more background on the production of *Border Brujo* see Gómez-Peña, "A Binational Performance Pilgrimage," 40–42; and Jason Weiss, "An Interview with Guillermo Gómez-Peña," *Review: Latin American Literature and Arts* 45 (July–December 1991): 8–13.

18. Other examples include *Border Realities* (1986), *I Couldn't Reveal My Identity* (1988), and *Backyard to Backyard* (1988).

19. *Border Brujo*'s altar/set also emphasizes the cultural aesthetic enacted by the Brujo throughout his performance. A citation of the home altars honoring the dead that are especially associated with the observation of El día de los muertos (Day of the Dead) in southern Mexico, Gómez-Peña's altar also quotes the transformations that this form has undergone in recent decades by Chicano *altaristas*. Perhaps most notable among this latter group of artists is Amalia Mesa-Bains, who is known for introducing icons of vernacular and mass culture to her altars, and who has also highlighted the altar's capacity to signify hope, rejuvenation, and communal memory. It is the use of the vernacular and mass culture that Gómez-Peña exploits to its most impressive effect in *Border Brujo*'s set. The *títere, calavera,* and other border souvenirs displayed alongside emblems of U.S. consumption, such as a humongous plastic hamburger, wryly point to the commodification of Mexican "folk art," but these juxtapositions also assume an audience that, though spatially dispersed, is united in its thorough saturation by mass-media images of Mexican and U.S. culture. See Amalia Mesa-Bains, "Artist's Statement," *Imagine* 3.1–2 (summer–winter 1986): 141–42.

20. Weiss, "An Interview with Guillermo Gómez-Peña," 12.

21. Speaking of the U.S. Latino arts community, Gómez-Peña wrote: "We come from a culture which doesn't venerate irreflexively the principle of newness, or better said, a culture which considers that an apolitical reverence for originality carries dangerous ideological implications. What we consider 'avant-garde' or 'original' generally deals with extra-artistic concerns and precisely because of this, it never seems 'experimental enough' for the art world" (Gómez-Peña and Kelley, eds., *The Border Art Workshop,* 57. See also his piece in Lilly Wei, "On Nationality: 13 Artists," *Art in America* (September 1991): 159.

22. The character of Border Brujo was "born" at a BAW/TAF installation entitled "Casa de Cambio." See Shifra Goldman's review essay of the installation in Gómez-Peña and Kelley, eds., *The Border Art Workshop,* 8–9.

23. Grant Kester, "Rhetorical Questions: The Alternative Arts Sector and the Imaginary Public," *Afterimage* (January 1993): 14.

24. Ibid.

25. See Gómez-Peña, "The Multicultural Paradigm," for example.

26. Gómez-Peña "A Binational Performance Pilgrimage," 49–66; Guillermo Gómez-Peña, "Border Brujo," in *Being América: Essays on Art, Literature, and Identity from Latin America*, ed. Rachel Weiss and Alan West (Fredonia, N.Y.: White Pine, 1991), 194–236; and Guillermo Gómez-Peña, "Border Brujo," in *Warrior for Gringostroika* (Saint Paul, Minn.: Graywolf Press, 1993), 75–95. The script was often modified in performance.

27. For example, he deleted the voice of a member of the Latin American oligarchy, a Central American war victim, and many of the transvestite's lines. He also left out a section about affirmative action and a critique of Chicano nationalism and radicalism at the end of the performance, which greatly changes the tone of the ending.

28. I am grateful to Chon Noriega for providing background information about *Son of Border Crisis*.

29. Gómez-Peña subsequently relocated to Los Angeles in 1993.

30. Gómez-Peña, "Death on the Border," 9.

31. For more information, see Avalos, "A Wag Dogging a Tale," as well as the Foreword by Larry T. Baza and Hugh M. Davies, ix–xvi, and Madeleine Grynsztejn, "La Frontera/The Border: Art about the Mexico/United States Border Experience," 23–58, all from *La Frontera/The Border*.

32. Weiss, "An Interview with Guillermo Gómez-Peña," 11; see also Gómez-Peña, "The New World Border," 63.

33. Gómez-Peña, "From Art-mageddon to Gringostroika," 24.

34. Ibid.

35. Gómez-Peña, "A Binational Performance Pilgrimage," 43; Weiss, "An Interview with Guillermo Gómez-Peña," 10.

36. Giroux, *Border Crossings*, 224.

37. On the importance of "dialogue" with "Others," see Chambers, *Border Dialogues*, 50, 76, 104–5; Giroux, *Border Crossings*, 28–35. On reading and writing as "border crossing," see Hicks, *Border Writing*, "Introduction: Border Writing as Deterritorialization," xxiii–xxxi. See also Gómez-Peña, "The Multicultural Paradigm," 21; and, his quote of Carlos Fuentes, "A Binational Performance Pilgrimage," 44.

38. Kester, "Rhetorical Questions," 13.

39. Roger Rouse, "Mexican Migration in the Social Space of Postmodernism," *Diaspora* 1.1 (spring 1991): 8–23.

40. Louis Uchitelle, "America's Newest Industrial Belt," *New York Times*, March 21, 1993.

41. Many of those organizations are listed in Ricardo Hernández and Edith Sánchez, eds., *Cross-Border Links* (Albuquerque, N.M.: Inter-Hemispheric Education Resource Center, 1992).

The Forbidden Kiss: Raúl Ferrera-Balanquet and Enrique Novelo-Cascante's *Mérida Proscrita* (1990)

Christopher Ortiz

In 1986 Raúl Ferrera-Balanquet, who emigrated to the United States as a part of what has been called the Mariel boat rescue operation in the early 1980s, formed the Latino Midwest Video Collective as a workshop and support network so that Latino media artists studying at the University of Iowa could share ideas and resources.[1] The collective's manifesto, authored by Ferrera-Balanquet, explains that "the textual construction of some of our videos ... takes as a point of departure the socio-political, psycho-sexual and economic set of relations in Latino culture, allowing us as Latino videomakers to critique elements of the world in general as well as those relations that work specifically within our culture" (1991: 149). Although not all of the collective's work deals with issues of sexuality, a large number of videos explore issues that, as Cherríe Moraga notes in "A Long Line of Vendidas," have been looked at as separate: "Sexuality, race, and sex have usually been presented in contradiction to each other, rather than as part and parcel of a complex web of personal and political identity and oppression" (1983: 109). In comparison to Latina lesbians and other gay men of color, Latino gay men have been surprisingly silent in articulating the political and personal meaning of their cultural and sexual identities. Exploring these complex webs of identity and oppression, Ferrera-Balanquet is only one of a few Latino media artists to deal specifically with gay identity *and* cultural identity as the formal and aesthetic concerns of his work.

In "Reflections on Latin American Gay Representation," Ferrera-Balanquet addresses the issue of how such work is exhibited and received: "Today, with the recent trends of Multiculturalism, our works are categorized by our ethnicity and separated from other audiovisual texts. As 'other' we are seen as anthropological objects. Our audio-

244

visual texts are categorized and displaced in a theoretical discourse which pretends to keep its lost hierarchic position" (1992: 3). This process can be seen in the reception of Ferrera-Balanquet's own work in gay and lesbian film and video festivals. For instance, *We Are Hablando* (1991, 10 minutes) was shown as part of "An Evening of Latino/ a Video" at the 9th Annual Gay and Lesbian International Film and Video Festival in Los Angeles. In the review of *Mérida Proscrita* within the 1990 San Francisco Lesbian and Gay Film Festival, Warren Sonbert situates the film against an exotic backdrop, calling the video "a moody glance ... at some heady passions between two macho boys around anachronistically scenic south of the border settings" (no page number).

Rather than being interpreted as works that can offer a more complex and politically conscious view of the communities they represent, the work of artists like Ferrera-Balanquet is placed in a traditional documentary and ethnographic mode; that is, it becomes a document that purports to provide "truth" about gay identity in another cultural context rather than work that can question ethnic and racial stereotypes and that, more often than not, works critically within its own set of artistic and cultural practices. As Frances Negrón-Muntaner points out in this volume, "The disavowal of Latino gay and lesbian cultural production is also reproduced at the level of film scholarship, where queer theorists and feminists alike continue to ignore its existence and specific aesthetic strategies." This disavowal, both at the level of film scholarship and in its public reception, is often caused by the inability of the non-Latino spectator to read the multiple codes — cultural, historical, political, linguistic — at work in these texts.[2] For Ferrera-Balanquet, this includes his experience as a sexual exile from Cuba. This essay will analyze *Mérida Proscrita* as a means to understanding its critical and artistic relation to movements such as the New Latin American Cinema and gay and lesbian liberation as well as the multiple (mis)readings offered by their various and different codes. As the United States becomes more multiethnic and multilingual, there is an increasing need to analyze the ways in which we (mis)understand each other.

Mala Noche versus *Mérida Proscrita*

Shot in Mérida, the capital of the Mexican state of Yucatán, *Mérida Proscrita* (1990, 8 minutes, 8mm film edited on video) traces the relationship between a young man and a hustler. The narrative revolves around the issue of a kiss. The young man, credited as the "Lover," wants the "Hustler" to kiss him. Although the video does not explicitly state the reason for his reluctance, within the context of Mexican culture the Hustler would not want to kiss the Lover because to do so would be to admit his homosexual desire. At the end of the video, the Lover tells the Hustler that he no longer can tolerate the situation and is going to end their relationship, whereupon the Hustler asks for one more chance. Rather than offer a pat ending, the video suggests that changing attitudes and social roles requires ongoing dialogue. The video's open-ended conclusion is a narrative strategy employed in a number of films from the New Latin American Cinema, a relationship I will explore in a later section. First, I will analyze the way in which Ferrera-Balanquet positions *Mérida Proscrita* within the context of gay and lesbian liberation discourse in the United States.

In speaking of *Mérida Proscrita*, Ferrera-Balanquet has used touted gay filmmaker Gus Van Sant's *Mala Noche* as an example of the way in which "we [as Latino gay men] are seen from the outside.... Again, gay Latino sexuality is constructed here based on the notion of maleness" (1992). For Ferrera-Balanquet, this comparison makes his own work into "a subversive gesture which denounces the appropriation of our representation by white gay image makers and critics."[3] As an oppositional strategy, a number of Latino gay works deconstruct the white gay male as the universal subject of gay identity through the formal and aesthetic exploration of culturally specific gay identities. Although not an explicit dynamic in the representational strategies of the video, Ferrera-Balanquet's oppositional stance operates in a similar fashion at the contextual level. By taking an oppositional stance in relation to a well-known and popular gay film, Ferrera-Balanquet is acknowledging that a non-Latino gay audience will also be viewing his work, and that, in fact, such an audience constitutes the very basis for his "subversive gesture." But, as I will expand upon later, such a stance is not an end point, but rather becomes the precondition for an international gay and lesbian solidarity organized around cultural difference.

Van Sant's *Mala Noche* is about a young working-class Anglo-American who works in a liquor store and befriends two young Mexican immigrants working illegally in the United States. The young man becomes enamored of one of the Mexicans, who is heterosexual, and attempts to woo him unsuccessfully. The other Mexican immigrant is apparently bisexual and expresses his interest in the protagonist, who continues to be enamored of the other. The film ends tragically with the death of the desired young Mexican and the continued existential malaise of the Anglo protagonist from whose point of view the film is narrated. The tragic death, of course, fits into the doomed white/nonwhite love narrative of countless Hollywood films.

Like *Mérida Proscrita, Mala Noche* deals with the question of frustrated desire; however, Van Sant's film frames the young Mexican immigrants as outsiders and exotic Others to a gay identity and community. In commenting on this, Ferrera-Balanquet refers to the way in which dominant gay culture in the United States has often coded Latino gay men as straight trade—heterosexual men who can be picked up for a same-sex encounter. Albeit beautifully photographed and moving (if the spectator chooses to take the point of view offered by the film), Van Sant's *Mala Noche* perpetuates dominant U.S. stereotypes about Latino men, wherein Mexican/Latino machismo becomes symptomatic of the underdevelopment of Latin American societies and U.S. Latino communities, and vice versa.

Of Machismo and Men

Challenging this causal linkage, *Mérida Proscrita* examines machismo as a particular way in which power is exercised in gender and sexual relations rather than being *only* symptomatic of underdevelopment. In Latin American/Latino culture, the sex act, rather than the object choice, are looked at as indicative of one's position in the power hierarchy. The *pasivo,* the penetrated one (or, the *chingado* in Octavio Paz's formulation) is the *efeminado* or effeminate one. The *activo,* or penetrator, remains a man; he is not homosexual. Both sociocultural and economic, the ambivalent position of the Hustler—as the one who seems to take the role of *activo* in the relationship and as someone who sells his body for a living—becomes the site in which power takes shape in class and race discourses that are themselves at the foundation of the construction of sexuality and sexual difference. *Mérida Proscrita* not only charts this relationship, but also excavates the social and political reality in which the relationship takes place.

In depicting a social landscape, the video juxtaposes shots of construction workers engaged in labor, of the Mexican flag atop a pole in the central plaza, and of activity in front of the main cathedral. These shots occur throughout the video and often serve as transitions in the narrative. In the beginning of the video, the two characters narrate the story of their relationship. Their images, shown in freeze frame with voice-over narration, are alternated with the shots of these various scenes. Thus, the story of the young men is one that is embedded in a particular system of discursive and economic structures. The flag and the cathedral represent the church and the state as two central institutions that have shaped Latin American social reality and history. The construction workers represent the economic sphere—the alienated labor and surplus value of capitalism—and the way in which it is constituted in racial difference. In this part of Mexico, Indians do most of the menial jobs such as construction. The church, the state, and the system of production keep everyone in his or her assigned place. The video represents gay sexuality with this social backdrop and through the juxtaposition of images makes an implicit equation between racially defined labor and homosexuality/prostitution.

By critiquing machismo in the context of a sexual and emotional relationship between two men, Ferrera-Balanquet is addressing a social and political dynamic at a structural level. The church and the state possess real power to regulate behavior; and the Other, whether racial (Indian) or sexual (prostitute or homosexual), is a category both institutions use to maintain their power. For the Hustler, then, the kiss implies a breakdown in the barrier between subject and object. If the Hustler kisses the young man, he will have allowed their relationship to move beyond the active/passive dichotomy *and* an economic exchange; thus, he will have relinquished the power to control the Lover that those prescribed roles give him—as man, as commodity.

Although the Lover is a student, his rented room indicates that he is from a lower-middle-class or working-class background. Thus, the fact that the Lover is a student does not indicate economic or class inequality between him and the Hustler. Rather than class rise, the Lover's occupation acts as a metaphor for the process of *concientización* or coming-to-consciousness, but only if education is viewed against the backdrop of the film's class analysis and Ferrera-Balanquet's own educational experience in the Cuban Revolution. But if the Lover's status as a student remains *within* the system of production analyzed by the video, then the Lover's status actually reemphasizes the way in which the church and the state shape and regulate behavior. The traditional role of education has been to reproduce the dominant ideology, which allows the state to maintain the status quo. At the same time that the Lover resists the gender roles prescribed for him, he is also implicated in the same system that produces those roles. *Mérida Proscrita* cannot be expected to solve this double bind, but by raising the issue it reveals the way in which the transformation of culture and of human relations is a slow and difficult process.

In the video, the Lover and the Hustler relate their histories in similar voice-over narrations. Their individual stories are framed as a dialectic of desire that constructs the text. The Hustler's sense of identity is upset as the Lover voices his own demands and needs. The Lover says, "Why don't you kiss me? I am tired of your refusal. I am tired of waiting." The Hustler responds, "Give me a chance. I need more time." Their dialogue is punctuated by scenes of Mérida and by their individual narrations of who they are and how they met. The dialogue and story center on the Lover's refusal to play the role of *pasivo* or *efeminado* and on the Hustler's fear of committing to a gay relationship. The Lover's refusal is also the text's refusal of the way in which Latino gay desire has been proscribed by Latino culture and defined by the dominant "ethnographic" modes of North American and European representation.

This reading raises questions about the function of the Indian laborers within the text. Throughout the video, the Hustler is juxtaposed with the construction workers. Does this imply equivalence — as I have suggested — between their labors and his in terms of exploitation, alienation, marginalization? After all, the image of the laborers punctuates important moments of the video, such as when the two young men are engaged in dialogue or the Hustler is seen plying his trade. Or do the Indian workers provide a metaphor for gay liberation that is congruent with *concientización*, but perpetuates the workers' silence? In digging foundations and constructing buildings, the construction workers provide a metaphor for the video's self-reflexivity as well as an archaeology of gay desire. In this vein, consciousness of internalized homophobia and of one's sexual desire requires an "excavation" of one's individual and cultural history. The answer is by no means a simple one. Despite the formal equivalence between laborers and the gay couple, there is also a telling difference in the first section: the still images of the gay speaking subjects contrasts with the moving images of the silent Indian laborers. The answer requires that we consider Ferrera-Balanquet's cultural and political influences in the New Latin American Cinema.

The New Latin American Cinema

New Latin American Cinema is a film movement that emerges out of the struggles for liberation in Latin America during the 1960s and 1970s. As Zuzana M. Pick notes in *The New Latin American Cinema: A Continental Project,* "The unfolding of the New Latin American Cinema — as an ideological project and a cinematographic practice — is the result of its capacity to conceptualize the social and political impact of cinema as a cultural practice" (3). Pick concludes, "The movement has explored marginalized aspects of social experience with the goal of empowering groups excluded from official representations" (97). After the revolution, Cuba offered financial support, technical education, and ideological inspiration for many filmmakers in Latin America (including Chicanos).

As a member of the first generation of children raised in the Cuban Revolution, Ferrera-Balanquet was exposed on a regular basis to New Latin American Cinema. If viewed from within this political and cinematic context, the image of the construction workers (some of whom are bricklayers) alludes to the Colombian documentary film *Los chircales* (1972; The brickmakers), directed by Jorge Silva and Marta Rodríguez. The documentary deals with a poor community of indigenous brickmakers on the outskirts of Bogotá. Commenting on the film, Pick says, "Confirmed by the omniscient voice-over narration, the impoverished conditions under which the Tunjuelito community manufactures bricks invalidate the democratic modernity of state discourse" (45). Ferrera-Balanquet's equivalence between indigenous labor, on the one hand, and the homosexual and the prostitute, on the other, allows him to link the issue of sexuality and sexual difference explored in *Mérida Proscrita* to the social and political project of the New Latin American Cinema. Read in this way, gay identity becomes an extension of that project and its concern with critiquing official versions of history and presenting the histories of groups that have been silenced and marginalized.

The fact that Ferrera-Balanquet chose to make his work in Mérida has both a personal and a historical significance, which returns the film to that image of the construction workers and the larger project of the New Latin American Cinema. In an unpublished manuscript, he explains, "The position of insider/outsider which I experience when I am there [Mérida] has helped to heal the longing for my Caribbean island and to understand the sexual politics of the Latin American culture" (1992: 1). What he describes is a condition of exile, a condition that many of the directors of the New Latin American Cinema have experienced: Miguel Littín, Raúl Ruiz, Valeria Sarmiento, Fernando Solanas. What differentiates his exile from that of some of these well-known directors, most of whom fled dictatorships, is not political identification per se, but rather that he fled because his sexual orientation marginalized him within socialism. As he says in his notes, "I ... questioned why I was expelled from school every time my sexual preference became known" (ibid.). As Ferrera-Balanquet discovered from his own experience, state discourses — whatever their color — attempt to use the Other as a means of maintaining political control and power. Ironically, during the years of the Mexican Revolution, many of Mérida's leading citizens, who were members of Yucatán's landowning upper class, went to Havana in exile. They fled because of their failed armed attempt to form their own republic in order not to have to obey the agrarian and social reforms that Mexico City began to impose on their medieval economic structure. A half-century later, Mérida (along with Miami) became an important point of arrival for many Cuban exiles to Mexico after the Cuban Revolution.

These histories become the basis for the video's effort to link private and public space. The two men's dialogue in the bedroom becomes linked to public space through crosscuts with the various scenes described earlier. The men cannot relegate their relationship to the private sphere in order to be free of church and state, especially insofar as these institutions use the family as a discursive trope and an administrative structure. By placing the narrative in Mérida with its historical relation to Cuba and its problematic relation to the Mexican Revolution of 1910, Ferrera-Balanquet reveals the discourses of nationalism and state-church control as intimately related to the regulation of sexuality, gender, and family. He provides a way in which

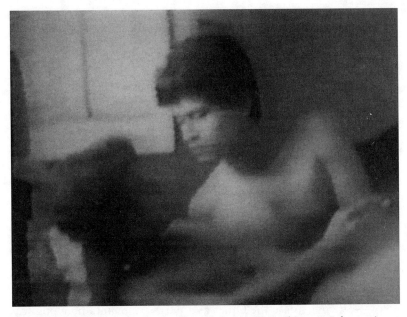

The Student and the Hustler discuss their relationship in Raúl Ferrera Balanquet's *Mérida Proscrita.*

the homophobia and discrimination of both the Cuban Revolution and nonsocialist countries such as Mexico can be understood in a larger historical context.

Ferrera-Balanquet's critique is in keeping with the New Latin American Cinema's intellectual and political project of *concientización.* The New Latin American Cinema wanted to provide audiences with analytical tools and a historical understanding of their condition so that they could take action and empower themselves. Although many filmmakers believed that they should first address themselves to their local, regional, or national audience, they also needed to build solidarity with other groups in struggle throughout the hemisphere. They believed that *concientización* could best be achieved through using the codes and conventions already at work in a particular culture. Some of those codes would only be understood by a local or regional audience and others would be understood by both national and international audiences. This, then, becomes the process by which Ferrera-Balanquet speaks from the position of cultural and intercultural specificity (as Cuban, Latin American, and exile) to U.S.-based and international audiences. In the next section I will analyze some of the aesthetic and narrative strategies that Ferrera-Balanquet uses in the video.

Generic Borrowings

Mérida Proscrita's narrative is foregrounded by codes borrowed from other generic forms central to gay/Latino culture such as opera, the melodramatic structure of the *telenovela,* and the bolero. Although he does not explicitly acknowledge New Latin American Cinema, Ferrera-Balanquet's understanding of the Latino Midwest Video Collective's critical practice is similar to that described in such documents as Julio García Espinosa's "For an Imperfect Cinema." In the manifesto of the collective, Ferrera-Balanquet says that its critical practice is

> an aesthetic practice which developed out of an understanding that the conventional distinctions between reality and fiction and their related genres such as fictional dramatic narrative, social documentary and surrealism no longer sufficiently represent the Latin American experience; it is a hybrid form of all three of these categories which when integrated and even blurred comes much closer to approximating the complexity of our lives. (1991: 149)

Ferrera-Balanquet's video is not the substitution of one fetish for another — for example, a white universal subject of gay identity for a Latino one — but rather the exploration of sexual identity within Latin American aesthetic-artistic practices and sociopolitical contexts. He comes out, as it were, within the terms of the New Latin American Cinema — but for multiple audiences. Thus, the video is neither separatist nor nationalist, but rather acknowledges shared codes and images within international gay culture as well as the differences.

At one point in the video, the Lover seeks advice from a friend, who then proceeds to introduce the closing encounter between the two young men with an aria from Puccini's *La Rondine,* "Che Il Bel Sogno Di Doretta." Doretta's song mirrors the action of the video as well as the words of the bolero, "Historia de un amor," which frames the video. In Puccini's *La Rondine,* the protagonist, Magda, sings the aria in the first act when she meet her true love. The aria tells the story of Doretta, who one day is seen by a king who then pursues her. Doretta, a courtesan, rejects the advances of the king because she is in love with a poor student. (Likewise, in *Mérida Proscrita*, the Lover is a student, and the Hustler is a prostitute.) Doretta says that one must defend one's love and one's heart. Just as Doretta sacrifices social position and riches for the love of her poor student, Magda too sacrifices her true love, Ruggero. He wishes to marry Magda, but she abandons him, because she feels that her previous life as a courtesan has made her unfit to marry him.

In the last section of *Mérida Proscrita,* the friend roams about in an internal courtyard wearing a sheetlike covering that serves as faux cape while the aria soars to a melodramatic climax. His performance serves as a prologue to the final encounter between the two young men. At the end of the friend's performance, a group of women and children is seen on a balcony while we hear auditorium clapping on the sound track. This clapping is a humorous moment and at the same time reemphasizes the performative nature of gender roles.[4] As an intermediate space, the courtyard connects the seemingly private discourse of intimate relationships (women and children/family) with the public sphere (men/work). The video reemphasizes this connection by following the courtyard and bedroom scene with the closing shots of the two young men walking in the public park as they continue their dialogue.

If the video emphasizes the performative nature of gender, it must nonetheless define subversion in relationship to these same roles. For this dual critique and alternative, the video turns to genre with its recurrent locations, narrative structures, character types, and audience expectations. Thus, for example, the operatic aria is not only a quotation of the melodramatic distantiation devices used in Cuban films such as *Lucía,* but also reflects the way musical forms such as the bolero and the opera have been appropriated in specific and often subversive ways by gay culture.[5] Melodrama often ends with the ambivalent or uneasy restoration of the status quo, which has been disturbed by some event, usually within the family structure. Operas often end tragically with the death of the woman. In opera, *telenovelas,* and boleros, the melodrama is characterized by an excess — improbable situations, exaggerated behavior, and the suspension of belief — which can result in the conventions of realism being exposed and questioned.[6] In writing about camp, Susan Sontag and Wayne Koestenbaum note that gay artists and spectators use melodramatic excess both as

The "melodramatic" climax to *Mérida Proscrita.*

a form of identification and as a distantiation device, which allows access to the social critique operating in the text. Michel Foucault provides insight into this phenomenon when he observes that hetero- sexual literature can be characterized by the mating ritual or the con- quest of the object of desire, but that gay literature has been charac- terized by the remembrance of the object of desire after the sexual and emotional connection (19). In other words, gay relationships are marked by a loss that comes from the prohibitions and repression of a heterosexist society; thus, the memory is often what remains of a sexual and emotional experience.

Carlos Almarán's bolero, "Historia de un amor," sung by Pedro Infante, is used as the framing music for *Mérida Proscrita.*[7] What is interesting about the lyrics is that they follow the pattern Foucault identifies of remembrance after the fact. As in the actual dialogue of the Lover and the Hustler, the bolero is sung by a first-person narra- tor to an absent second person, for, as the bolero tells the listener, the addressee is no longer present. Because a first person addresses an absent second person, the bolero also becomes gender-neutral (as is the case with many famous boleros), providing a musical space of iden- tification for gay men's relationships, albeit one based on loss. Ferrera-

Balanquet, however, changes the bolero's narrational pattern by having both the Lover and the Hustler engage in a two-way dialogue. The two protagonists' dialogue breaks the traditional dynamic of power/powerlessness inherent in many boleros (the same one inherent in the *pasivo/activo* dichotomy). The dialogue between the two protagonists acts as a distantiation device that critiques the bolero's narrative conventions, even as it also draws upon its melodramatic effect.

The main verse of the bolero, "This is the story of a love unlike any other / that made me understand everything / that is good and that is bad," is rather ironic and biting in the context of the video's social and political critique. The video pokes fun at heterosexual society by literalizing the first line of the verse and making it a story about two gay men. By using two gay men as the protagonists and thus making it truly "unlike any other love" for a heterosexual audience, the video also focuses attention on how often the bolero itself as a genre is trite and repetitious, thus exposing its conventions and tropes. Unrequited love and its variations are all alike. In terms of the video's political critique, the last two lines of the main verse continue the ironic gesture of the first. By subverting gender expectations and exposing the heterosexism of the bolero as well as its long-suffering acceptance of the status quo, the video leads the spectator to think about those structures that create oppression and discrimination.

If *Mérida Proscrita* were a traditional melodrama that followed uncritically the narrative patterns of a bolero or a *telenovela,* the issue of the forbidden kiss and the problem of a committed gay relationship would probably be solved by having the Hustler meet a young woman who would redeem him and save him from a life of prostitution. The Lover would fade into the background or be punished for his desire to break the socially constructed norm of *pasivo/activo*. Ferrera-Balanquet does not follow a heterosexual story line, but neither does he simply make a gay version in which the two lovers overcome their obstacles and find eternal love. Rather, the familiar melodramatic narrative of love becomes one of the means by which the artist critiques the social roles and restrictions that have defined gay existence in a Latino cultural context. By using artistic codes and re-creating a cultural and social dynamic—*pasivo/activo*—familiar to gay audiences, Ferrera-Balanquet politicizes this dynamic and inserts it into both an international and a culturally specific struggle for gay rights. The dual address itself finds symbolic expression in the video's open-ended conclusion. The two lovers have not resolved the issue of the kiss, but they have begun to communicate and to express their fears and desire ... in public.

Notes

1. Raúl Ferrera-Balanquet has BGS (1987) and MFA (1992) degrees from the Fine Arts program at the University of Iowa, where he formed the collective with Latino videomakers such as Joseph Castel and Poly Chang-Barrera. The collective lasted until 1991, when its members began to graduate and leave the area. Although members shared ideas and helped each other in various capacities in their respective productions, each received authorial credit for his or her work. Ferrera-Balanquet currently teaches video production at Columbia College in Chicago. Although the collaboration of Enrique Novelo-Cascante, a gay activist and theater director who resides in Mérida, is acknowledged in the production of the video, this essay discusses *Mérida Proscita* in the context of Ferrera-Balanquet's overall work as a video artist. Ferrera-Balanquet has actively discussed and theorized his own video production in essays such as "The Videotapes of the Latino Midwest Video Collective: A Manifesto," *Cinematograph* 4 (1991): 149–52, and "Sites of Struggle: Exile and Migration in the Cuban-exile Audiovisual Discourse," *FELIX: A Journal of Media Arts and Communication* 2.1 (1995): 46–55. For a discussion of Cuban media artists in exile, see Ana López, "The 'Other' Island: Cuban Cinema in Exile," *Jump Cut* 38 (June 1993): 51–59, also included in this volume. For a general discussion of Latino/a video artists, see Christopher Ortiz, "Ni de aquí, ni de allá:/Latinos/as in the Imagination of Southern California," *FELIX: A Journal of Media Arts and Communication* 2.1 (1995): 171–76.

2. For a discussion of spectatorship in terms of linguistic codes, see Carl Gutiérrez-Jones, "Legislating Languages: *The Ballad of Gregorio Cortez* and the English Language Amendment," in *Chicanos and Film: Representation and Resistance,* ed. Chon A. Noriega (Minneapolis: University of Minnesota Press, 1992): 195–206.

3. For a discussion of Latino representation and sexuality, see Christopher Ortiz, "Hot and Spicy: Representation of Chicano/Latino men in gay pornography," *Jump Cut* 39 (June 1994): 83–90; and Tomás Almaguer, "A Cartography of Desire: Chicano Gay Men," *differences: A Journal of Feminist Cultural Studies* 3.2 (1991): 75–100.

4. On the performativity of gender, see Judith Butler, *Gender Trouble: Feminism and the Subversion of Identity* (New York: Routledge, 1990); Marjorie Garber, *Vested Interests: Cross-Dressing and Cultural Anxiety* (New York: Routledge, 1992); and Eve Kosofsky Sedgwick, "Queer Performativity," *GLQ: A Journal of Lesbian and Gay Studies* 1.1 (spring 1993).

5. Humberto Solas's *Lucía* (Cuba, 1968) is an excellent example of how New Latin American Cinema has deconstructed genres such as melodrama

in order to reveal ideological and social contradictions. For example, part 1 of *Lucía* takes place in 1898 and uses excessively romantic music during the protagonist's reverie, often prompting laughter that breaks audience identification with the melodramatic narrative. See Negrón-Muntaner's discussion in this volume on the use of the bolero and other popular forms in Latino gay and lesbian film/video.

   6. See Ana M. López, "The Melodrama in Latin America: Films, Telenovelas, and the Currency of a Popular Form," *Wide Angle* 7.3 (1985): 5–13; reprinted in *Imitations of Life: A Reader on Film & Television Melodrama*, ed. Marcia Landy (Detroit, Mich.: Wayne State University Press, 1991): 596–606.

   7. "Historia de un amor" (A love story) is narrated by someone who has lost the love of his life, though the lyrics do not specify why this is the case. I have included below the main verses with my own translation. There are variations on this bolero.

> Ya no estás más a mi lado, corazón.
> En el alma solo tengo soledad.
> Y si ya no puedo verte, ¿por qué Dios
> me hizo quererte para hacerme sufrir más?

> Siempre fuiste la razón de mi existir.
> Al dejarte no podía vivir más.
> En tus besos encontraba el amor que
> brincaba el calor de tu pasión.

> Es la historia de un amor como no habrá igual
> que me hizo comprender todo el bien, todo el mal.

> You are no longer at my side, dear one.
> In my soul I only have loneliness.
> And if I am no longer able to see you, why did God
> make me love you only to make me suffer more?

> You were always the reason for my being.
> Upon leaving you I could no longer live.
> In your kisses I found the love that
> emanated from the heat of your passion.

> This is the story of a love unlike any other
> that made me understand everything
> that is good and that is bad.

Although the bolero serves as the framing device, it is not subtitled within the video. To a gay international audience familiar with Almodóvar films such as *La ley del deseo* (Law of desire), the bolero's exact content may not be understood, but its use as an emotive device and textual gloss would be recognizable. The full meaning and function of the bolero, however, is reserved for a Spanish-speaking audience. My analysis of the bolero's function is directed at both audiences.

References

Ferrera-Balanquet, Raúl. "Reflections on Latin American Gay Representation: Contextualizing *Mérida Proscrita.*" Unpublished manuscript, 1992.
———. "Sites of Struggle: Exile and Migration in the Cuban-exile Audiovisual Discourse," *FELIX: A Journal of Media Arts and Communication* 2.1 (1995): 46–55.
———. "The Videotapes of the Latino Midwest Video Collective: A Manifesto." *Cinematograph* 4 (1991): 149–52.
Foucault, Michel. "Sexual Choice, Sexual Act: Interview with Michel Foucault." *Salmagundi* (fall 1982–winter 1983): 10–23.
García Espinosa, Julio. "For an Imperfect Cinema." In *Twenty-Five Years of the New Latin American Cinema,* ed. Michael Chanan. London: British Film Institute, 1983: 28–33.
Koestenbaum, Wayne. *The Queen's Throat: Opera, Homosexuality, and the Mystery of Desire.* New York: Poseidon Press, 1993.
Moraga, Cherríe. *Loving in the War Years: lo que nunca pasó por sus labios.* Boston: South End Press, 1983.
Paz, Octavio. *El laberinto de la soledad.* México: Fondo de Cultura Económica, 1993; 1st ed., 1950.
Pick, Zuzana M. *The New Latin American Cinema: A Continental Project.* Austin: University of Texas Press, 1993.
Sonbert, Warren. "Film Fest: A Valentine for Tom." *Bay Area Reporter,* June 14, 1990.
Sontag, Susan. "Notes on Camp." In *The Susan Sontag Reader.* New York: Vintage Books, 1983.

(Re)constructing Chicana, Mestiza Representation: Frances Salomé España's *Spitfire* (1991)

Carmen Huaco-Nuzum

Values and beliefs that were once held to be universal and transcendental have indeed been relativized and historicized; but far from being the end of the world, this predicament has brought a whole range of experiences and identities into view for the first time.[1]

Kobena Mercer's discussion of the dissolution of "fixed" identities may well serve to introduce the politicized videos of Frances Salomé España, which examine chicana, mestiza identity politics and the reconstruction of female desire.[2] Mercer adds that the archaeological view of identity and subjectivity of the 1960s and 1970s is no longer desirable or plausible because this view fails to take into account the contradictions and conflicts that "arise in the relations within and between the various movements, agents and actors in contemporary forms of democratic antagonism."[3] Like Mercer, other cultural theorists of color (Stuart Hall, Rosa Linda Fregoso, Norma Alarcón, Tomás Ibarra Frausto, Homi Bhabha, and others) have also pointed out the demise of fixed identities in a postmodern world that is continually interpellating, mediating, and appropriating cultural resources from any given group or community. In *The Bronze Screen,* Rosa Linda Fregoso clarifies this distinction between two models of identity politics, separating the archaeological model, dependent on uncovering the colonial experience and rediscovery of an "authentic" self "fixed" in time and space, from the postmodern view that relies on process, production, and the continual change of the subject's identity as she/he is mediated by time, culture, experience, and history.[4]

Born in the United States of Mexican parents, España produces feminist, sociopolitical videos that force us—as chicanas, mexicanas, and latinas—to confront a history of disenfranchised patriarchal colonization in an effort to rediscover and retrieve important parts of our his-

260

tory. España's preoccupation with the rediscovery of the historical past in connection to the present is demonstrated in *Spitfire* (1991), which incorporates both the archaeological and the postmodern aspects of cultural identity politics. (The five-minute video is complete, except for "abstracted" or manipulated readings of contemporary Chicana poetry on the sound track.) However, España is not concerned with uncovering a "fixed essence" of a core chicana mestiza identity, but rather with showing how both models of cultural identity qualify each other.[5]

Spitfire introduces the notions of time, memory, history, and desire through image manipulation to represent chicana, mestiza identity as a process of continual reevaluation and change. España's earlier work wrestles with similar contextual preoccupations. *El Espejo/The Mirror* (1991) draws on the personal *testimonio* to examine how, through the cultural redefinition of the past and present, one can uncover a new form of chicana, mestiza subjectivity. In *Anima* (1989), ancestral rituals are investigated through formal stylistic techniques to convey how ritual (El día de los muertos, or Day of the Dead) can be mobilized to reaffirm chicana, mestiza identity.[6] Both the interest in reconceptualizing time (temporal and historical) and the remobilization of ritual reappear in *Spitfire*.

España utilizes the term "reinvention" to describe new ways of "imaging" the relationship between chicana, mestiza representation and pleasure.[7] In *Spitfire*, a "reinvented" pleasure emerges from the positioning of the chicana, mestiza as chronicler of her own story and from the reinterpretation of her historical connection to the past. España characterizes *Spitfire* as a "work" that attempts to define "who we are as subjects": "What we know are male interpretations of the native woman's legacy. We need to draw from our own history to redefine ourselves."[8] This is precisely what *Spitfire* achieves: a new form of chicana, mestiza iconography that subverts popular sexualized female images. Toward this end, the video juxtaposes "live" shots of a young chicana, mestiza with still images of la Virgen de Guadalupe and Mesoamerican female deities. Initially, the images of the chicana, mestiza are depicted through slow motion, extreme close-ups, and manipulation of the color (which enhances the curves and outlines of her body and face), while the Virgin and the deities are abstracted through pixelization into color blocks. After a series of alternations between these sets of images—against suspenseful and, at times, ominous music—*Spitfire* ends with an image of the chicana, mestiza slightly abstracted through pixelization and staring into the camera. This conflation of images suggests the compression of time and space, and positions the chicana, mestiza in a continual state of flux between a historical past and a self-redefining present.

In "Minimal Selves," Stuart Hall writes that "looking at new conceptions of identity requires us also to look at re-definitions of the forms of politics ... the politics of difference, the politics of self-reflexivity, a politics that is open to contingency but still able to act."[9] Through the politics of self-reflexivity, España examines how a new postmodern chicana, mestiza might emerge from a collective social-historical awareness of her subaltern divided subject position to patriarchy and white culture. Gloria Anzaldúa attributes the fragmentation of the chicana, mestiza subject to internalized oppression, patriarchal appropriation, and reinterpretation of cultural female archetypal symbols that inscribe and impose values on the chicana, mestiza.[10] The resident of Anzaldúa's "Borderlands," then, straddles the fence between two cultures as she demands her turn to speak. For the chicana, mestiza, this liminal space can be both privileged and unprivileged, providing her with more objectivity and self-reflection; however, her journey is also more precarious because she must dodge the dominant cultural bullets that threaten to erase her difference. *Spitfire* contextualizes mexicana archetypal images with those of a contemporary chicana, mestiza, encouraging the chicana, mestiza spectator to get in touch with the autochthonous past that also constitutes part of her present identity. In the end, both Anzaldúa and España call for the chicana, mestiza to retrieve mexicana cultural symbols of resistance that will help her (re)invent and (re)define identity in her own terms.

How Hollywood Turned Her into a Spitfire

As Alvina Quintana informs us, the post-sixties feminist chicana was trapped in a yet more liminal space, "resisting not one but two oppositional discourses which denied her visibility"—namely, those of mainstream white feminism and chicano patriarchal ideology. It was from this precarious, marginalized position "between ideologies," she notes, that a new form of aesthetics emerged for the chicana writer "characterized by a multiplicity of voices and experiences."[11] In "La Quinceañera of Chicana Counter-Aesthetics," Rosa

Linda Fregoso draws on Quintana's notion of the new chicana aesthetic to point out how chicana independent filmmakers have forged a "counteraesthetics" in opposition to white culture and chicano patriarchy, both of which engage in phallocentric practices that render the chicana invisible and/or react to her creative process as a threat.[12]

Throughout the history of Hollywood filmmaking, the cultural specificity of latinas, mexicanas, and chicanas has been absent or overshadowed by racism and sexism. In the Hollywood of the late 1930s to early 1940s one finds the epitome of the sexually provocative generic latina played by the mexicana starlet Lupe Vélez, best known in Hollywood as the "Mexican Spitfire." Typecast as a dumb brunette (who with time became more blonde), Vélez was packaged as the embodiment of the sexual in ten formula films and sequels until her suicide in 1943.[13] The image of Vélez as an "exotic" object of desire is exemplary of Hollywood's depiction of the latina as an "exotic" commodity.[14] In a pointed reference to Vélez and her circumscribed roles, the title of España's video alludes to the *Mexican Spitfire* series, and participates in the reclamation of chicana, mestiza representation from centuries of racial patriarchal containment. The chicana, mestiza has been unable to escape from the fixed position of her historical "imaging," which, as I show later, can be traced to the pre-*encuentro*. In the context of visual production of the last twenty years, it is the intervention of chicana, mexicana, and latina theorists, writers, artists, and filmmakers like Sylvia Morales (*Chicana* [1979]), Loudes Portillo (*Después del Terremoto* [1979]), Salomé España (*Spitfire*), and others, that chicana, latina representation has been led out of a historical darkness to reclaim her rightful place and voice within the culture.[15]

Like España's previous work, *Spitfire* returns to the ancestral past in order to salvage lost female archetypes and rituals. However, as Stuart Hall reminds us, "There can ... be no simple 'return' or recovery of the ancestral past which is not re-experienced through the categories of the present—no base for creative enunciation in a simple reproduction of traditional forms which are not transformed."[16] Similarly, through computerized graphics and rapid editing that capture fragmented images of Coatlicue, Cihuacoatl, and la Virgen de Guadalupe, España suggests that these mexicana archetypes, through their fragmentation, must undergo dialectical change that may or may not lead to an eventual synthesis. These fragmented cultural signifiers interpellate the chicana, mestiza spectator in a process of self-revalidation, providing her with points of identification through which to renegotiate those lost aspects of her cultural history. Given the video's concerns with history, before I examine the text further, I will provide a short historical analysis of mexicana female archetypes and how these have constructed chicana, mestiza subjectivity at the intersection of gender, race, and class.

Socially Constructed Mexicana Archetypes

In "La Mujer y la Familia en la Sociedad Mexica," María de Jesús Rodríguez gives a detailed account of the patriarchal colonization of the female noble Mexica in the pre-Columbian period. Cut off from all forms of social exchange or positions of power outside the home, the female *cihuapilli* was chosen as sacrificial virgin to appease the gods, or brought up to become a breeder of nobles and soldiers.[17] Once identified with the role of the maternal, the *cihuapilli* became a venerated commodity whose only source of recognition was death through childbirth. Sexual inequality follows the female *cihuapilli* even after death. Transformed into a bird, the male warrior returns to earth in the company of the sun god, allowed to languish in the eternal bliss of the ambrosia flower. By contrast, the *cihuapilli* returns to earth only to find that she has been tricked. Denied the company of the sun, she is afforded only his reflection as guide. Back on earth, the *cihuapilli* is transformed into a phantasmagoric specter, feared for her gaze and malignant powers to promote "illness and render men insane."[18] It is not surprising that this cultural construction of the female Mexica would influence the emergence of the folk myth of La Llorona as the central representational trope of mexicana identity. Feared by the men who caught her gaze, La Llorona, like her ancient Greek counterpart Medusa, is given power to destroy men with her gaze.

In Mexican mythology, Coatlicue, a Nahuatl bisexual deity known as the mother of all gods, emerges as the duality of two aspects of cosmic force: life and death.[19] In *Psicología de las Mexicanas* Juana Armanda Alegría notes that when Coatlicue gives birth to Huitzilopochtli, her autoimpregnation is contested by the male gods. They dethrone her in favor of Huitzilopochtli, who then assumes the role of patriarchal god of sun and war over the Aztecs.[20] From this point on, Alegría writes, Aztec women find themselves with two main functions in life: procreation in the private social sphere and/or prostitution in the public service of the male.[21] It is safe to assume that it is at this historical juncture that the Madonna/whore construction of female identity is first inscribed in the culture, a historical legacy that, in time, would witness the mexicano self-appointment as guardian of mexicana desire. The advent of Catholicism, predicated on male power and the subservience of all women, only helped to reinforce hegemonic gender positions of inequality as social practice.

The figure of Malinalli Tenepal—also known as Tonantzin, la Malinche, and Doña Marina—appears as a tragic misreading of history by male chroniclers bent on defaming the character of this female symbol of *mexicanidad*. Malinalli's role in the *encuentro* phallocentrically inscribes her as a "vendida" (sellout) traitor to the indigenous race: she is blamed for having given birth to the first mestizo, even though historical documentation shows that prior to the *encuentro* a mestizo population existed in other areas of Central America.[22] "El malinchismo ... made Doña Marina a scapegoat," Alegría writes, questioning why history has failed to hold "Moctezuma Xocoyotzin responsible for handing over the country to the colonizer."[23] In recent years, Malinalli (as well as La Llorona and Coatlicue) has been rediscovered and her history reinterpreted by Norma Alarcón, Adelaida del Castillo, Cordelia Candelaria, and others, who have provided feminist counterreadings of resistance. In "Chicana Feminism: In the Tracks of the Native Woman," Norma Alarcón, by way of Anzaldúa, notes that "the most relevant point in the present is to understand how a pivotal indigenous portion of the mestiza past may represent a collective female experience as well as 'the mark of the Beast' within us—the maligned and abused indigenous woman."[24]

La Virgen de Guadalupe emerges as a Mexican archetype that, according to Roger Bartra, personifies the Mexican spirit and the conflation of two female representational myths: la Virgen de Guadalupe recognized as protector of the abandoned sector of society, and Malinalli as the violated mother, "la chingada."[25] Bartra traces the construction of these female symbols to the *encuentro,* when Cortés first presented the Mexican people with an image of a virgin and son (the son Malinalli had by Cortés out of wedlock). However, after

Malinalli is inscribed as a "vendida," the image of a virgin later reemerges as la Virgen de Guadalupe. Bartra writes that la Virgen de Guadalupe and Malinalli have come to represent the duality of the mexicana — "powerful yet dominated ... a queen yet a slave" — and claims that this is the modular paradigm by which the postmodern mexicana will be constructed.[26] The conflation of these two Mexican archetypes, Bartra further notes, expresses the projection of a patriarchal preoccupation to conquer the mexicana.[27] For many chicanas, mestizas, however, la Virgen de Guadalupe remains a powerful symbol of *mexicanidad* and an inspiration against oppressive hegemonic social forces that threaten to obliterate cultural identity. Gloria Anzaldúa writes: "La Virgen de Guadalupe is the single most potent religious, political and cultural image of the chicano/mexicano. She, like my race, is a synthesis of the old world and the new, of the religion and culture of the two races in our psyche, the conquerors and the conquered."[28] For Anzaldúa and others, the representation of la Virgen de Guadalupe as sociopolitical symbol of dissent must continue to be rearticulated by mexicana, chicana feminists in order to challenge established forms of patriarchal knowledge. As mexicanas, chicanas become more cognizant of their social inequality within the culture, they recognize that ideological institutions of power remain invested in maintaining female subjectivity tied down to the shadow of Eve and the religious legacy of original sin that utilizes la Virgen de Guadalupe as regulator of female sexuality and desire.[29]

Reestablishing Chicana, Mestiza Feminist Representation

Ultimately, chicana, mestiza subjectivity is a composite of these mexicana archetypes from which the Madonna/whore dichotomy was established to maintain the chicana, mestiza in a position of historical servitude. What makes *Spitfire* important is the manner in which these mexicana archetypes are (re)introduced and visually reconstituted to interpellate the chicana, mestiza spectator in a process of (re)evaluation through which she must confront this aspect of her history, which she previously either dismissed or internalized as a sign of oppression.

Spitfire opens with a red screen, which is sustained for a few seconds, then quickly followed by the title. In popular culture, the color red has connoted tempestuous emotion, passion, aggression, and sexuality ascribed to women, and, more specifically, has been associated with chicanas, mestizas, latinas as passionate objects of "exotic" male fantasy. This form of intertextual cultural coding alerts the spectator of the filmmaker's intention to offer a deconstructive reading that undercuts traditional forms of chicana, mestiza, latina representation. If ideology is, as Althusser argues, a social construction continually interpellating the subject, *Spitfire* functions as a self-reflexive, ideological *testimonio* providing the chicana, mestiza spectator with a recognizable social context through which she can be interpellated. Well crafted, each shot in *Spitfire* is aesthetically balanced and culturally coded to engage the chicana, mestiza spectator in a process of inquiry and self-empowerment.

Spitfire does not mimic reality; rather it produces new terms for chicana, mestiza representation through the reinscription of familiar mexicana images and sounds into a different signifying system. In this manner, experimental stylistic elements such as oblique camera angles, computerized images, and synthesized musical score both engage and challenge the spectator's relation to preexisting cultural icons and visual codes. Thus, for example, the lightness of the female body is contrasted to the solidity of Mesoamerican female sculptures and the historical legacy they embody through the contrapuntal play between a close-up of a woman's shoulder and the massive qualities of Coatlicue's curbed stone head. Similarly, flutes and drums on the sound track function as a recurrent cultural motif that evokes an ancestral, pre-Columbian past, connecting past and present spaces of collective historical experience as the basis for a new type of visual pleasure. The rapid succession of cultural imagery and sounds works to interpellate the spectator while also distancing her from the object on the screen, thus encouraging the spectator to reevaluate her gender and social placement within the culture.

España intercuts close-up and medium shots of a young chicana, mestiza with rosary beads against computerized images of la Virgen de Guadalupe, Coatlicue, Cihuacoatl, Ixtacihuatl, Mesoamerican female deities, and cultural artifacts that suggest the need for reintegration and redefinition of chicana, mestiza subjectivity. This is achieved through computerized graphics, which are interspersed between the mexicana deities and la Virgen de Guadalupe, and the manipulation

Close-up of young chicana, mestiza. Scene from Frances Salomé España's *Spitfire*.

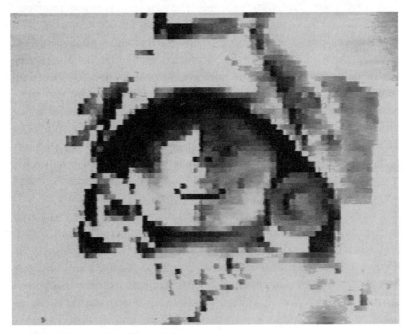

Coatlicue, Mesoamerican female deity.

of the chicana, mestiza image that conveys the subject's reintegration with her cultural past.

The video relies on a recurrent use of fragmented close-up shots of a chicana, mestiza's ear as she listens to her story. This iconography undercuts established forms of viewing the chicana, mestiza as a functional object of male desire and the male gaze. España refuses to portray the chicana, mestiza as a sexualized object, and positions her as the narrator of her own story. Through the deliberate use of dismembered close-up shots of a chicana, mestiza shoulder, torso, and the nape of her neck that emphasize her sensuality, *Spitfire* comments on the chicana, mestiza's need to recapture those fragmented aspects of her sexuality that she must now integrate as agent of her own desire. These fragmented body close-up shots of a chicana, mestiza are often transformed into pixelated, abstract compositions, at times diffused by the camera lens to suggest a reclamation of the female body from phallocentric imprinting. In contrast to a phallocentric visual pleasure and Eurocentric rationality, *Spitfire* uses recurring sound motifs of water, and a chicana, mestiza image reflected against water as a metaphor for the fluidity of movement and rebirth of chicana, mestiza identity in a process of redefinition and change. The representation of a chicana, mestiza captured in negative print and traditional Mexican costume suggests the reintegration of social-historical spaces, a fusion of collective experiences that ultimately determine that the chicana, mestiza as an oppositional feminist social construct will no longer be silenced. Indeed, the final close-up shot of *Spitfire* reveals a chicana, mestiza's gaze half parted in shadow, indicative of the multiple and divided subject position from which she now gazes to (re)address her newfound subjectivity.

Spitfire is reminiscent of Cauleen Smith's *Chronicles of a Lying Spirit* (1991), a contemporary African American feminist video that also relies on cultural coding to convey new forms of meaning. Both texts displace "fixed" representations of the chicana, mestiza or African American female images through the use of a densely coded iconographic context and stylistic techniques that rely on the rapid succession of edited and manipulated images to destabilize traditional forms of chicana, mestiza and African American female representation. But whereas *Chronicles of a Lying Spirit* relies on an ironic voice-over narration that works against misreadings of history, *Spitfire*

Divided subject as agent. Final shot of chicana, mestiza in *Spitfire*.

transforms the cultural icons and music that are the underpinnings of logocentric narratives about the chicana, mestiza.

Implications of Identification and Pleasure

Spitfire's contested voice allows the chicana, mestiza to emerge as a politicized chronicler of her own history and potential agent of resistance. From this subaltern position, España articulates or visually renders forms of interpretation other than those assigned by patriarchy and white culture, which are based on new readings of the cultural meaning of "otherness" and "difference." Chela Sandoval has elaborated this point in her essay on "oppositional consciousness" in which she argues that an interpretational shift has to come from within a culture, for its authenticity cannot be validated if it is constructed outside of cultural and historical specificity.[30]

Spitfire, as an ideological visual text, suggests a reframing of perception through the manipulation and positioning of chicana, mestiza iconography in relation to pleasure. But, as feminist film theorists have pointed out, the terms of cinematic pleasure imply that a mechanism of identification must be operative for either direct or indirect pleasure to be possible. For the chicana, mestiza spectator, the notion of cinematic pleasure poses additional complications, since she has generally been excluded from the cinematic contract and cut off from any form of primary identification. This exclusion only leaves the possibility of pleasure through indirect identification, and this poses a problem, for when separated from the more direct forms of access, that pleasure is vastly reduced. In addition, the fragmented pleasure available to the chicana, mestiza spectator through the "classical" cinematic apparatus also depends on the assumption that this apparatus functions universally across racial boundaries, and fails to take into account semiotic differences in the interpretation of cultural codes and symbols. It also assumes that the chicana, mestiza spectator has acculturated into white culture to such a degree that she derives some aspect of pleasure from white-imposed iconographic constructs (which often is not the case). By contrast, *Spitfire* offers the chicana, mestiza spectator a direct form of access to primary identification through culture-specific and recognizable chicana, mestiza images.

If one cannot escape ideology, as Althusser suggests,[31] then the chicana, mestiza subject needs to reaccess how she is positioned and constructed in ideology and the relation of that positioning to white culture and patriarchy. The chicana, mestiza must temporarily learn to negotiate some form of pleasure, not only through the mobilization of greater degrees of fantasy (than her white female counterpart), but also through her articulated dissent against her subaltern placement in Hollywood films. Jacqueline Bobo proposes an innovative reading of how African Americans are interpellated by a film's "interdiscourse." The interpellation is mediated by what Bobo calls "cultural competencies" on the part of the spectator, or the "range of knowledge that a viewer brings to the act of watching a film and creating meaning from a work."[32] Bobo breaks down cultural competency into binary opposites:

> One is a positive response where the viewer constructs something useful from the work by negotiating her/his response, and/or gives a subversive reading to the work. The other is a negative response in which the viewer rejects the work. Both types of oppositional readings are prompted by the store of negative images that have come from prior mainstream media experience.[33]

As I see it, Bobo's schemas of "cultural competencies" can also function for the chicana, mestiza experience, for I agree with Bobo that
the viewer's "range of knowledge" and the social conditioning of the
subject ultimately determine the spectator's ability to embrace or re-
ject a film. What is paramount, however, is that the level of "cultural
competency" begin to be encouraged at the primary level of education in order to help offset popular media representation of inappropriate images that continue to circulate and interpellate the subject.

Relations of power and knowledge between chicanas, mexicanas,
latinas, patriarchy, and white culture must continue to be articulated,
especially to the extent that power does not just oppress, but also
"induces pleasure, forms knowledge and produces discourse."[34] In
the end, oppositional discourses — by chicana/o cultural theorists, film/
video critics, and media artists — must continue to challenge relations of power and knowledge in which the chicana, mestiza image
becomes the site for the production of phallocentric racial pleasure
and fantasy.

Notes

I am grateful to Rosa Linda Fregoso and Carmen León for their responses
to an earlier version of this essay.

1. Kobena Mercer, " '1968': Periodizing Postmodern Politics and Identity," in *Cultural Studies,* ed. Lawrence Grossberg, Cary Nelson, and Paula
Treichler (New York: Routledge, 1992), 424.

2. The term "mestiza" is not meant to signify a biological, racialized
subject. Instead, I employ the term solely as trope. Unavoidably, however,
the designation mestiza/o is problematized by issues of race, class, and power
relations on both sides of the Mexican border. In the last ten years, however,
Norma Alarcón, Gloria Anzaldúa, and others have reappropriated the term
"mestiza" to redefine chicana subjectivity. Thus, the semiotic connotations
ascribed to the mestiza imply that crossing and recrossing the border create
new terms of power and social relations from which racial or metaphorical
semiotic meaning can be derived. In addition, when I use the term "mestiza"
alongside that of chicana, latina, mexicana, I do not imply that they are in-
terchangeable or that they represent one essentialized monolithic subject.

3. Mercer, " '1968,' " 425.

4. Rosa Linda Fregoso, *The Bronze Screen: Chicana and Chicano Film
Culture* (Minneapolis: University of Minnesota Press, 1993), 31. Fregoso explains how the two views of identity politics function in the process of mediating the subject: "This second view consequently emphasizes a notion that
privileges the concepts of *becoming* within cultural identity, rather than of

being, of *process* as opposed to structure, and of *production* contrary to re-discovery or archaeology" (ibid.).

5. Drawing from Stuart Hall, Fregoso points out that the two forms of cultural identity do not cancel each other, noting that "the importance of Hall's theoretical insights rests in his recognition that this second notion of cultural identity 'qualifies even though it does not replace the first' " (ibid.).

6. For scholarship on España's previous work, see Fregoso, *The Bronze Screen,* and Chon A. Noriega, "Talking Heads, Body Politic: The Plural Self in Chicano Video," in *Resolutions: Contemporary Video Practices,* ed. Michael Renov and Erika Suderburg (Minneapolis: University of Minnesota Press, 1996).

7. Teresa de Lauretis, *Alice Doesn't: Feminism, Semiotics, Cinema* (Bloomington: Indiana University Press, 1984), 38–39. De Lauretis's notion of imaging and how images are constructed calls for a change in the visual codes of representation that go beyond visual pleasure (Laura Mulvey's initial contention for circumventing cinematic objectification). What is important for de Lauretis is not the erasure of pleasure, but the relation of the subject's position to pleasure.

8. Interview with Frances Salomé España by Carmen Huaco-Nuzum, 1993.

9. Stuart Hall, "Minimal Selves," *Identity: The Real Me,* ICA Documents 6 (London: Institute of Contemporary Arts, 1987), 45.

10. Gloria Anzaldúa, *Borderlands/La Frontera: The New Mestiza* (San Francisco: Spinsters/Aunt Lute, 1987), 27–37.

11. Alvina Quintana, "Politics, Representation and the Emergence of a Chicana Aesthetic," *Cultural Studies* 4.3 (October 1990): 258–59.

12. Rosa Linda Fregoso, "La Quinceañera of Chicana Counter-Aesthetics," *Centro Bulletin* 3.1 (winter 1990–91): 87–91.

13. Emilio García Riera, *México visto por el cine extranjero* (Guadalajara: University of Guadalajara, 1988), 51–53.

14. In the last forty years, mexicana, chicana, latina representation in popular cinema has undergone another restrictive reclassification of subservient domestic to a white master (for example, *Basic Instinct* [1992]) or assume an anglo-masquerade. In the television series *The Commish,* for example, the commissioner's white wife is played by the latina actress Teresa Soldana.

15. It is important to note that in the 1960s and 1970s latina, chicana feminist community grassroots organizations on the East and West Coasts (latina legal services, health care, and union activists) were active in helping to reverse the disadvantaged socioeconomic position of the chicana, latina — work that often failed to gain them the recognition they deserved.

16. Stuart Hall, "New Ethnicities," *Black Film, British Cinema,* ICA Documents 7 (1988): 30.

17. María de Jesús Rodríguez, "La Mujer y la Familia en la Sociedad Mexica," *Presencia y Transparencia: La Mujer en la Historia de México* (México: El Colegio de México, 1987), 16–19.

18. Ibid., 17–18.

19. Adela Fernández, *Dioses Prehispánicos de México, mitos y deidades del panteón náhuatl* (México: Editorial Panorama, 1983), 54–95.

20. Juana Armanda Alegría, *Psicología de las Mexicanas* (México: Editorial Samo, 1977), 51–56.

21. Ibid., 65.

22. Ibid., 73.

23. Ibid., 73–76 (my translation).

24. Norma Alarcón, "Chicana Feminism: In the Tracks of 'the' Native Woman," *Cultural Studies* 4.3 (October 1990): 248–56, 251.

25. Roger Bartra, "A la Chingada," in *La Jaula de la Melancolía* (México: Grijalbo, 1987), 205.

26. Ibid., 209–17.

27. Ibid., 211–24.

28. Anzaldúa, *Borderlands/La Frontera*, 30.

29. One need only look at contemporary Mexican and Latin American *telenovelas* (*Cara Sucia, La Picara Soñadora, Dos Mujeres un Camino, Más Allá del Puente, Mari Mar,* and others) to find the commodified portrayals of *mexicanas*, latinas as venerated virgins devoid of agency and desire that reinforce male positions of power and racial hegemony. In addition, these *telenovelas* promulgate established positions of class and race that separate mexicanas, latinas of "clase decente" (criollas) from those of "clase baja" (the racially mixed underclass campesinas).

30. Chela Sandoval, "U.S. Third World Feminism: The Theory and Method of Oppositional Consciousness in the Postmodern World," *Genders* 10 (spring 1991): 1–24. See also Ramón Saldívar, *Chicana Narrative: The Dialectics of Difference* (Madison: University of Wisconsin Press, 1990), 7.

31. Louis Althusser, "Ideology and Ideological State Apparatuses," in *Lenin and Philosophy* (New York: Monthly Review Press, 1977), 160–70.

32. Jacqueline Bobo, "The Color Purple: Black Women as Cultural Readers," in *Female Spectators: Looking at Film and Television,* ed. E. Deidre Pribram (London: Verso, 1968), 102–3.

33. Ibid., 103.

34. Michel Foucault, *Power/Knowledge: Selected Interviews and Other Writings* (New York: Pantheon Books, 1972), 119.

Distributors

Art Com
P.O. Box 193123 Rincon Center
San Francisco, CA 94119-3123
415-431-7524
415-431-7841 (fax)

Video artists: Compilation tape, *Chicano Art Video,* includes short videos by six artists: Harry Gamboa Jr. (*L.A. Merge*), Frances Salomé España (*Anima*), Sandra P. Hahn (*Slipping Between, Replies of the Night*), Sandra Peña-Sarmiento (*Crónica de un ser*), Luis Valdovino (*Work in Progress*), Isaac Artenstein (*Son of Border Crisis*)

Canyon Cinema
2325 Third Street, Suite 338
San Francisco, CA 94107
415-626-2255

Filmmaker: Super-8 films of Willie Varela, 1974–92 (some films are available on video)

Cinema Guild
1697 Broadway, Suite 802
New York, NY 10019
212-246-5522
212-246-5525 (fax)

Filmmakers: Isaac Artenstein (*Ballad of an Unsung Hero*), Affonso Beato (*Puerto Rico: Paradise Invaded*), Estela Bravo (*Miami-Havana*), Diego Echeverria (*Los Sures*), Paul Espinosa (*The Lemon Grove Incident, The Trail North*), Ana María García (*La Operación*), José García Torres (*The Nationalist*), Zydnia Nazario (*The Battle of Vieques*), Frances Negrón-Muntaner (AIDS *in the Barrio*), Pedro Rivera and Susan Zeig (*Manos a la Obra: The Story of Operation Bootstrap*), Jesús Salvador Treviño (*Yo Soy Chicano, Yo Soy*)

Direct Cinema
P.O. Box 10003
Santa Monica, CA 90410
310-396-4774
310-396-3233 (fax)
Filmmaker: Lourdes Portillo (*La Ofrenda: The Days of the Dead*)

Electronic Art Intermix
536 Broadway, 9th Floor
New York, NY 10012
212-966-4605
212-941-6118 (fax)
Video artists: Edin Vélez, Tony Labat

El Teatro Campesino
P.O. Box 1240
San Juan Bautista, CA 95045
408-623-2444
408-623-4127 (fax)
Filmmaker: Luis Valdez

Flower Films
10341 San Pablo Avenue
El Cerrito, CA 94530
510-525-0942
510-525-1204 (fax)
Video artist: Enrique Oliver (*Photo Album*)

Frameline
346 Ninth Street
San Francisco, CA 94103
415-703-8654
415-861-1404 (fax)
Video artist: Raúl Ferrera-Balanquet (*Mérida Proscrita*)

New Yorker Films
16 West 61st Street
New York, NY 10023
212-247-6110
212-307-7855 (fax)
Filmmakers: Nestor Almendros and Orlando Jiménez-Leal (*Improper Conduct*)

Third World Newsreel
335 West 38th Street, 5th Floor
New York, NY 10018
212-947-9277
212-594-6417 (fax)
Filmmaker: Newsreel Media Collective (*El Pueblo Se Levanta*)

Women Make Movies
462 Broadway, Suite 500
New York, NY 10013
212-925-0606
212-925-2052 (fax)
Filmmakers: Osa Hidalgo de la Riva (*Mujeria*), Sylvia Morales (*Chicana*), Susana Muñoz (*Susana*), Frances Negrón-Muntaner (*Brincado el Charco: Portrait of a Puerto Rican*), Lourdes Portillo (*Después del Terremoto*), Ela Troyano/Ana María Simo (*How to Kill Her*)

Individual artists

Karim Aïnouz
175 Thompson Street, #12
New York, NY 10012
212-614-0454 (also fax)

Isaac Artenstein
Cinewest Productions
700 Adella Lane
Coronado, CA 92118
619-435-5582

David Avalos, Louis Hock, and Elizabeth Sisco
c/o Sisco, Hock, Avalos
903 26th Street
San Diego, CA 92102

The video component of the installation *Welcome to America's Finest Tourist Plantation* has never been shown on its own. For inquiries or information on collaborative videos, contact address above.

Frances Salomé España
P.O. Box 4044
Alhambra, CA 91803
213-881-9454

Raúl Ferrera-Balanquet
Latino Midwest Video Collective
P.O. Box 47343
Chicago, IL 60647
312-342-6047

Pablo Figueroa
321 West 22d Street, #4B
New York, NY 10011
212-243-4383

Harry Gamboa Jr.
P.O. Box 862015
Los Angeles, CA 90086-2015
213-508-1679

Ana María García
Pandora Films
Calle 4, F-2 Alturas del Río
Bayamón, Puerto Rico 00959
809-731-7237 (also fax)

Raphael Montañez Ortiz
315 Harper Place
Highland Park, NJ 08904
908-846-2690 (also fax)

Sylvia Morales
Sylvan Productions
12104 Washington Place
Los Angeles, CA 90066
310-391-0070 (also fax)

Lourdes Portillo
Xochitl Films
981 Esmeralda Street
San Francisco, CA 94110
415-255-7399
415-255-7704 (fax)

Felix Rodriguez
668 Warren Street, #2
Brooklyn, NY 11217
718-622-9454

Ela Troyano
594 Broadway, Suite 908
New York, NY 10012
212-431-4550
212-431-4608 (fax)

Willie Varela (videos since 1992)
7868 Juliet Way
El Paso, TX 79915
915-592-2972

Contributors

Marcos Becquer is a Ph.D. candidate in cinema studies at New York University. His work has appeared in *Third Text* and *Wide Angle*.

Charles Ramírez Berg is associate professor and graduate adviser in the Department of Radio-Television-Film at the University of Texas-Austin. He is the author of *Cinema of Solitude: A Critical Study of Mexican Film, 1967–1983* (1992) as well as articles on Mexican cinema, Chicano cinema, and issues of stereotyping and representation in film and television.

C. Ondine Chavoya has taught at the University of New Mexico and worked on Chicana/o exhibitions at the Mexican Museum, San Francisco, San Jose Museum of Art, and Galería de la Raza. Currently, he is a Ph.D. candidate in visual and cultural studies at the University of Rochester.

Marvin D'Lugo directs the Screen Studies program at Clark University. He is author of *The Films of Carlos Saura* (1991) and writes frequently on issues of national identity in Spanish-language cinemas. He is currently completing a book on theories of national cinema.

Claire F. Fox is an assistant professor in the Department of Spanish and Portuguese at Stanford University.

Ilene S. Goldman recently completed her doctoral degree in the Department of Radio/Television/Film at Northwestern University. Her essay on recent Colombian cinema is forthcoming in the next volume of *Hispanic Issues, Representing Locations, Locating Representations: Transformative Spaces & Latin American Cinema*. She is currently working on *Americas without Borders/Américas sin Fronteras*, a catalogue of U.S. Latino and Latin American video art titles available for rental at the Video Data Bank.

281

Carmen Huaco-Nuzum is a U.C. President's Fellow, Department of Chicana/o Studies at the University of California, Davis. She has published articles on Chicana, Latina feminist film culture and presently is completing a book on Mexican, Chicana cinema entitled *The Dialectic Politics of Hybridity.*

Lillian Jiménez has been involved in independent film and video for twenty years. In that time, she has served as a producer, media art center administrator, funder, exhibitor, educator, and writer. She is currently an independent media and management consultant in New York City.

Alisa Lebow is an independent videomaker and Ph.D. candidate in cinema studies at New York University. In 1994 she completed a video on questions of gender and sexuality entitled *Outlaw,* featuring transgender activist and writer Leslie Feinberg.

Ana M. López is associate professor of communication at Tulane University where she teaches film, Latin American, and cultural studies. She was a visiting professor at the School of Cinema/TV, University of Southern California, spring 1995. She is coauthor of *Mediating Two Worlds: Cinematic Encounters in the Americas* (1992) and the author of numerous articles and book chapters.

Scott MacDonald is author of *A Critical Cinema* and *A Critical Cinema 2,* an ongoing series of interviews with independent moving-image makers whose work critiques conventional media, published by the University of California Press. *A Critical Cinema 3,* which includes an interview with Raphael Montañez Ortiz, is in preparation. MacDonald's discussion of fifteen major independent filmmakers, *Avant-garde Film/Motion Studies,* was published in 1993. He teaches and programs film series/exhibitions at Utica College in Utica, New York.

José Esteban Muñoz is an assistant professor in the Performance Studies Department at New York University. He is coeditor of *Politics in Motion: Culture, Music and Dance in Latin America* (forthcoming) and *Pop Out* (forthcoming). He is currently completing a book on contemporary American identity practices in film, video, and performance titled *Disidentifications.*

Frances Negrón-Muntaner is a media maker, writer, and scholar based in Philadelphia. She holds an MFA from Temple University and is a Ph.D. candidate in comparative literature at Rutgers University-New Brunswick. She has recently edited an anthology on Latino poets in Philadelphia, *Shouting in a Whisper,* and completed an experimental narrative film on Puerto Rican identities titled *Brincado el Charco: Portrait of a Puerto Rican.*

Kathleen Newman teaches Latin American and Chicano cinema at the University of Iowa. She is author of *La violencia del discurso: el estado autoritario y la novela política argentina* (1991) and is working on a book on State theory and cultural studies.

Chon A. Noriega is assistant professor in the Department of Film and Television at the University of California, Los Angeles. His previous books include *Chicanos and Film* (Minnesota) and *The Mexican Cinema Project.* He has curated numerous film and visual arts exhibitions, and recently produced and wrote the documentary *Revelaciones/Revelations: Hispanic Art of Evanescence.*

Christopher Ortiz is a graduate of Vassar College and holds an M.A. from Brown University in Hispanic Studies and a Ph.D. in Film and Television from the Department of Film and Television at UCLA, where he completed a dissertation on contemporary Mexican cinema. He has published on a wide variety of topics including contemporary Spanish literature and U.S. Latino/a media arts and has been active as an independent curator for a number of festivals and arts organizations. He resides in West Hollywood, California.

Index